Building Fortress Europe

DEMOCRACY, CITIZENSHIP, AND CONSTITUTIONALISM

Rogers M. Smith, Series Editor

Building Fortress Europe

The Polish-Ukrainian Frontier

Karolina S. Follis

PENN

UNIVERSITY OF PENNSYLVANIA PRESS

PHILADELPHIA

Published by
University of Pennsylvania Press
Philadelphia, Pennsylvania 19104-4112
www.upenn.edu/pennpress

Printed in the United States of America on acid-free paper
10 9 8 7 6 5 4 3 2 1

Library of Congress Cataloging-in-Publication Data

Follis, Karolina S. (Karolina Szmagalska-)
    Building fortress Europe : the Polish-Ukranian frontier / Karolina S. Follis.—1st ed.
        p.   cm. — (Democracy, citizenship, and constitutionalism)
    ISBN 978-0-8122-4428-1 (hardcover : alk. paper)
    Includes bibliographical references and index.
    1. European Union—Boundaries. 2. Immigrants—Poland. 3. Immigrants—Ukraine.
4. Polish people—Ukraine. 5. Ukrainians—Poland. 6. Poland—Boundaries—Ukraine.
7. Ukraine—Boundaries—Poland. I. Title. II. Series: Democracy, citizenship, and
constitutionalism
DK4185.U38 F65   2012
943.8'6057—pcc   2012008452

To my parents

Contents

Chapter 1

Introduction: Rebordering Europe

We are like travelers navigating an unknown terrain with the help
of old maps, drawn at a different time and in response to different
needs.

—Seyla Benhabib

The expansion of the European Union on May 1, 2004, to incorporate eight
new member states in postsocialist Eastern Europe, and its second act of
including an additional two in 2007, have been the latest in the centuries-
long sequence of border shifts in Europe.[1] Contours of European maps have
usually changed in the aftermath of wars. This time, however, the shift was
peaceful, and the territorial outlines of the countries involved remained un-
touched. Instead, their borders were refitted for a new purpose. Where the
new members bordered on each other, or on old EU member states, frontiers became the open "internal EU borders," as, for example, between Poland
and the Czech Republic, Slovakia and Hungary, Hungary and Austria. Where
they touched countries that so far have not received the invitation to join
the European Union, the boundaries became "external EU borders" and thus
subject to a whole new order of regulation and policing (for example, Poland-
Ukraine, Poland-Belarus, Slovakia-Ukraine, Estonia-Russia). Between 2003
and 2008 I returned to Poland and Ukraine regularly to study the human
consequences and political implications of this peculiar shift.

It affected the daily routines of state practice—border control and policing, traffic, and immigration bureaucracy—as well as the larger issues of
geopolitics and foreign policy. The changes insinuated themselves also into

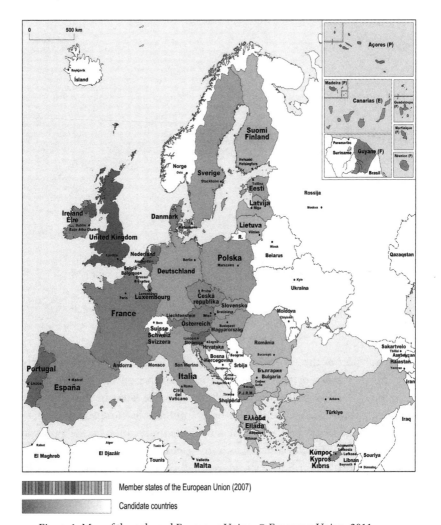

Figure 1. Map of the enlarged European Union. © European Union, 2011.

the lives of many people—Poles, Ukrainians, and other non-EU citizens, in the borderland and beyond. Among such people were Anna Sadchuk and her family and friends.[2] Anna was an itinerant Ukrainian worker in Warsaw. She was twenty-nine years old when I first met her in 2005, through a chain of encounters with other itinerant workers. Anna went to a vocational school to become a hair stylist, but in Poland she worked as a cleaning lady. She was a petite brunette with freckles and spoke in a soft voice that made her initially seem shy. That impression, however, dissipated halfway through our first conversation, at a café in her neighborhood one spring afternoon. She was a cheerful person with a penchant for telling stories, many of them having to do with the hazards and tricks of negotiating the border between Ukraine and Poland, the EU-imposed visa requirements, and the day-to-day perils of being an illegal migrant worker. "People here need us," she told me,

> everyone in Warsaw has their *Ukrainka*, to do the work they don't want to do. Polish women work in nice offices, wear nice clothes, they don't have time to clean and cook. And so what are these visas for? Everybody knows that we're going to come anyway. If we have to pay [bribes] we pay. If we have to lie [to the officials], we lie. . . . They [border guards] are not so stupid to think that we are coming on vacation. They know why we are here. They must check the visa, we must show the visa. And what? It changes nothing.

Anna, her brother, his wife, and her sister all come from a small town in the Lviv *oblast'* (district) in western Ukraine. Together with two more female friends, they share a couple of boarding rooms in the attic of a neglected building in a centrally located neighborhood in Warsaw. Every morning they commute to their multiple, ever-changing, and unauthorized jobs all over the city. Anna was the youngest; her brother Dima was the oldest at forty. She has lived and worked in Poland intermittently since 1998, when she came for the first time with her brother to look for a job. Dima, like most male Ukrainian workers, has held mostly short-term jobs in construction. She started out picking and canning fruit and with time moved to better-paid urban house-cleaning jobs, where she was able to earn up to six hundred U.S. dollars per month (in 2006).[3]

Anna and her roommates, like thousands of other Ukrainians from their region and beyond, could not make ends meet back home. This has been due to persistent high unemployment that has marred the region since the collapse of Soviet-era industry and collective agriculture (official figures in 2008 were 8.3 percent for Lviv *oblast'*, but it is thought to be higher).[4] The partial attempts at economic reform undertaken since 2005 have failed to address an overall scarcity of economic opportunity, felt acutely particularly in the rural areas of western Ukraine. Therefore, thousands of Ukrainians, primarily from the west, have been relying on the Polish *szara strefa* (gray zone, i.e., shadow economy) for employment. They come, because, as Elżbieta Matynia wrote

in 2003, "even within 'the East' there is some place more west . . . enjoying
relative economic success, proximity to the European Union, higher density
of international transit on major highways, or greater strength of the local
currency in relationship to the Euro" (Matynia 2003: 501).

The precise number of such migrants is subject to some dispute, but informed estimates range from 300,000 to 500,000.[5] Poland's young capitalism
generates demand for cheap labor, especially in agriculture, construction, and
private households.[6] Because of its proximity, coming to Poland does not require the personal investment, risk, and expense that migrating farther west
would entail.[7] Yet Anna and others still negotiate a border regime which has
thickened on EU's eastward expansion, and which is built on the assumption
that every non-EU traveler is a potential undesirable migrant.

But Ukrainian workers continue to cross the border.[8] They adjust to the
increasing constraints imposed by border regulations, but they also subvert
and resist them. They exploit the economic opportunities enhanced by EU's
closeness, simultaneously connecting the Polish and Ukrainian societies
through a web of relationships that are asymmetrical, but vital to both sides.
At the same time they develop new ways of living away from their families, yet
in permanent connection to a home where they cannot be physically present.
"Every time I come here, I hope it's the last time," Anna told me one Saturday
night when I visited her and her three roommates, Halyna (her sister-in-law),
Nadia, and Ola. Permanently settling in Poland is neither their desire nor a
real possibility. Ultimately, the objective is to go back to Ukraine, for Anna,
her friends, and the vast majority of other itinerant workers. As we drank
inexpensive Moldovan wine and ate Ukrainian cookies, the women told stories of their repeated border crossings and the scary, unpleasant, and funny
things that happened in the course of their journeys. They recalled hustlers
who hang out at border crossings and bus terminals and sign up women for
"prestigious" jobs at nightclubs and escort services; all four women dismissed
the possibility of ever doing such work, but they claimed to have had acquain-
tances who did. They talked about the bribes they needed to pay to customs
agents when their hard-earned cash was found on them during return trips
home. They explained how one can circumvent the border regulations and
overstay the visa without running into trouble by altering the passport stamp,
having the passport illegally stamped without leaving the country, or pur-
chasing forged documents.

Some time after my encounter with Anna, and after having already completed several months of fieldwork and many trips across Poland's eastern

border, I attended a meeting of Polish and Ukrainian border professionals (which I discuss in detail Chapter 5). At that meeting, one of the Polish speakers, an NGO expert, started his presentation on combating illegal immigration across the new external border of the European Union with the following statement: "Let me tell you a secret: Poland does not have an immigration policy." I wondered at the time why should that be a secret—after spending time among Ukrainian migrants, and learning about their lives beyond the official gaze, I was well aware that there was no policy to speak of that would lend any predictability or order to their arrivals and their work. Was the expert's declaration just rhetoric to spark interest, or did it signal recognition of a serious problem? The remainder of the presentation covered in great detail the current ways of policing Poland's eastern border and preventing illegal migration, but the speaker did not revisit the issue of the lack of an immigration policy. As this study progressed, however, I began to understand that the answer was implicit in his presentation, and was confirmed by the activities of multiple agencies, such as the Border Guard and the Aliens Bureau, involved in border issues. Poland indeed did not have an immigration policy, or, for that matter, one pertaining to the broader realities of postsocialist mobility; the "secret" was that the new border regime, developed in the context of joining EU and the Schengen territory without internal frontiers, was a surrogate for one. This elision of vital matters of human mobility, legality, and territoriality within the new border regime has become the central theme of this ethnography.

This book is about the rebordering of Europe on the Polish-Ukrainian frontier between 2003 and 2008. I connect experiences such as Anna's to the complexities and intrigues of the new border regime, as I have reconstructed them from my encounters with border guards, officials, and experts involved in its formation. This research supports my contribution to the larger scholarly conversation addressing the question of what borders are today, in a time when European states are engaged in a project of supranational integration and traditional sovereignty is being redefined; when capital, goods, and people move transnationally in staggering numbers and at an unparalleled speed; and when populations and individuals are subjected to the workings of the variable modes of post-9/11 securitization. The dismantling of the Iron Curtain in 1989 had a massive impact on the social and political geography of the continent, human mobility, and ways of thinking about territory and populations. With the post-2004 reconfiguration of borders in Europe, these adjustments and rearrangements call for reassessment.

Borders as Objects of Social Inquiry

This project began with the observation that in the post-Cold War world, few other political artifacts have been at the core of quite as many pressures and hopes as that of an international border. The state's exclusive control over its territorial boundaries has been one of the key markers of state sovereignty (Anderson 1996; Andreas and Snyder 2000; Balibar 2002, 2004; Benhabib 2004; Chalfin 2003; Donnan and Wilson 1999; Dudziak and Volpp 2006; Giddens 1985; Hobsbawm 1990; Krasner 1999; Sassen 1996, 1999; Torpey 2000; Walters 2002, 2006). However, in the late twentieth and early twenty-first centuries, a complex of social, economic, and political transformations complicated the terms in which modern sovereignty has been understood. Has globalization, thought of loosely as the rise of transnational flows, combined with increasing flexibility of capital and growing power of corporations and other non-state entities, undermined sovereignty? Or rather, has it forced the state to reassert its power in new ways by different means? (Appadurai 1996, 2001; Chalfin 2003, 2004; Anderson 1992; Kearney 1995; Sanders and West 2003; Sassen 1996; Trouillot 2000). Notwithstanding the importance of this debate, I bracket, for the time being, the question of sovereignty's contemporary modalities, the status of the nation-state, and its possible future. Instead, I want to focus on the fact that in this context international borders are fundamentally changing their character. They are being reinvented as sites of mobility and enclosure (Cunningham and Heyman 2004), broadening the scope of transnational possibilities but also indicating their limits.

Scholars across disciplines have asked whether international borders are opening up or closing. Are they becoming more or less permeable, more or less important, for whom, when, and why? This wide-ranging research has yielded a set of partial certainties. Globalization, technological progress, and contemporary "fast-capitalism" (Holmes 2000) do spur transnational flows and a circulation of people, objects, and ideas to which international borders are no obstacle (Appadurai 1996; Castells 1996). The ability to experience the world as borderless is, however, a privilege whose distribution hinges on the variables of class or economic status, nationality and citizenship, gender, ethnicity, race, religion, politics, and geopolitics. (Anderson 2000; Ehrenreich and Hochschild 2004; Balibar 2002; Blank 2004; Bornstein 2002; Cunningham 2004) First World democracies have been erecting walls around themselves since long before the planes hit the Twin Towers (Andreas 2000b; Andreas and Snyder 2000). Afterward, a new "governmentality of unease" (Bigo 2002) has crept into international border controls and fears of terrorism, meshed with older anxieties about excessive immigration and the ostensibly rampant "abuse of asylum" (Lavenex 1999; Bohmer and Schuman 2007). We have thus seen a progressive securitization of borders (Rumford 2006; De Genova and Peutz 2010). This in turn entails a rapid advancing of biometric technologies to control human mobility as well as an erosion of freedom of movement, and of human rights guarantees to vulnerable groups and individuals in transit. In this context, some scholars have presented compelling Foucaultian and Agambenian analyses of the specific biopolitics involved in deploying borders as enclosures, and of the zones and states of exception emerging at the limits of the normal legal order (Foucault 1990; Agamben 1998; De Genova 2010; Fassin 2005; Giorgi and Pinkus 2006; Landau 2006; Minca 2006). Refugee camps, detention centers for illegal migrants, and other holding spaces for the unwanted and the deportable have been placed on a historical continuum with other states of exception, where the "suspension of the usual social norms is accepted . . . because it is implemented for 'undesirable' subjects" (Fassin 2005: 379). The historically and contextually specific constructions of "undesirability" have also been studied and critiqued, often with respect to their legal production (Coutin 2003, 2005; De Genova 2002; Kelly 2006; Silverstein 2005).

These works differ in critical emphasis, but by and large they highlight antidemocratic, ethically dubious, and socially unjust elements of state and policing practice, often relating them to the historical trend of contemporary states to withdraw from responsibility for human welfare, broadly associated with the ideology of neoliberalism. My project is indebted to this scholarship, but it attempts to chart its own path. I draw on empirical data collected in Poland and Ukraine to ask how borders, as both gateways and enclosures or exceptions, fit into the larger process of the expansion and evolution of the European Union as a novel type of a supranational, ostensibly democratic political community. Which forms of agency, belonging, and habitation do they enable or disallow? Which social and spatial imaginaries do they support and which support them?

I pose these questions because borders and border zones are not merely margins of polities, but play a central role in their constitution. Given that the European Union appears to be an entity in a perpetual state of emergence, I shall focus on how it is actualizing itself through the complex efforts of establishing its own eastern external border. I will look at the frictions these efforts produced in a particular place, at the particular moment of expansion.

Some of these frictions—for example, between national and EU authorities; local community and national government; economic and security interests; human rights commitments and exclusionary tendencies—are emblematic of the larger tensions and contradictions in the construction and consolidation of the enlarged European Union.

Addressing these questions requires a dynamic concept of the border, one that would account for both its inherent connection to territory, as a frontier or a borderland, and the fact that today this connection is being (partially) severed. Beyond the material, such a concept must capture also the symbolic and discursive life of borders, that is, their relationship to boundaries understood, in the classic Barthian vein, as the separation of self from other which lends meaning to identity (Barth 1969, 2000; Cohen 1986, 2000; Stolcke 1995).

In 1995 Robert Alvarez noted à propos the literature on the U.S.-Mexico border that "some scholars feel that to take a metaphorical approach to borderlands distracts us from social and economic problems on the borders between the nation-states and shifts the attention away from the communities and people who are the subject of our inquiry" (Alvarez 1995: 449). He pointed out that "literalists" focused on what they saw as "the actual" problems of the border, such as migration, policy, environment, identity, labor, and health. 'A-literalists' in turn account for social boundaries on the geopolitical border and for the contradictions, conflict, and shifting of identity characteristic of borderlands (Alvarez 1995: 449, see also Cunningham and Heyman 2004). In recent years the dichotomy of literalist and a-literalist approaches has blurred (Donnan and Wilson 1999; Berdahl 1999; Inda 2006; Pelkmans 2006), and new conceptualizations of borders are at their richest when they draw on both of these distinct genealogies.

Hastings Donnan and Thomas Wilson suggested a definition that names and systematizes the domains wherein borders operate:

> Borders are signs of the eminent domain of the state, and are markers of the secure relations it has with its neighbors, or are reminders of hostility that exists between states. Borders are the political membranes through which people, goods, wealth and information must pass in order to be deemed acceptable or unacceptable by the state. Thus [they] are the agents of a state's security and sovereignty. . . . Borders have three elements: the legal borderline which simultaneously separates and joins states; the physical structures of the state which

exist to demarcate and protect the borderline, composed of people and institutions which often penetrate deeply into the territory of the state; and frontiers, territorial zones of varying width, within which people negotiate a variety of behaviors and meanings associated with their membership in nations and states. (Donnan and Wilson 1999: 9)

The parsing of the constitutive elements of borders facilitates thinking about the connections between their legal and spatial aspects. At the same time, however, this definition seems too static to account for transnationality, securitization, and the emergence of entities such as the European Union that transcend the nation-state. In the globalized world borders operate in ways that can potentially affect not just those who "pass through them" and those who inhabit frontier zones, but everyone inside and outside the territories that they mark. The question then ought to be how they have become devices for remodeling citizenship, and hence entire societies and polities.

Étienne Balibar captured the nature of this change with particular acuity. In his essay "What Is a Border?" he shows how throughout the history of modern political systems borders have operated in a differential manner. His key point is that today, in times of unprecedented human mobility, they are becoming increasingly heterogeneous. The old tendency of nation-states to make political, cultural, and socioeconomic borders coincide is falling apart. The result is that "some borders are no longer situated at borders at all":

> they are in fact elsewhere, wherever selective controls are to be found, such as for example health and security checks. . . . The concentration of all these functions . . . at a single point—along a single line which was simultaneously refined and densified, opacified—was a dominant tendency during a particular period, the period of the nation state . . . but not an irreversible historical necessity. For quite some time now it has been giving way, before our very eyes, to a new ubiquity of borders. (Balibar 2002: 84)

This ubiquity, or proliferation, of borders across societal domains is the concrete manifestation of what has been called the dislocation of state boundaries (Andreas and Snyder 2000; Walters 2006). It entails the emergence of new sites, spaces, situations, and events for the making of distinctions between citizens and aliens. These distinctions are ever more profuse, and they no longer happen at birth or at physical borders (i.e., points of admission to a given state territory). Persons in transit are no longer classified simply as citizens, visitors, immigrants, or refugees. Instead, we are witnessing the ascendance of a growing number of forms of (non)*being* relative to boundaries, that is, ways in which to be, or not to be, a citizen and an alien. The difference is not simply between being "legal" or "illegal." Possibilities range from EU and national citizenship with a full scope of rights, to being an undocumented alien without the right to asylum, suspended in a state of uncertainty while awaiting deportation in a detention center located within or outside the EU territory. In between, a spectrum of other situations render individuals and groups dependent on ad hoc life provisions and arbitrary forms of social control. These in turn, as Carol Greenhouse observed, "appear to intensify the discriminatory effects of status differences (gender, age, nationality, . . .), with only the most uneven—if any—protection of the law" (Greenhouse 2006: 195). This proliferation of categories is a historical development, in the sense that it can be traced back to the traumas and breaking points of Western modernity which gave birth to modern citizenship and human rights in the first place. Needless to say, it is also dynamic, in that the inscription of categories and assignment of status is never fixed. It can slip or be adjusted many times over the course of a person's life, as she changes location and as new categories are invented. This categorization of subjects is not absolute. It constrains agency, but doesn't block it, unless, of course, it terminally thwarts it, as, for example, with those unwanted migrants who are left to die at sea (Fekete 2004; United Against Racism 2011).[9] In any case, however, the proliferation of categories has subjective and material consequences that can be traced back to the variability and ubiquity of borders.

Bordering and Rebordering

Reflecting on political change on the continent after the watershed year of 1989, one notices a striking paradox. Since the end of the Cold War, formidably represented in the collective imagination by the collapse of the Berlin Wall, Europeans on both sides of the former divide have been captivated by the idea of a continent without borders. The trademark ideas of Europeanization, such as travel with no passports, freedom to settle in any EU country, or one currency for all had a tremendous appeal for the heterogeneous publics of the formerly divided continent (Favell 2008b, 2009; Kaelble 2009).

Simultaneously, these same publics continue to be exposed, via media representations and political rhetoric, to the direct and immediate images of borders as insurmountable walls, barbed wire fences, and hostile shores. But are these two visions truly at odds? Even a cursory reading of the basic EU legal texts reveals that they are indeed two aspects of one Janus-faced principle. This holds that to practice cross-border exchange of goods, services, ideas, and people safely within European boundaries, the EU territory and population must be effectively shielded from without. Unbordered space is only possible within borders.

What accounts for the emergence of this tension? The idea of a Europe devoid of internal divisions has a history that some date as far back as the Kantian ideal of cosmopolitan republicanism (Harvey 2001: 274).[10] But at the same time it has always depended on the "externalization or creation of negative others" (Borneman and Fowler 1997: 489), embodied at times by the Oriental stranger (Said 1994), at times by the not-quite-civilized East European (Wolff 1994; Todorova 1997) or, more recently, by the ubiquitous phantom of the Muslim fundamentalist potentially lurking within any nonwhite immigrant. It is therefore possible to read the tension between the drive to "de-border" (Habermas 2003) and that to protect Europe within a secure enclosure as an expression of a fundamental contradiction at the heart of the European integration project—that between its long-standing universalist claims and its strong exclusionary tendencies.

For centuries, the peoples of the European continent experienced instability and war. The devastation and carnage of World War II prompted the initial steps to foster peace among European nations through economic and political integration. The EU expansion into Eastern Europe was a continuation of this process, propelled by the desire of the Western European leaders of the late twentieth century to affirm the ultimate end of the Soviet socialist experiment.[11] The accession of new member states in 2004 and 2007, the abolishing of internal borders, and the effort to reinforce external ones are events that bring to the fore urgent questions concerning the future of the European Union as a novel type of political body. Although reforms stipulated by the Lisbon Treaty do simplify governance and introduce the new positions of President of the European Council and High Representative of the Union for Foreign Affairs and Security Policy, it seems unlikely that Churchill's vision of a "United States of Europe" will ever materialize. But even though the defenders of traditional national sovereignty are vociferous and many, the EU is plodding along, and gradually impressing its mark on a broadening range of everyday matters, from food to education, from energy to travel, borders, and human rights.

In the absence of a grand scheme, one way to understand European unification is to see it as a gradual reconfiguration of the relationship between populations and territory. In the modern nation-state a government has sovereign power within a defined territorial area, and the majority of the population are national citizens. By introducing the concept of EU citizenship, with such privileges as the right to live, work, study, and enjoy some measure of social security anywhere in the EU, and by creating a territory without internal borders but secured around its perimeter, the European Union significantly challenges the nation-state model.[12]

To get at the lived and practical ramifications of this challenge, and at the same time to avoid relying on concepts that reify and excessively emplace borders, throughout this book I use the concept of *rebordering*. It denotes both the talk and the practice of defining and enforcing the boundaries of the European Union. Rebordering is a hegemonic process that is nevertheless contested by many agents and from many angles. It unfolds within public discourse as well as in concrete actions and practices of politicians and state officials. As discourse, rebordering refers to challenging, expanding, or otherwise altering the idea of Europe in order at once to accommodate Eastern Europeans, and potentially other neighbors, as new citizens of the European Union, and to define its new spatial, cultural, and conceptual boundaries. As action, rebordering includes the bureaucratic, legal, and police practices aimed at establishing a tight perimeter around the European Union, while opening up the internal EU borders.

The rebordering of Europe is a historically specific instance of the broader phenomenon of *bordering*, that is, the discursive and material construction of border regimes. I draw here on John Borneman's concept of the *Grenzregime*, developed in the context of the division of East and West Berlin, as the entire system of rules and regulations intended to demarcate political entities, police inclusion and exclusion, senses of belonging and citizenship itself (Borneman 1998). Border regimes are always products of what Malcolm Anderson calls "territorial ideologies," namely, "sets of beliefs about the relationship of the population to the area that it inhabits" (Anderson 1996: 34). This ideological component further underscores the need to attend to both material and symbolic manifestations of (re)bordering.

Thus rebordering, as I conceive of it, is at once about inclusion and exclusion, expansion and its limits. Hand in hand with the opening of internal borders and the closing of external ones goes the more surreptitious process of introducing various forms of border controls *within* EU territory—Balibar's "ubiquity of borders" (2002). The combination of these developments establishes the terms of belonging, mobility, and legal status for both resident populations and immigrants within unified Europe.

Rebordering entails significant power shifts between citizens of member states and those of the excluded adjacent countries. The former are granted stakes in the new idea of European citizenship, with the freedom to move about and, with only some restrictions, to settle in an area encompassing most of the continent and its islands. In this way the demand for migrant labor in the wealthier countries of the West of Europe can be satisfied almost entirely thanks to East-West mobility within the EU. This engenders what Favell calls "a tempting racial logic," that is, "opening to populations from the East may enable the more effective closing of Europe to the South, filling the structural need for which Western Europe had historically to turn to colonial and developing country immigrants from more distant societies and cultures" (Favell 2009: 172). Whether that makes a substantial difference in terms of the degree of anxiety that immigrants provoke is another matter, as illustrated, for example, by the 2005 controversies in France around the notorious figure of the "Polish plumber" and his supposed assault on French wages and, indeed, on the French way of life.[13] Non-EU citizens must contend with new limitations on their freedom of movement and right to enter any of the twenty-seven EU states. What are the specific human consequences and local social dynamics that these shifts engender? The Polish-Ukrainian border shall serve as a laboratory case of rebordering, and in the chapters that follow I address these questions by shedding light on the local experiences, debates, and resistances that unfolded there in the wake of Poland's EU accession in 2004.

The Political History of Rebordering

Decades have passed since the end of the Cold War, and Eastern European victories over bankrupt socialisms no longer inspire jubilation.[14] Instead, the unfolding aftermath has perplexed and challenged East and West Europeans alike. Democratic futures where human rights marked the inviolable standard of human dignity ceased to be regarded as certain. This paradigm has suffered both in spite and because of EU expansion, in ways that this book endeavors to document, primarily by paying attention to the ramifications of a novel territorial arrangement inextricably bound with the European Union: the Schengen territory without internal borders.

In 1951 France, Germany, Italy, Belgium, the Netherlands, and Luxembourg founded the European Coal and Steel Community. The initial narrow economic focus translated into an ambitious political goal: to achieve lasting peace between France and Germany (Dinan 2005: 2). The projected European Community had a decisive Franco-German center of gravity and no a priori demarcated borders. But the Iron Curtain, already firmly in place, constituted an unquestioned barrier and contributed to equating "Europe" with its Western "core" (Dinan 2005: 144; see also Habermas and Derrida 2003; Case 2009).

Subsequent treaties broadened the extent of economic integration and articulated more forcefully its political goals. The Treaty of Rome envisioned an "ever closer union among the peoples of Europe" and "common action to eliminate the barriers which divide Europe" in order to ensure enduring peace and economic and social progress (Preamble to the 1957 Treaty of Rome). But economic integration proved easier than eradicating obstacles to the movement of people.[15] In 1985 the Schengen group (France, Germany, Luxembourg, Belgium, and the Netherlands) initiated the project of establishing a shared territory without checks on internal borders. But the proposition that people move freely between separate nation-states was politically contentious and legally daunting. It took several more years before the Schengen agreements became operational and were expanded to the majority of EU states.

Meanwhile, the rapid collapse of Soviet socialism in 1989 led to a redefinition of the existing European Community. Polish authorities, and those of other newly democratic states in Central Europe, quickly articulated their strategic goal of joining the evolving European project (Geremek 1990; Michnik 2003). The Treaty of Maastricht (1992) established the European Union, and together with the Treaty of Amsterdam (1997) it prepared the ground for extending integration eastward. Overcoming the legacy of conflicts which have taken millions of lives had been the abiding moral and historical premise of "building Europe"—not only in the sense of establishing common institutions, but also as a project of crafting a cultural identity that could bolster the legitimacy of the integration process (Shore 2000). Now, not without tension and internal and external opposition, this commitment was extended to formerly Soviet-dominated countries of Eastern Europe.

As of May 2004, the "area of freedom, security and justice" proclaimed in the Amsterdam Treaty was expanded to cover territories from the Portuguese shores to the northern coast of Estonia, swamps of eastern Poland, and western slopes of the Carpathian Mountains. In 2007, with the inclusion of Bulgaria and Romania, it reached the Black Sea. The status of the novice states was not, however, fully equal to that of the original fifteen. With few exceptions (Ireland, United Kingdom, and Sweden) old member states imposed limitations on the right of citizens of the new member states to work anywhere in the EU. Moreover, at the time of the 2004 expansion, the Schengen zone was not enlarged to include the new ten, and checks continued to be applied to incoming traffic as before, on the borders of Germany, Austria, and Italy.[16] The new members were fully incorporated into Schengen only in 2008, following repeated postponements caused by problems inherent in the complex project of constructing a shared database, known as the Second Generation Schengen Information System, SIS II, that was becoming a crucial tool in the policing of the European Union's external borders.[17]

At the same time, larger prospects of further integration of the European "area of freedom, security and justice" through an EU constitution were abandoned in favor of the less ambitious but more realistically achievable reforms of the Lisbon Treaty. Following the 2005 French and Dutch rejections of the Constitutional Treaty in national referenda, European leaders demonstrated little eagerness to defend, much less promote, what many have promptly called a "dead" document.[18] The word "constitutional" was dropped from its subsequent iterations, but the new treaty, renegotiated and adopted in June of 2007 in Lisbon, had to overcome yet another nearly lethal hurdle—the Irish "no" vote in 2008. It was only in 2009 that a second referendum in Ireland yielded an approval for the reform and convinced the remaining resisters, Presidents Lech Kaczyński of Poland and Vaclav Klaus of the Czech Republic, to complete the process of ratifying Lisbon.

The rapid and anticlimactic passing of what has been called Europe's "constitutional moment" (Walker 2004) and the obstacles in expanding Schengen were only two of the many setbacks suffered by the EU in the recent past. The leaders at the European Commission had to contend also with the mounting skepticism toward integration demonstrated by political elites in both old and new EU countries, which laid bare some old problems of European integration. Combined, these problems directed the spotlight at the dubious democratic credentials of the bureaucracy in Brussels (Shore 2006); second, they revealed a resounding uncertainty as to the ultimate ends of constructing the elaborate machinery of the European Union (Walker 2004; Ferrara

2007; Fligstein 2009). These questions and criticisms continue to reverberate in Europeanist scholarship, media debates, and electoral campaigns and between the often mutually disconnected nodes of European civil society. Together with controversies concerning future enlargements, particularly the possible inclusion of Turkey (Robins 2003; Firat 2009; Kirişci 2006), they signal an enduring ambivalence concerning Europe's ultimate political and cultural identity as well as its boundaries. Yet despite such obstructions, close collaboration was increasingly seen as a matter of necessity demanding pragmatic policies and efficient governance.

This ambivalence on a political level imbues the practical aspects of day-to-day maintenance of the expanded EU with dilemmas and contradictions. I contend that, while there are unresolved political and philosophical questions regarding the precise contours and limits of the EU integration endeavor, in the course of its six-decade history it has acquired its own momentum, and the expansion of Schengen is one of its examples. The process of rebordering unfolds faster than, and to a large extent independently from, the political debate about constitutional treaties, the future of Europe, and the role and place of immigrants within it. Technical progress advances, yet the normative realm has not caught up. Thus one of the key strategies that the EU and national bureaucracies resort to is governance by exclusion, that is, a practice of integrating the national and the supranational by means of laws, processes, and institutions involved in the strict regulation of mobility and migration.

Securing the external borders of the Community while ensuring openness inside it is one of the many areas of EU activity where change occurs in a piecemeal manner, without a predetermined outcome and in response to variable pressures. The official blueprint for "strengthening freedom, security and justice in the EU" between 2005 and 2010, known as the Hague Programme, articulates the aims of border policy thus:

> The European Council considers that the common project of strengthening the area of freedom, security and justice is vital to securing safe communities, mutual trust and the rule of law throughout the Union. Freedom, justice, control at the external borders, internal security and the prevention of terrorism should henceforth be considered indivisible within the Union as a whole. (Hague Programme 2004: 4)[19]

Throughout this text, I probe the substance of this "indivisibility." What instruments, protocols, and techniques are being deployed to forge it? What material, living, and kinetic forms does it mask or legitimate? Which are the novel forms of managing populations and governing life undertaken in the name of freedom, justice, control, security, and prevention?

Defining the Ethnographic Object

During my first visits to the borderland in the summers of 2003 and 2004, in towns and villages and at the Poland-Ukraine border crossings, the social landscape revealed itself as one of patchy employment, haphazard migration, smuggling, and trafficking in people, a loosely organized underground economy distributing profit from the pushing of illegal goods, and intense consumption of tobacco and alcohol. But the ubiquitous blue EU flags with the circle of yellow stars, flown next to the white and red Polish flag on the Polish side of the border, emblazoned on electronic equipment, billboards, and glossy NGO pamphlets, signaled a new and unrehearsed order of intervention.

Borders in the Eastern bloc used to be patrolled by the military subservient to the geopolitical agenda of the Soviet Union. After 1989, following the model already adopted in the West, military patrols were replaced by dedicated border police. The members of these police forces had a reputation for colluding with the often illegal cross-border transactions that flourished as capitalism was taking root in the region. But with the impending EU enlargement and the need gradually to adjust the border to the standards of Schengen, what transpired on the roads, bridges, marshes, and forests of the Polish-Ukrainian borderland came to be seen as the business of all Europe.

Besides Poles and Ukrainians, other people began to appear in the borderland, usually on their way from somewhere farther east (Chechnya, Afghanistan, Pakistan, Central Asian Republics, China, Vietnam) to somewhere farther west (Germany, France, Spain, UK).[20] They crossed the new EU frontier as workers, refugees, asylum seekers, and economic migrants. Their encounters with the new regulations and their agents were decidedly different from those of the white, recognizably Slavic inhabitants of Poland, Ukraine, or the neighboring states. They were the ones subject to most careful surveillance as potential security threats, especially as post-9/11 fears elevated security to a high position on the EU agenda.

I had arrived in the borderland with the idea of studying the transformation of the Polish-Ukrainian frontier into an external border of the EU.

But this acceleration and intensification of traffic originating in locations near and far, as well as the refining of control now orchestrated by central European agencies, revealed the "awkward scale" of the phenomena I was confronted with (Comaroff and Comaroff 2003). A traditional single-sited ethnography did not seem adequate for the task. The decisive shifts reconfiguring life on the borderland, I observed, had less to do with the inherent dynamics of local relations between Poles and Ukrainians, and more with the larger transformations that have swept across Europe in the last twenty years. Given that the border between Poland and Ukraine was becoming enveloped in the larger process of rebordering, a different optic was required. Governance by exclusion, which I had begun to observe, demanded ethnographic study and analysis in the sites and contexts where it is crafted and where its effects are most profoundly experienced.

If contemporary borders are dislocated and ubiquitous, then to understand the contemporary rebordering of Europe from an ethnographic vantage point is to abandon the certitude of territorial borders as clearly locatable political artifacts, markers of sovereignty, and privileged locations for the articulation of difference. Instead, it requires conceptualizing them as key sites in a tentative, mutable, and situated regime, which proliferates the categories and regulations for the sorting out of people, things, and territory in Europe today.[21] To write the border is to attend to the specific places, agents, and practices whereby the sorting out is performed on a day-to-day basis. This includes but is not limited to the borderline itself. It is to interrogate the material and symbolic force of the emerging categories and practices of citizenship, entry rights, residence, and other forms of (non)being relative to boundaries (see Appendix on Methods).

An ethnography of the border regime must show not only how it administers legal status within populations so as to reproduce political communities, but also how in so doing, it produces new modes of conduct, self-discipline, and self-understanding. Exposing such novel ways in which individuals are made and become subjects of governmentality (Foucault 1991) sheds light on the operation of the border regime as a state-making machine. At the same time, it allows for an insight into the subtle and cumulative shifts informing the redefinition of citizenship, migrant subjectivity, and political communities. Following other scholars interested in the particular ways in which groups and individuals stake citizenship claims in the context of manmade disaster and political transition (Petryna 2002; Phillips 2005, 2008), migration (Fassin 2005; Hall 2002; Ong 1999; Ticktin 2006) or incarceration (Koch

2006), I join those who assert that the normative understanding of citizenship as membership in the political community must be complemented by an empirically and historically grounded account of its strategic and circumstantial uses, as well as its discontents.

Naturally, shifts in the uses of and exclusions from citizenship are framed not only by the changes which sweep across Europe, but also by globalization more generally. In her analysis of social regulation at this new conjuncture, Nancy Fraser has argued that it is important to recognize the historical differences between particular forms of governmentality. She points out that the organization of social relations in the conditions of post-1989 transnationalization relies on a different set of mechanisms from the ordering of older, nationally bounded societies of mass production and mass consumption:

> No longer exclusively a national matter . . . social ordering now occurs simultaneously at several different levels. . . . Thus although national ordering is not disappearing, it is in the process of being de-centered as its regulatory mechanisms become articulated (sometimes cooperatively, sometimes competitively) with those at other levels. What is emerging therefore is a new type of regulatory structure, a multilayered system of globalized governmentality whose full contours have yet to be determined. (Fraser 2003: 165)

It is within this system of globalized governmentality that the border regime operates. The key to analyzing profitably such multilayered arrangements "from a quasi-Foucaultian point of view" is to "identify the characteristic ordering mechanisms and political rationality of the emerging new mode of regulation" (Fraser 2003: 167). Cris Shore concurs, adding that what is particularly useful about the concept of governmentality, is that "it decouples 'government' from the idea of 'Government'" (Shore 2006: 721). It does so in much the same way as the idea of governance, which he defines as "a system in which power is located not in bounded, singular or sovereign states, but in rules, processes and multi-level institutions" (712). He prefers however, the Foucaultian notion of governmentality to analyze power in the European Union for its ability to draw attention to "the myriad ways in which governing takes place beyond the state, that is, the various technologies, actions and calculations that are used by authorities for the exercise of political rule" (721).

In this analysis of rebordering, I will rely on the narrower term of governance to refer to processes, rules, and institutional practices deployed in the production of new European inclusions and exclusions. I reserve the notion of governmentality to signal the larger dynamics that Fraser and other theorists write about. Ethnography, as a mode of engagement that privileges close encounter and attention to local and historical particularities of experience, is especially well suited for examining the different levels at which the global and the European are being constructed and governed. The following chapters explore this issue by attending to the vexed but under-scrutinized practice of "building Europe," not from its bureaucratic heart outward, but rather through the processes of enclosure within new boundaries (cf. Shore 2000). Since the ultimate political form and spatial boundaries of the European community do remain uncertain, my approach to understanding the project of continental unification has been to assume the existence—to paraphrase János Kornai—of an "actually existing EU."[22] This entails attending to EU integration as an assemblage productive of the new sociopolitical realities that frame the lives of some half billion people in the Old World.[23] The "actually existing EU" emerges not from formal legal state processes of harmonization and enlargement, but from the tensions and overlaps between national and supranational modes of knowing and governing territory and population. It is, as Douglas Holmes argued, "not a matter of 'studying up' or 'studying down,' but, rather, studying 'through' this emerging European space along dynamic tangents that link the abstract knowledge work of EU officialdom with countless domains of existential struggles and intimate experiences of Europeans" (Holmes 2003: 466).

The Rhetorics of Civilization

My interlocutors involved in adjusting Polish eastern borders to "European standards" (Border Guards, state officials, nongovernmental experts) often brought up the concept of civilization. I shall unpack these claims at the outset, for they illuminate key dynamics that I observed in the field. First, reforming border-related legislation and upgrading border services and surveillance were to represent "civilizational progress." In this context, to civilize is to modernize. It is to align with what is seen as a pinnacle of civilization, that is, Western European institutions and policies. Laws, procedures, bureaucratic and policing practices are things that lend themselves to "civilizing." Signing international treaties is an expression of the wish to appear "civilized" (Merry 2006). Orderly, polite, and efficient management of cross-border mobility was both a requisite condition and a sign of belonging to the elite club of politically and socially advanced European nations.

Second, in the wake of EU enlargement Poland's border was sometimes cast as the frontier of "European civilization." We must note that the notions of the *frontier of civilization* and of *civilizing the border* rely on two different implicit understandings of *civilization*. The phrase *frontier of civilization* (*granica cywilizacji*) carries distinctly Huntingtonian undertones, in the sense of implying that the line separating today's European Union from what once was the Soviet Union divides two essentially different "cultural groupings" (Huntington 1993). The idea that Poland's eastern border is a civilizational boundary that shields Western societies and their values from the barbarian East, or that Poland, with its staunch commitment to Latin Christianity, represents the last bastion of those values, is an old nationalist-messianic trope. It has been consistently mined, primarily but not exclusively on the Polish political right, for irrefutable evidence of Poland's European credentials. Hence the enthusiasm of some commentators for the reinforcement of this frontier as an external boundary of the EU (e.g., Najder 2003).

This ethnography, conducted on both sides of the new Euro-border, brings evidence that contradicts any such ideas of a sharp divide. The legal borderline has been reasserted and tightened, but it does not coincide with any decisive West-East chasm. Rather, it cuts across a contested terrain of ambiguous and competing allegiances to both East and West. *East* and *West* themselves are not monolithic or unequivocal categories here, but perpetual subjects of reinterpretation, strategic deployment, and ideological projection. It is one of the aims of this text to show that the contrasts and discontinuities articulated along the Polish-Ukrainian border are not reflections of any essential difference, civilizational, cultural, or otherwise. Whether expressed in national, religious, or other terms, any disparities are contingent products of perpetually contested histories.

History, especially that of the twentieth century, remains the key reservoir of images, ideas, and events that define the border region in the minds of both Poles and Ukrainians. But today the European Union is emerging as an increasingly more important force and symbol in the region. It is an object of desire and aspiration, and sometimes of fear and loathing. On the one hand, by its enlargement and neighborhood policies it is fostering pragmatic regional cooperation. Through formal integration (enlargement) and association activities (European Neighborhood Policy) it draws new members and their neighbors into its orbit (Seeberg 2010; Scott 2005; Kubicek

2007; see also Chapter 6). On the other hand it advances a bordering agenda that leaves no doubts as to who is in, and who is out. The EU attracts and repels; it cultivates proximity and creates distance. It is primarily these contemporary tensions that frame the stories of people, places, and institutions in the chapters that follow. But that doesn't mean that one can tell those stories without grounding them in more remote and still unsettled pasts, from the pre-1914 era of Central European empires through two World Wars and forty-odd years under Soviet domination. The centuries-long succession of changing rule, wars and revolts in the territory between Poland and Ukraine has marked it with fractures, discontinuities, and uneven development. These legacies live on and account for some of the specific local responses and challenges to the wider process of rebordering. I draw attention to such distinctive experiences throughout the book. I bring them together in Chapter 7 to consider whether the history of the Polish-Ukrainian borderland, with its intensely politicized memory battles and earnest attempts to imagine a better future, can inform a vernacular politics that would eschew the discourse of "civilizational frontiers" and help make sense of the European Union, rebordering, and the new divide that it engenders.

Meanwhile, the border can be described simultaneously as an external obstacle and, as the contemporary lives of Ukrainian migrant workers illustrate, a feature of both space and time. Through inducing personal adjustments and illicit practices—discussed at greater length in subsequent parts of this book—the border becomes a spatiotemporal object thoroughly integrated into personal life and the sense of self (Chapters 2 and 3). Law and policy might construct the border as tight and impermeable to unauthorized breach. However, I observe that it is better conceptualized as an interface for a range of interactions, encounters, and events. Positing that the eastern external boundary of the European Union is a sharp civilizational divide obliterates these subjective and intersubjective experiences and the social dynamics that they produce.

Nevertheless, the discourse of civilizational or otherwise essentialized difference will probably continue to inform the debate on what are the boundaries of Europe. Decisions on future possible enlargements—most notably the contested candidacy of Turkey for EU membership—will be made based on the legal, economic, technical, and bureaucratic preconditions laid out in the Copenhagen Criteria for EU membership, but also amid variously articulated claims of culture and civilization.[24] This book describes events and experiences that challenge the idea that "European civilization" might have a clearly demarcated border. Talk of European civilization makes sense only insofar as it refers loosely to an amorphous and hugely diverse area on the continent and beyond whose constituent parts are connected by shared stakes in certain ideas and traditions—and those ideas and traditions, the Enlightenment, Christianity, Judaism, democracy, or liberalism, are in any case perpetually contested and in many ways contradictory. The territory of the European Union is far from being coterminous with European civilization understood this way—for that to be the case it would have to include Ukraine, Georgia, Israel, and parts (if not all) of the United States, to name just a few heirs to civilizational ideas and ideals usually referred to as European.

Notwithstanding the import of the debates on what is Europe and where does it end, this ethnography shows that civilization in a third sense—not as an entity, but as a process—is indeed at stake in rebordering. Norbert Elias observed that the civilizing process "is a change of human conduct and sentiment in a quite specific direction" (Elias 1994: 365). In his landmark analysis of the sociogenesis of the concepts of culture and civilization and their role in state formation, he pointed out that in the course of the civilizing process,

> physical violence is confined to the barracks; and from these storehouses it breaks out only in extreme cases, in times of war or social upheaval, into individual life. As the monopoly of certain specialist groups it is normally excluded from the life of others; and these specialists, the whole monopoly organization of force, now stand guard only in the margin of social life as a control on individual conduct. (Elias 1994: 372)

There is no predetermined end to the civilizing process. According to Elias, it is neither a random coming and going of orderless patterns, nor a premeditated rational affair. But what remains constant (and crucial for this inquiry) is that it advances through piecemeal adjustments of rules and behaviors, with the unsightly and the abominable gradually banished from sight and from the direct experience of average citizens.

The echoes of such an Eliasian civilizing dynamic are very much at work in the rebordering of Europe. The EU bureaucracy takes great care to train and prepare its "specialist groups" for the task of containing and warehousing illegal immigrants, asylum seekers, and other unwanted pariahs, whose very presence within EU borders upsets racialized notions of Europeanness and is deemed to carry a potential for violence. The increasing specialization of border services, as well as the growing tendency to "process" immigrants outside the EU's borders, are about more effective and targeted limiting of their access to European territory and resources (Chapters 5 and 6). But it would be a mistake to take the claims of EU border and immigration policy at face value. The common immigration and asylum systems which are currently under construction are not simply pragmatic measures for the protection of the EU market, nor common-sense steps toward increased security. At the same time it is not adequate either to conceive of them, as some critics of "fortress Europe" do, solely as a repressive bureaucratic design for the distribution of hardship and injustice. Rather, they are a product of uneasy compromises, an evolving and contested machinery designed to meet the political, social, and cultural needs of the European body politic (Chapter 4).

Rebordering does not guarantee protection from external threats, however defined. It is not about constructing a new iron curtain, or "a fortress of impenetrable rules" (Riabchuk 2005). This study shows that it engenders governance by exclusion whose aims reach beyond the policing of borders, and encompass the entire realm of relationships between EU citizens and noncitizens, as well as their connection to territory. It is, however, far from being a total regime; it is rather one under perpetual construction which responds to shifting political agendas, and which distributes its benefits, hardships, and violence, physical as well as symbolic, in a highly differentiated manner. It introduces selective and specialized modes of granting legal recognition and economic opportunities associated with legal status, while neglecting important manifestations of postsocialist and other mobilities. Viewing it solely as a tool of repression would lead to overlooking the multiple ways its designers actively engage with the changing realities of transnationality, the democratically and undemocratically expressed social anxieties concerning otherness, and in which they respond to existing legal regimes, including international human rights conventions.

This engagement occurs on multiple levels. Brussels policymakers, in their work of crafting the border regime, attempt to address an array of divergent needs and end up embracing conflicting and contradictory agendas. On the one hand, they aim to harmonize EU approaches; on the other they seek to leave a significant degree of autonomy to states. In this way individual governments are bound by shared legal standards, while they can exercise their own approaches to regulating the influx of labor. They can introduce special programs to invite workers (both high- and low-skilled) for temporary or permanent employment in specific sectors of the economy, while limiting competition in others. They can pander to politically influential anti-immigrant constituencies by promising restrictive enforcement of asylum and immigration laws, while remaining bound by existing human rights commitments that their countries have signed (such as the 1951 Convention on the Status of Refugees). In practice, both EU authorities and national politicians and bureaucrats straddle the thin line between respecting the humanist spirit of rights recognized as fundamental and inventing new ways of simulating, deferring, and externalizing concern for those rights.

The chapters that follow take the reader through the various dimensions of rebordering described in this Introduction, from the lives of migrant workers to the daily duties of border guards and the dilemmas of officials and nominally independent experts. They reflect my methodological approach, which I think of as ethnographic zooming in and out—from close focus on particular lives affected by rebordering to a panoramic picture of national strategies of Europeanization. Above all, it is my purpose to show how headline-making European issues—in this case the restricting of immigration into Europe—play out in one corner of the newly expanded Union, and how the people who live there, steeped in their distinctive history, selectively affirm and vigorously contest "the area of freedom, security and justice" assumed to be in the interest of everyone across the twenty-seven member states.

Chapter 2

Civilizing the Postsocialist Frontier?

[Borderlands are places where] . . . personal histories . . .
intersect the major currents of twentieth-century European
experience: nationalism and state building, the two world wars, the
confrontation between fascism and socialism, the Cold War and its
end, and troubling questions where Eastern Europe . . . belongs in
a union of European states.

—Pamela Ballinger, on the borderland between
Italy and Slovenia in Istria

It was summer 2003 when I first arrived in the border area between Poland and Ukraine. In June that year, in a two-day accession referendum, Poles had voted overwhelmingly in favor of joining the European Union.[1] The country was gearing up to become an EU member state, and in Warsaw and other major cities "Europe" was the talk of the town. But I was interested in finding out what people thought of these developments in more peripheral locations, especially in the neglected and impoverished eastern borderland that was to become the external boundary of the expanded EU—a place where it would meet the former republics of the former Soviet Union. I had been following the media portrayals of the area as Poland's untamed "wild east" and the arguments casting the eastern border as a civilizational boundary dividing Europe from the ostensible chaos of the post-Soviet world. I had become interested in the counternarrative that Poland and its eastern neighbors had a fraternal connection, and in the Polish foreign policy discourse of a "strategic partnership" with Ukraine. Politicians, pundits, and assorted policy experts worried that the European Union was about to sever the emerging connections by drawing a "new iron curtain."

I was curious how these different but coexisting definitions of the situation reverberated in towns and villages along the border and what would happen to the vibrant traffic between Poland and Ukraine that had been growing year after year since the opening of this border in the aftermath of the Soviet Union's collapse and the declaration of Ukrainian independence in 1991. I wanted to know what local people—on both sides of the emerging divide— were making of the looming imposition of a visa regime for Ukrainians to enter Poland and, more generally, of the government's announcements that the frontier would be *uszczelniona* (sealed) to protect the territory of the European Union from the expected surge of unwanted immigration.

At the time of my first visit to the Polish-Ukrainian borderland (*pogranicze*) I didn't yet know what I would come to fully grasp later: that the border as a physical location is only one of the many sites where the rebordering of Europe was taking place. I traveled from Przemyśl (Peremyshl in Ukrainian), a town on the Polish side, via the pedestrian crossing in Medyka/ Shehyni, to Lviv in Ukraine, and back, a few days later, on the train via the small border town of Rava Russkaya. What struck me the most was the contrast between the rhetoric of EU-driven modernization, order, and efficiency resonating from all corners of Polish media and officialdom, and the lively, and at times desperate, chaos of the border crossings and disorderly town and village marketplaces that seemed to escape any form of control.

The border itself teemed with cargo and passenger traffic. At the road crossings, there were cars, buses, and trucks, loaded with people and goods, making a continuous two-way flow. The ubiquitous TIR semi-trucks carried cargo between Poland and Ukraine, Europe and Asia.[2] At all times of night and day they formed long lines on both sides of the border, giving the multinational crowd of drivers an opportunity to socialize and conduct more or less shady business as they awaited control for an average of ten or twelve hours at a time. These vehicles were subject to thorough scrutiny. Many were innocent transports of construction materials, furniture, or other basic stock. But, as I soon found out, at times the border guards would discover people being clandestinely transported across the border in the TIRs' massive containers, or underneath their chassis. Customs authorities regularly seized contraband worth hundreds of thousands of Polish *złoty* concealed, in highly creative ways, in the trucks' nooks and crannies. Criminal organizations found a well of opportunities to exploit. Using local freight and wholesale companies across the continent as fronts, the smuggling business spanned transnational networks where "violent entrepreneurs" (Volkov 2002; see also Ledeneva 2006; Humphrey 2002) in collusion with state agents contributed to the accumulation of capital that fueled Europe's and Eurasia's shadow economy.

Next to the grand smugglers, there were cigarette runners, who marked their trails with discarded empty cigarette cartons and tangled bundles of tape they used to affix contraband to their bodies. There were the meat and onion pushers, keen students of the laws of supply and demand, who would buy bulk in Poland and sell retail in Ukraine.[3] These people of the market, the majority of them female, did not work on their own accord. They were also entangled in hierarchically organized networks where they did the legwork for middlemen and their bosses who owned the wholesale establishments and reaped the bulk of the profits.

At the pedestrian crossing in Medyka/Shehyni both Poles and Ukrainians walked across the border several times a day, usually carrying cigarettes and alcohol from Ukraine to Poland. As I stood with them in the hours-long line, one elderly man showed me his passport filled tightly page after page with dated border stamps. "I don't need a calendar, this is my calendar!" he said, and joked that the border guards miss him on days he doesn't show up. The checkpoint's opening and closing hours dictated the rhythm of daily life in the towns and villages adjacent to the border. Most of the men and women populating the crossings would show up, as if to work, in the morning and make a return crossing twice or three times until early evening, openly bringing the legal allowance of alcohol and tobacco each time (one carton of cigarettes and one liter of spirits), and additionally two or three times that amount concealed in their clothes and on their bodies. The difference in prices and taxation allowed for potential profit margins of up to 100 or even 150 percent on resale on the black market, which far outweighed the risk of being caught with the contraband.

In the bathrooms and waiting rooms at the checkpoints and bus and train stations I watched women in loose, layered outfits hide plastic baggies filled with 90 proof spirit under their skirts and in their brassieres. Later, the alcohol would be decanted to plastic soda bottles and sold clandestinely at markets or to illegal purveyors. Packs of cigarettes were removed from cartons, wrappings discarded and strewn about. Women of all ages, who appeared to make up the majority of this itinerant population, attached individual packs to their legs and waists with cellophane tape. Men tried the same technique or stuffed them in their knee-high socks. No one made a particular effort to be discreet; everyone was doing the same thing and there seemed to be no shame or danger in it. Occasionally, in an unruly line or on a crowded train a baggie filled with spirit would burst. The smell and squealing of the person whose skin was burning from the alcohol would attract no more than passing laughter.

The people engaged in this petty contraband were commonly referred to as *mrówki* (ants) in Polish and *chovnyky* (shuttles) in Ukrainian. Border guards and customs officers treated them with impatience and sometimes contempt, but it was an open secret that many extracted substantial payoffs from the flow of this traffic. This in turn contributed to the bad reputation of border services in the eastern districts.[4] The media at the time often broadcast sensationalist reports about "anarchy" and "corruption" on the Polish-Ukrainian frontier, which contributed to the perception of the area as the "wild east," and justified the need to "clean up" and "civilize" it, and to "tighten" the border. This form of contraband, however, although it constituted the most visible symptom of the economic woes of the region, was only one of the many facets of the traffic and movement that rapidly intensified on the borderland in the years after the Soviet Union's demise. From the early 1990s on, tourism and business travel—previously all but impossible—began to mix with long- and short-term semi-legal and unauthorized migration, asylum seeking, and trafficking in people. On the eve of EU expansion, the efforts to regulate and control all this movement started to clash with the needs and desires of people inhabiting both sides of the border.

People's experience of the region's complicated history supplied the terms for the discussion of the changes on the border and the consequences of EU enlargement. For example, while many of my Ukrainian interlocutors (day traders, migrant workers, migrant advocates, and some officials) feared the crafting of a new iron curtain and compared Evrosoyuz (the European Union) to Radiansky Soyuz (the Soviet Union), people I spoke to in Poland believed the new restrictions would not be quite as rigid. "The new border is not an iron curtain," I was repeatedly told, as my informants struggled for apt metaphors. "It is a velvet one," insisted one NGO professional involved in supporting Polish-Ukrainian business exchange. An EU grant administrator emphasized that the border would remain permeable and claimed that it is not a curtain at all but a *firanka*, a dainty lace drape. A different and altogether less glamorous take was offered by one elderly man engaged in a small tobacco-smuggling operation. "It's going to be," he exclaimed to me, "a fence with holes in it!" These perceptions indicated to me early on that all the actors involved or caught up in rebordering had trouble with thinking about borders. They were exposed to contradictory claims about the border's openness and closure—assurances that on the one hand "legitimate" traffic would continue to flow, while "illegal" movement would cease. Sensing that clear-cut distinctions would be difficult to make, they were grappling, in their own ways, with the tension between the frontier's new role as a marker of Europe's definite limits, and that of a gateway for the flow of people and goods between a "here" and an "over there."

From the "Belt of Mixed Peoples" to Nation-States

But discontent with frontiers and the constraints they impose was nothing new in the history of this region. Less than a hundred years before EU's expansion to Eastern Europe, another pivotal moment in European history and politics generated a different set of ideas and practices of delineating borders in the area. In the early twentieth century, at the end of World War I and the time of the Paris Peace Treaties, European politicians referred to Eastern Europe from the Baltic to the Balkans as "the belt of mixed peoples" (Arendt 1951: 271; see also Hobsbawm 1990). They struggled mightily to develop a formula that would restrain the freshly awakened competing nationalisms of the multitude of ethnic groups previously contained within the Austro-Hungarian, Tsarist, and Ottoman empires. The area of today's eastern Poland and western Ukraine was as representative a stretch of this "belt" as any. It was home to five main ethnic groups—Poles, Ukrainians, Jews, Germans, and Russians—and several smaller ones, such as Gypsies, Armenians, and Tatars.[5]

The post-World War I decision concerning Poland's eastern boundary, reached in 1921 in the Treaty of Riga between Poland, Soviet Russia, and Soviet Ukraine, which ended the Polish-Soviet war of 1920, was a result of a compromise that ultimately satisfied neither Polish nationalists, nor the minorities, nor the Soviet Union. The Treaty settled the interwar eastern Polish boundary approximately 200 kilometers east of the 2011 borderline. "It reflected," according to historian Kate Brown, "no demographic nor political realities, but rather an uneasy truce between warring parties" (2004: 7). Consequently, in the subsequent two decades, the Polish-Ukrainian borderland changed hands five times, before in 1945 Poland's eastern border was demarcated in Yalta roughly along the line of the river Bug (pronounced *Boogh*) and the western slopes of the Carpathians.[6] Thus most of what constituted the historical borderland between Polish and Russian territories was included in the Ukrainian, Belarusian, and Lithuanian Soviet Socialist Republics, and since 1991 it makes up the western territories of states that have constituted themselves after the Soviet Union's collapse.

It is this repeatedly shifting status that prompted Brown to call this "amorphous corridor between historic Poland and Russia" a "no place," by which she means "a place that has never been a political polity nor possessed any historical notoriety" (2004: 1). Instead, as she and other historians have amply documented, this "no place" seems to have been cursed by a relentless succession of violence, wrought by competing empires, nation-states, and nationalist armies that saw it as a proper part of their domains and that struggled to establish viable rule over its incomprehensible mosaic of ethnicities, languages, and religions. Timothy Snyder zeroes in on the violence and offers a different name for this area. In his remarkable history of the political mass murder committed by Hitler and Stalin, he calls it "the bloodlands"— the place where "in the middle of Europe, in the middle of the twentieth century, the Nazi and Soviet regimes murdered some fourteen million people" (Snyder 2010: vii).

Part of the legacy of Central European conflicts that have deeply scarred the borderland is the difficulty of demarcating the boundaries of this "no place" itself. Snyder places the bloodlands between central Poland and western Russia, from the areas around Gdańsk, Poznań, and Kraków in the west, to those around St. Petersburg, Smolensk, and Kharkiv in the east (Snyder 2010: 2). The Polish term for the eastern region of historical Poland, Kresy, roughly translates as "margins" and implies an unspecified distance, the line on the horizon. Depending on who is speaking, Kresy can mean Volhynia and Galicia, the districts which in the nineteenth century were peripheries respectively of the Russian and the Austro-Hungarian empires and, after 1918, of the Polish state, or it could include the entire territory of western Ukraine up to Zaporozhia—the eastern boundary of the historic Polish-Lithuanian Commonwealth that ceased to exist in the seventeenth century. Either way, Kresy falls within the bloodlands, and between the early 1930s and mid-1940s they were the scene of shooting, gassing, group executions, and mass starvation.

Today, however, most of the historical Kresy is western Ukraine, and the term itself has proved incendiary. Tinged with nationalist sentiment and connoting Polish nostalgia for eastern territories lost to the Soviet Union, it has

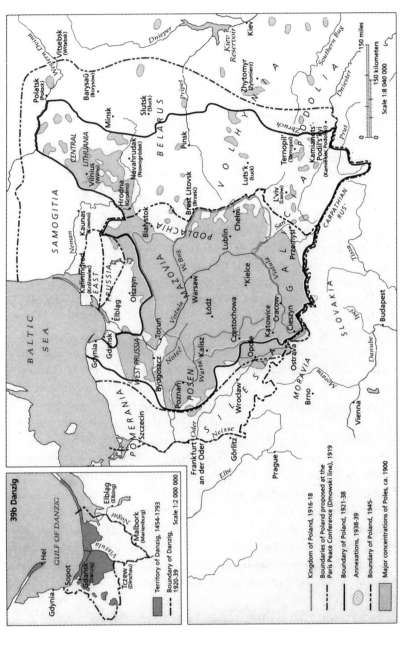

Figure 2. The changing borders of Poland. Paul R Magocsi, *Historical Atlas of Central Europe* (Seattle: University of Washington Press, 2002); reprinted by permission of the University of Washington Press.

become, as I show in Chapter 7, too divisive for the era of Polish-Ukrainian strategic partnership. Instead, politicians, NGOs, and think tanks focus on what has been reframed as "border area" or "border zone." Bracketing history, they see a region in need of development, an arena for investment and infrastructural, social, and cultural projects.[7]

But the dry language and rigid geography of contemporary governmental reports, EU programs, and NGO activities coexist with a complicated politics of memory, where all boundaries are contested and each patch of land is the object of somebody's deep emotional investment because it carries the bones of loved ones or because it had soaked up ancestors' blood. Overgrown cemeteries with sinking graves, ruins of churches, synagogues, houses, and farms, wartime memorials, and abandoned military installations are a ubiquitous feature of the landscape and a focal point of many people's accounts of the past. Most ruins in the area—be they of manors, places of worship, or garrisons—can also be read as an ambivalent record of the specific forms of exercising power practiced by a succession of overlords. Thus, as I have emphasized elsewhere, it is productive to view the contemporary borderland as a palimpsest where new modes of living overlap with material and mental residues of old systems of rule and suppression (Szmagalska-Follis 2008; also Huyssen 2003).[8]

During World War I, the Russian Revolution, and the Polish-Soviet war of 1920 the borderland was an active theater of war and an object of the Red Army's conquest, loss, and reconquest. After the Riga Treaty, the area became the scene of constant tensions between the majority population and national minorities—a problem that was handled differently on each side of the divide, and one that was a constant source of destabilization until 1939. That year's Soviet incursion into the borderland was followed by the Nazi occupation, from 1941 until 1944.[9] However, after the German defeat in the battle of Stalingrad (1943), the Soviets pushed back and recaptured most of their previously lost territories. In the late 1940s the area was divided anew. By then, subsequent victors had systematically and purposefully destroyed its fantastically complex ethnic, linguistic, and religious diversity.

In the early years of World War II, the Soviets deported most of the historical borderland's Poles and Germans. The Nazis annihilated the region's vast and vibrant Jewish population. In 1943 Polish and Ukrainian nationalist armies entered into a protracted conflict whose objective was ethnic purification and seizing control over contested land. In 1943, in the villages of Volhynia, UPA partisans perpetrated mass killings of Polish inhabitants. The numbers of victims are contested. Such historians as Timothy Snyder (2003), Yaroslav Hrytsak (2000) and Grzegorz Motyka (2008, 2011) offer the estimate of 50,000 to 60,000 dead.[10] These events, and the subsequent Polish retaliation, which is said to have taken another two to three thousand dead (Motyka 2008), represented a grave escalation of the mutual hostility on the borderland, which had been intensifying since the launch of the 1930s policies of the interwar Polish state designed to intimidate the Ukrainian minority.[11] (I shall discuss the enduring implications of these events in Chapter 7.) The attempts of the nationalist fighters on both sides to settle the territorial limits of their respective future nation-states were as tragically brutal as they were futile, given that the final shape of the postwar map of Central Eastern Europe was ultimately not up to them. Poland's territorial outline changed beyond recognition after its boundaries were shifted 200 kilometers to the west as a result of agreements between the Allied Powers in Yalta and Teheran. Between 1945 and 1948, large-scale forced resettlements of Poles into the newly established Polish People's Republic and Ukrainians into the Soviet Union completed the dogged, but up until that point unsuccessful, effort of subsequent regimes to realign national populations with national territories.[12] Finally, having, in the Polish case, achieved a near-perfect national homogeneity,[13] the new Communist authorities considered the problem of ethnic minorities solved. At the cost of mass murder, immense suffering, and destruction the newly divided territory was molded for Soviet governance finally unthreatened by constant ethnic unrest.

"Whatever might be said about the settlement of 1945," says Norman Davies, "it is as final as any such political arrangement can be" (1982: 517). At a time of his writing in the late 1970s, the settlement he had in mind was the establishment of the Polish People's Republic located between the German Democratic Republic, Czechoslovakia, and the USSR. So much for finality—none of those countries exist any more. Between 1989 and 1992 the GDR ceased to exist as it became reunited with West Germany; the USSR fell apart; Czechoslovakia peacefully split in two; and the Polish People's Republic reconstituted itself as Rzeczpospolita Polska, the Polish Republic. However, the territorial boundaries between those refurbished states remained the same, as did, by and large, the composition of their populations. In other words, the political system installed in Eastern Europe in 1945 proved anything but final. But the ethnic and territorial divisions marked out in the mid-twentieth century outlived the politics that created them in the first place. Davies's remarks from three decades ago remain broadly correct:

[The] finality does not derive from the wisdom of its perpetrators, but from their ruthlessness. Frontier problems were not so much solved as destroyed. Throughout Eastern Europe, national minorities who may or may not have been responsible for intercommunal tensions, were physically removed. From the point of view of modern governments . . . the result is extremely tidy. But the human cost was terrible. (Davies 1982: 517)

Peculiar Neighborhood

Over the forty-plus years that followed the 1945 settlement, the population of today's borderland inhabited two neighboring socialist states. It was a peculiar neighborhood, however, and a distinctly unfriendly border. Barbed-wired and heavily patrolled, to both sides it suggested the definite spatial limit of their world, rather than a meeting point of two apparently allied countries. The division ossified over the years, further distancing the two already hostile populations. Michał, a Polish translator of Ukrainian literature who guided me during my first trip across the border in 2003, recalled a mid-1990s encounter with a Polish border guard that captured the lasting sense of void projected onto the other side. As Michał approached the pedestrian crossing during a trip to Lviv and it became apparent to the guard that he was a bona fide traveler, not a contraband-carrying *mrówka*, the guard reportedly asked, *A po co pan tam idzie? Panie, przecież tam nic nie ma!* [What are you going there for? Sir, but there's nothing there!].

Theorist of boundaries Fredrik Barth encourages the following thought experiment:

Reflect for a moment on the scene of two English neighbors, conversing over the garden fence. The territorial boundary of their properties separates them but it gives shape to their interaction in a way that I suspect positively enables it, since it frames and defines the nature of the opportunity. Thanks to that boundary, the conversation can proceed in a more carefree and relaxed way, and be elaborated and pursued with less risk of other entanglements—a consideration that may loom large in shaping the role performances of neighbors. (Barth 2000: 28)

Reconnecting what has been separated is a pervasive human tendency, Barth argues. The neighborly fence as a site of circumscribed but productive potential interactions (what he calls "affordances") is one of the expressions of boundaries as connections. It can be extrapolated to uncontested borders of nation-states in times of peace, when trade and other forms of exchange can thrive precisely because a clear boundary separates their two domains (Barth 2000: 29). Although one might think that a shared political doctrine and the ostensible "brotherhood" between Poland and the Soviet Union would have made for such an amicable neighborly fence between them, nothing was farther from the truth. Soviet institutions enforcing territorial boundaries were permeated with the paranoia of external infiltration and dedicated to ensuring and sustaining isolation.[14] As Andrea Chandler put it, "Soviet Union's leaders knew that control of knowledge, information, and contact with the outside world was power" (1998: 5).

Implementing the post-Yalta territorial order meant that long-established social and economic ties between towns and communities were severed and transportation links cut off. Cities—in particular the once thriving Lviv (Lwów in Polish, Lemberg in Yiddish and German)—lost their organic connection to the surrounding areas, now separated by the border (Krok and Smętkowski 2006: 180). While declarations of Polish-Soviet friendship were an obligatory part of state propaganda and political ritual throughout the socialist era, the actual intergovernmental and bureaucratic relationships were suffused with mutual historically sedimented distrust. This reciprocal hostility was rooted in the history of Tsarist relations with the Polish monarchy and nobility, including the nineteenth-century uprisings against Russian rule, and bolstered by the Polish-Soviet war of 1920 with its potent anti-Bolshevik and anti-Polish propaganda on respective sides.[15] The undercurrent of distrust carried over to the socialist period, hardly ameliorated by the joint fight, in the latter years of the war, of the procommunist Polish People's Army and the Red Army against Hitler. Vast segments of Polish society, after all, remained more or less openly loyal to the prewar bourgeois-democratic idea of Polish statehood. Aware of that, the Soviet leadership, particularly under Stalin, but later as well, regarded even the Polish Communist Party and the People's Army with enduring suspicion, to say nothing of institutions that had survived the war, such as the Church or universities.

The practices of border maintenance and control represented very well the contradiction between political alliance on the one hand, and isolation on the other. As far as the Soviet authorities were concerned, Soviet citizens had no business traveling to Poland, save for the selected few sent on Party-approved missions. Nor were the Poles welcome in Soviet territory, unless their identities and itineraries were thoroughly vetted by designated security services. The actual reasons why people would want to travel—to reunite with family or visit graves or sites of religious observance—were politically inconvenient and would have served as unwelcome reminders both of the erstwhile connectedness and of the violence perpetrated on the borderland populations. Such contacts were thus banned outright or made maximally difficult, for fear that they would stir up sentiments that could unsettle the socialist order.

In 2005 in Korczmin, a village directly on the frontier, I witnessed an emotional cross-border religious gathering of precisely the kind that would have been anathema to the Communist authorities. On an August Sunday a procession of Ukrainian Greek Catholics came to the Polish side of the border to celebrate the Assumption of Mary at the recently restored seventeenth-century wooden Greek Catholic church.[16] At the time of dividing Polish and Soviet territory, the church remained in Poland, about 600 meters from the actual boundary line. Most of the Ukrainians who would have attended it and kept the parish alive were resettled to the other side, separated by coiled barbed wire from their place of worship. The church and the adjacent cemetery with its nineteenth-century graves fell into disrepair, ignored for decades by both preservationists and the Roman Catholic inhabitants of Korczmin. It wasn't until the 1990s that, thanks to the efforts of the Greek Catholic parish in the nearby city of Lublin, an important cultural center for the Ukrainian minority in Poland, the church was gradually restored. Finally, starting in 2003 Ukrainians from the other side were allowed to make an annual cross-border pilgrimage to celebrate the Assumption. Local authorities sponsor on the occasion a day of Polish and Ukrainian festivities with concerts, food and drink, and educational events designed to promote mutual understanding. For one day in August, local border guard units establish a makeshift checkpoint to enable Ukrainian pilgrims to cross the border and carry an icon of Mary between the church on one side and a holy spring on the other.

The festival I witnessed attracted more than 1,500 people, some of them children at the time the border was drawn. At the checkpoint I watched an elderly woman being led across the border by her twenty-three-year-old granddaughter Svetlana. It was a sheer coincidence that I had met Svetlana previously in Warsaw as part of a circle of Ukrainian students who support themselves by cleaning in private homes. She was enrolled in a part-time psychology program at a Catholic college and hoped to return to Ukraine and become a primary school counselor. At the time she was very critical of what she referred to as the Polish "consumerist life." She was affirming values other than those promoted in the course of postsocialist economic reforms, telling me that church and family life, having "borscht after mass on Sunday," and baking cakes were all very important to her, and how she and her room-mates (she lived with two other young Ukrainian women) tried to recreate these elements of home life in Warsaw. She had also commented bitterly on the Polish stereotype of the Ukrainka as someone who is so desperate for money that she would obediently agree to any "dirty work"; my notes from that conversation say that she had declined to discuss the specifics, but had alluded to being ill-treated by her employers.

Now that I ran into her in Korczmin, she was dressed in her Sunday best, wearing stylish sunglasses and walking with a confidence that was in striking contrast to the body language of the seniors in the queue. Svetlana's grand-mother's hands were shaking as she handed her brand-new Ukrainian pass-port to the guard, not looking up at him as she did so. The guard tried to make a lighthearted joke about the "virgin" passport but it fell on deaf ears. Having been one of the resettled former inhabitants of the area, the woman was overcome by emotions and eager to get to the church. Svetlana was sur-prised but pleased to see me. "Now you can see for yourself," she said as the queue moved on, "that we're not all about dirty work. We are spiritual people with faith and traditions." She was taking this symbolically powerful event as an occasion to reinforce the point that religious experience and belonging to a community and place were key elements of her identity. She was again rebuking the pervasive stereotype of Ukrainians in Poland as purveyors of the "dirty" labor of maids and cleaners, but in Korczmin that reality seemed distant. Inviting the Ukrainian pilgrims to Korczmin for the Assumption sig-naled a momentary symbolic suspension of the new border regime and of the economic order it protects, and the day of rituals, prayers, and festivities was the recreation of an ultimately ahistorical utopia where the village belonged to both Poles and Ukrainians and they belonged to it.

In Korczmin and elsewhere, a decade and a half after the Soviet Union ceased to exist, people continued to recall vividly its border security system, point out to me its material remnants, and speak of the personal, spiritual, and material deprivation they endured in its shadow. In Shehyni, the village on the Ukrainian side of the hectic Medyka/Shehyni pedestrian crossing, I once talked with a group of three women in their forties and fifties who used to work on a now defunct collective farm. Today they draw their income from running cigarettes across the border. On a November afternoon, my research assistant Andriy and I were invited for *chay* (tea) into the front room of a modest one-story house. The women, Halyna (the hostess) and her friends Ivona and Khrystyna, talked one over the other, interspersing their accounts of today's hardships and their speculations about the future of Ukraine with memories of the Soviet past. Khrystyna mentioned relatives in Poland, so we asked about visiting them before 1991.

> *Khrystyna*: It wasn't possible. [In our *kolkhoz*] you could pretend that you were going *turystychno* (as a tourist), on your annual vacation. They [the local officials] would tell you then exactly what to say [at the border]: "*tak mayete kazaty; tak mayete kazaty*" (this is what you have to say, this is what you have to say). God forbid you said anything about relatives. But if you wanted to see the sights [in Poland], they would sometimes let you go.
> *Ivona*: I had this neighbor who sometimes went. She was a secretary in the office [of the *kolkhoz*]. She would get this *lystek* (paper) that she was on delegation. For two days, three days and back home! And she went and she brought from Poland for me this cream for the face, *Gala* [laughter]. We didn't have that.
> *Khrystyna*: *Vlada* [the authorities] didn't want anybody going abroad. Only they [the officials] could go, not us.

The women recalled seeing *soldaty* (soldiers) in their village all the time, harassing people when they dug up potatoes in the fields too close to the border, or when they picked berries in the woods. The borderline used to be heavily militarized. Fences, barbed wire, underwater barriers, belts of plowed ground, and nuclear military facilities marked the perimeter of the empire. Observers of political life in the Soviet bloc commented on the obsessive nature of this fencing—as Ryszard Kapuściński noted in 1967, "keeping in mind that wherever it is technically possible, these borders were and are marked with thick coils of barbed wire (I saw such barriers on the borders with Poland, China, and Iran) and that this wire, because of the dreadful climate, quickly deteriorates and therefore must often be replaced across hundreds, no, thousands, of kilometers, one can assume that a significant portion of the Soviet metallurgical industry is devoted to producing barbed wire" (Kapuściński 1995: 85).

Wiring people in was part of a larger strategy. KGB-supervised military units protected the border against foreign attack, infiltration, and westward escapes of Soviet citizens. "Here we used to have the so-called *systiema* [Russian for system]," one Polish border guard in his forties told me as he was showing me around a particularly busy checkpoint on the Bug. He was referring to the now dismantled combination of barbed-wire fencing, observation towers, and plowed ground for easier tracking of human traces established on the Polish side, following the Soviet model. He recalled that

> people weren't allowed anywhere near it, and if they'd trespass they'd have to show ID, they'd be arrested or shot at. Now, Bug is a very clean river with lots of fish so it was very inconvenient for anglers [laughter]. . . . Until 1989 the bridge was closed to traffic. We opened it only for official delegations, but that was always a serious matter.

The *systiema* stretched along all sections of the border, including river banks and mountains. By the late 1950s barriers were erected on 90 percent of its length (Dominiczak 1997: 355). Few vehicles ever passed through the checkpoints, and one modest booth sufficed where today cars and trucks pass through in multiple lanes.

The isolation persisted despite the fact that the Polish-Soviet border was obviously not where the iron curtain was located. Berlin's Checkpoint Charlie and the Elbe were several hundred kilometers to the west. The stakes in crossing the Soviet-Polish border were relatively low compared to the border between the two German states. But the experience of living up against an impermeable fence, for the inhabitants of places like Korczmin or Shehyni, was similar to that of the people of the East German village of Kella, so compellingly portrayed by Daphne Berdahl as the place "where the world ended." (1999) In those and other villages (and also on the borders between Czechoslovakia and the USSR, and Hungary and the USSR),[17] the reality and materiality of the border was part of everyday life, (Berdahl 1999: 146; see also Pelkmans 2006) not just a concrete manifestation of Soviet politics, but also a constant reminder of the places and people on the other side to which access had been cut off.

Reopening

This closure and separation was undone only in 1991, when Ukraine (to the horror of some Polish nationalists), became independent. Poland immediately recognized its independence (it was, in fact, the first country to do so), and by May 1992 a new treaty had been signed by presidents Lech Wałęsa and Leonid Kravchuk regulating transit between the Polish Republic and Ukraine. These actions were diplomatically important, in that they signified a fresh start in Polish-Ukrainian relations. In being the first to grant independent Ukraine political recognition, the postsocialist Polish state not only sought to disown its lingering prewar reputation for imperial and colonial politics toward its eastern neighbor, but also affirmed the notion that, due to the proximity of the Russian Federation, it is in Poland's interest to border on a sovereign Ukraine. It was also the beginning of official post-1989 Polish eastern foreign policy, involving active support for democratic reforms and the pro-Western orientation in Ukrainian politics. (This strategically justified, but pitfall-ridden approach found its ripest expression in Polish support for the Orange Revolution in 2005, as discussed in Chapter 7).

The new geopolitics went hand in hand with what might be termed a new geopoetics (King 2000), that is an alternative expression of space and place through imagining the borderland as a quintessentially Central European space.[18] In this elite take on the Polish-Ukrainian (and Polish-Belarusian and Polish-Lithuanian) borderland, the area was no longer a forgotten Soviet "no place," but rather an inspiring, even enchanted land, rich with traces of lost cultural diversity waiting to be rediscovered, memorialized, and commodified (see Chapter 7).

While the liberal political and cultural elites were rediscovering and redefining the region, and inevitably clashing with the also reenergized nationalists, especially as they stumbled upon such conflict-generating subjects as anti-Semitism and Polish, Jewish, and Ukrainian wartime victimhood, the border was opened to a free flow of traffic. Inhabitants of the borderland promptly seized the opportunity. No visas were required of citizens of either country, and Ukrainian visitors needed only a passport with a tourist voucher or an invitation from a Polish citizen.[19] New border crossings were established and began to operate around the clock. A lax approach to border controls contributed to the rapid increase of traffic. Statistics from that period show that foreign arrivals on all borders in the first postsocialist decade grew more than tenfold—from 8.2 million in 1989 to 88.6 million in 1999.[20] The comings and goings of Ukrainians and other citizens of the former Soviet Union were largely responsible for those staggering numbers (Iglicka 2001: 507).[21]

This movement of Ukrainians to Poland, and to a lesser extent of Poles to Ukraine, was firmly bound up with the post-Soviet economic collapse and the concurrent emergence of the early postsocialist free market economy. In the early 1990s, when Ukraine was suffering hyperinflation and mass unemployment, petty cross-border trade offered decent profits and constituted a plausible survival strategy. One study conducted among citizens of the former Soviet Union (not just Ukrainians, but also Belarusians and inhabitants of more remote former republics) in the mid-1990s in Medyka and Terespol, on the Polish-Belarusian border, showed that participants in this trade who were at all employed earned salaries between $25 and $230 per month, depending on profession and country of origin. Meanwhile, net profits from one trip to Poland to sell inexpensive goods, mostly leftover products of Soviet manufacturing, such as household items, tools, and toiletries, which were successfully competing in local markets with more expensive western imports, amounted to 40–50 percent of expenditures, averaging about $750 (Iglicka 1999).[22] As sociologist Claire Wallace observed of this trade, "In understanding the economic well-being of the population, we should also take into account the economic situation of the population as people perceive it" (2002: 606) According to her research, in 1998, only 8 percent of Ukrainians believed that they could get by on their incomes. Even if people had jobs, they often were not paid for months at a stretch, and in any case their wages fell far behind inflation (607).

In the years following the opening of the border, Ukrainians and other citizens of the former Soviet Union visiting Poland to sell their wares and to buy selected products in Poland contributed to local economic growth. This was the case even though the bulk of their transactions unfolded in the untaxed shadows of the official economy known as *szara strefa,* the gray sector. For example, they generated demand for textile and leather products. According to one analyst, this was one of the main factors behind the boom in the small private textile and shoe businesses (Okólski 1999). Later, in the early 2000s, Polish home furnishings became popular. One could spot signs written in the Cyrillic alphabet advertising stores and warehouses selling *mebly* (furniture) along all the roads leading to the border. But the most characteristic venues where people engaged in the new economic activities became the ubiquitous open-air markets. Every borderland town had one, for the sale and purchase of goods ranging from food to hardware, from clothes to building materials, and from illegal imports such as tobacco and alcohol to fraudulent phone cards, pirated CDs and DVDs, weapons, and forged documents. Some of the larger markets, in Chełm, Lublin, Tomaszów, and Przemyśl, were known also as sites for informal job recruitment, mostly for seasonal workers in agriculture or day laborers in construction. The unruly nature of these spaces and the presence of organized crime, combined with the general (and historically warranted) perception of the east of Poland as less developed and more chaotic than other regions of the country, contributed to the common characterization of the borderland as Poland's "wild east." But the largest hub of all, the mother, so to speak, of all Polish markets, was located in Warsaw on the site of a defunct sports stadium. That market, which operated between 1989 and 2008 and was estimated to generate annual revenue of 12 billion Polish *złoty*, was known simply as the Stadion, even though, in a probably unintended act of mockery, the private company that rented space from the stadium administrator called it Jarmark Europa, the Europe Market (see Chapter 3). It attracted not only traders from post-Soviet countries, but also foreigners from other parts of the world. Its diverse multitude of traders and customers provided the most spectacular illustration of the fact that the new movement across open borders was by no means a phenomenon confined to the borderland, but rather a flow reaching the heart of the country and beyond.

But all this new cross-border movement did not meet the criteria of the traditional definition of migration. For the most part, it did not lead to settling, or even prolonged residence.[23] Most of the visitors never intended to move permanently to Poland and have never done so; if anything, as I show in Chapter 4, they treated Poland as a transit country on their way farther west. They traveled either for very short jaunts, like the petty traders whose comings and goings I described in the beginning of this chapter, or for slightly longer repeated periods of up to three months at a time, as low-wage laborers seeking jobs as cleaners, maids, and caregivers, as well as for seasonal work in agriculture and construction. Migration scholars sought to establish typologies of those movements and described them as "primitive" (Iglicka 2001), "circular" (Wallace 2002), "pendular" (Anderson 2000), and "incomplete" (Okólski 2001) migration. Wallace argues that

An important aspect of this migration, both into and out of the country, has been the fact that rather than permanent one-way migration (the dominant pattern until recently) there has been a predominance of *short-term, circulatory movements* backward and forward across borders. This would be better termed *mobility* than migration. (604)

"Mobility" might indeed be the better concept, insofar as it is more capacious and implies fewer presuppositions about the nature of the movement. According to John Urry, it encompasses many senses of moving or being capable of motion, including but not limited to "migration or other kinds of semi-permanent geographical movement" (2007: 8). There are many ways, Urry argues, in which our societies today are more mobile than ever. Mobility is a property of people and things, often enabled by modern technology. There is also mobility in the sense of *mob*—a multitude or an unruly crowd. There is social mobility, vertical ability to move through a hierarchy of social status. Social mobility is intertwined in complex ways with physical movement. Finally, there is the "horizontal sense of being 'on the move'" which "refers especially to moving country or continent often in search of a better life or to escape from drought, persecution, war and starvation and so on" (7–8).

Taking into account the multiplicity of ways to be "on the move" implied by the concept of mobility, there are good empirical reasons to choose it over "migration" to capture the bulk of the movements across Poland's eastern border (see also Morokvasic 2004). To keep things in historical perspective, we might term this "postsocialist mobility," bearing in mind that it was made possible by the lifting, in the early 1990s, of the politically motivated constraints on travel. But an important caveat applies: in EU documents and legislation the term "mobility" is usually reserved for the right of EU citizens to live and work in any country of the European Union. For example, in the Employment and Social Affairs section of the EU portal we read that "the EU encourages worker mobility for the benefits it brings to the individual in terms of personal and career development and as a means to match skills to demand." Moreover, "the new approach [embraced in the Lisbon Strategy for creating jobs] must combine flexibility and mobility in labor markets with robust social security safety nets, a concept known as 'flexicurity.'"[24] Of course mobility in this sense does not pertain to non-EU citizens—they are excluded from the continental freedom of movement and, needless to say, from "flexicurity." In the eyes of European policymakers as well as those of border enforcement agents, postsocialist mobility is nothing else but economic migration from outside the EU. As such it becomes a target of regulations and directives aiming to control it strictly, even if in theory member states have the freedom to shape their own economic immigration policy. As the EU expanded to the east of the continent, new member states were given little choice but to incorporate EU approaches to non-EU citizens into their national law and enforcement practice (Iglicka and Rybicki 2002).[25] The border was to be thickened without regard for the simultaneously unfolding delicate process of reknitting the borderland connections severed half a century earlier. As Timothy Snyder put it, "To convince the EU that they 'belong,' Poland must (among other things) show that it understands that other states, such as Ukraine and Belarus, do not" (Snyder 2000: 223). Just as many regional and local activists, artists and intellectuals worked to redefine the area as quintessentially Central European by virtue of sharing cultural commonalities and historical experience, it was to become, once again, sharply divided. Polish authorities attempted to soften the impact of the new laws by delaying the imposition of a visa requirement and, when it was finally introduced in 2003, by granting visas to Ukrainians liberally and free of charge, for as long as it was possible. But with the incorporation of Poland into the EU, rebordering entered a terrain of tensions of a long and, from the perspective of Brussels, a rather obscure lineage.

The Politics of Postsocialist Mobility

In the late 1990s Chris Hann (1998) described the city of Przemyśl as a prominent site for the re-emergence of Polish postsocialist nationalism. Like all urban centers in the region, before World War II it was home to Poles, Ukrainians, Jews, and small numbers of other ethnic minorities. After the war, with the once-strong Jewish presence wiped out and all but a small minority of Ukrainians expelled, it became an ethnically homogeneous provincial center ten kilometers west of the barbed-wire boundary of the Soviet Union.[26] In his work Hann analyzed the 1991 case of an intractable property struggle between the Ukrainian minority Greek Catholics and Polish Roman Catholics over the rights to the Carmelite Church. He described the feud between bishops and their respective Polish and Ukrainian supporters as an example of aggressive nationalist "politics of the past," a fomenting of a climate of mutual distrust and intolerance verging on the threshold of a violent outburst (Hann 1998: 853). The eventual resolution of the conflict was unsatisfactory for the inherently weaker Greek Catholic community. They were granted rights to a different church, while the Roman Catholics appropriated the one initially at stake and removed its dome in order to rid it of any traces of the Greek rite. Hann argued that the conflict took a dangerous turn because

> far from withering (or "freezing") under socialism, [nationalism] continued to grow in this period: overt promotion of political nationalism of the sort that typified the interwar period was precluded, but rigid control of education and culture helped to ensure that the nation, rather than any kind of sub- or supra-national entity became the dominant focus of loyalty and identity. Above all, it suited the Roman Catholic Church to promote the nation as the basic principle of cultural ordering. (842)

There is little to dispute in this diagnosis. Indeed, the stubborn resistance displayed by Polish politicians and the public to some of the more radical forms of Europeanization indicates that the nation as a source of identity remains more politically potent than any other type of political community.[27] But the more site-specific conclusion of Hann's Przemyśl case study, namely that the borderland climate of postsocialist nationalism precludes the Ukrainian minority from openly practicing their identity (1998: 862), appears to require an update.

Over the weeks that I spent in Przemyśl in early summer and fall 2005, I noted some isolated and subdued signs of the old Polish-Ukrainian hostility. A local bookstore carried anti-Ukrainian publications on the massacres in Volhynia in 1943. A washed-out piece of graffiti saying *Ukraińcy do domu* ("Ukrainians go home") was visible on the side of a blockhouse in a neighborhood on the outskirts. Were these signs of a brewing conflict or only vestiges of a receding anti-Ukrainian prejudice? As I pursued vernacular accounts of the city's recent past, one of the people I encountered was Jacek Gawin, a local radio reporter in his late forties. A passionate chronicler of local events, he invited me to his home studio and showed me an album of press clippings and fliers documenting the last two decades in Przemyśl and the region.

Jacek described how, before the introduction of a visa requirement for Ukrainians, Belarusians, and Russians, the border was virtually open. He recalled that indeed, between 1991, the year of Ukrainian independence, and 2003, the last year of visa-free traffic, passports and cash were required, but it was rare for guards to return anyone from a crossing. The traffic moved in both directions. Customs authorities performed the spectacle of fighting contraband, but only a fraction of the smuggled goods was confiscated. The ability to transact in informal markets provided a lifeline for the local unemployed and underemployed.

In his account of the play of the past in the present, Jacek connected the emergence of illicit and semi-illicit, economically driven cross-border mobility to the easing of local Polish-Ukrainian tensions:

> *Szara strefa* [the gray sector] is strong and developed here. I think that *szara strefa* fixed the relations between Poles and Ukrainians at this lowest level, between people. When the Ukrainian state was being established, it was the beginning of the 1990s, Polish-Ukrainian relations at the state level were excellent, the presidents kissed, gave each other bear hugs, but here. . . . But here the Balkans were in the making. In 1991–92 [because of the Church property conflict] blood could have flowed here.

Jacek suggested that the intensity of traffic and exchange revealed that the nationalists most vocal in the conflict were out of touch with the present. After the border was opened, he said, the old specters of Ukrainian retribution ceased to inspire fear. It turned out that "the Ukrainian Insurgent Army was not coming back after all" and that it was not going to "slaughter" the Poles:

> There was this stereotype here of a Ukrainian bandit who would come with a wooden saw and would hack women and children in half. This is how people were raised here, on the literature about [the] 1943 [killings]. . . . With that came the nostalgia for Lviv, the city that was taken away. . . . They thought in the early 90s that Lviv could still return to Poland. . . . Yes, it was really dangerous here. And this danger, among other things, was relieved by *szara strefa*. Because people noticed that instead of beating each other up they could smuggle vodka, cigarettes. . . . Poles could build a house for cheap with Ukrainian labor. Ukrainians could build one for cheap with materials smuggled from Poland. *Kurwy* [hookers] started coming because they saw there was money to be made off Polish businessmen. Everything now could be arranged cheaper. So what's the point of fighting?

Men and women would travel back and forth. Cross-border relationships and marriages began to form. Finally, Jacek said, referring to the interwar and Habsburg periods, "like before, blood started to blend."

In other words, unregulated activity around procurement of basic goods and services (including sexual ones) recouped, according to Jacek, some of the prewar heterogeneity of the border area. Older linguistic and ethnic ties were revitalized, and with them the capacity to engage in peaceful and pragmatic, if often brazenly illegal, transactions. But just like the "before" he had in mind, the present was far from idyllic. The specific causes and forms of symbolic and physical violence were different; they did not emerge from within the terror of virulent nationalism, but from the uncertainty and insecurity of postsocialist economies and illicit cross-border exchange.

Przemyśl had been a gray sector hub before Poland's EU accession and has remained one since. In 2005 and 2006 five buses per day departed for Lviv from the local bus terminal, in addition to countless minibuses, known as *busiki* in Polish, *marshrutki* in Ukrainian, shuttling between Przemyśl and the border crossing in Medyka, 10 kilometers away. The ride to the border was two *złote* (approximately 60 cents) and the inhabitants of Przemyśl and local villages, on both the Polish and the Ukrainian side, often made the trek across several times a day.[28] The price difference on cigarettes allowed for up to 50 percent profit, and even if each time a carrier, usually a woman, brought only the allowed one carton, bought in Ukraine for 20 *hryvnia* (15 *złote*, then about five U.S. dollars), she could still make up to 15 *złote* by immediately selling it to the local mafia buyers for 25 to 30, depending on the play of supply and demand on a given day. (Legal cigarettes of comparable quality would cost about 55 to 60 *złote*.)

At the unmarked minibus stops and inside the minibuses, people traded information about the guards and customs officers on duty on a given day. Ukrainians referred to them as *pohranychnyky*, an old way of referring to soldiers on border duty. The Poles used the word *wopki*, from WOP, the acronym for the long-gone socialist Borderland Protection Forces. There was one street lamp near the spot where the rides to the border departed, where people posted notes every day listing the names and aliases of officers who were currently on duty at the checkpoint: "Monday, 7am–1pm: *Baśka, Ruda* (Redhead), *Gruby* (Fatso)." These notes served as warnings for the border crossers who, intimately familiar with the habits and idiosyncrasies of the personnel, could infer from the schedule if the day was going to be one of hassles and possible trouble or smooth sailing. The movements of vendors, tobacco pushers, and itinerant workers appeared cautious but thoroughly routine.

I do not intend to argue that Poles in Przemyśl, or anywhere else for that matter, in spite of Hann's observations, suddenly shed ethnic and national prejudice and became rational economic actors focused on profit and tolerant of, or at least indifferent to, other identities. But even though that has not been the case, the dramatically altered political economy of the region and the opening of the Polish-Ukrainian border upset the dyadic "us versus them" dynamic of neighborly relations and provided a new context for making sense of ethnic, linguistic, and religious difference. The emergence of the gray sector and postsocialist mobility between Poland and Ukraine can be conceptualized as a historically and geographically situated transnational process "anchored in and transcending one or more nation states" (Kearney 1995: 548) and relying on "the condition of cultural interconnectedness and mobility across space" (Ong 1999: 4). Ong parses the term *transnationality* in order to tease out its multiple meanings and robust analytic potential:

> *Trans* denotes both moving through space and across lines, as well as changing the nature of something. Besides suggesting new relations between nation states and capital, transnationality also alludes to the *trans*versal, the *trans*actional, the *trans*lational, and the *trans*gressive aspects of contemporary behavior and imagination that are incited, enabled and regulated by the changing logics of state and capitalism. (1999: 4)

Indeed, the end of Soviet-era constraints, coupled with the launching of the free market, did open the space for individuals and groups to engage in transactions, translations, and transgressions, all of which profoundly altered relationships between people on both sides and shaped the cross-, or rather *trans*-border economy. For better or worse, migrants, vendors, and other participants became embedded "in multi-layered, multi-sited transnational fields, encompassing those who move and those who stay behind" (Levitt and Glick Schiller 2004: 1003). As Ukrainians forged new work and personal connections on the Polish side of the border, they usually remained in constant touch with families back home, maintaining emotional ties and providing material support. Poles venturing into business in Ukraine would locate their financial interests there, but keep their homes on the Polish side.

As a result, in Przemyśl and elsewhere, the late 1990s and early 2000s were a time when Ukraine ceased to be associated primarily with the prewar ethnic tensions and mass killings perpetrated in the region during World War II. Instead, collective perceptions of Ukrainians came to be shaped first by the petty traders and immigrant workers coming to Poland in ever-greater numbers, and second by the media images of Ukraine as a proximate and welcoming place that is in many ways like Poland, only somewhat economically more backward and more scathed by its Soviet experience. Hand in hand with claims of backwardness came the potent Arcadian trope of Ukraine as more "authentic" and unspoiled by fast-paced capitalism.

Through the daily interactions set off by mercantile exchange, employment, and other relationships, Poles began to develop a new intimacy with their neighbors, which transcended the border and complicated the nationalist narrative of lasting hostility, on the one hand, and the simplistic government-driven claims of "Polish-Ukrainian partnership" and the church idiom of "reconciliation," on the other. Competing nationalisms by no means disappeared, but they ebbed into the background. Claims of irreconcilable differences continued to be uttered and retained their destructive potential. They were, however, increasingly drowned out by a powerful new narrative where benevolent, if overly romanticized, notions of commonality intertwined with pragmatic claims of shared economic, political, and strategic interests.

Western Imaginaries at Eastern Borders

Thus the reopening of the Polish-Ukrainian border in the early nineties was the result of post-1989 politics that created affordances unseen in decades and allowed for the mending of old, and the forging of new, connections across the boundary. Between 1991 and 2003 a fuzzy zone of border-crossing interrelationships supplanted the sharp divide. One way to tell the story of what happened in this particular corner of Europe in the first decade of the twenty-first century could be through the prism of a dialectic of opening and closure. Post-World War II arrangements between the Soviets and the Allies led to a new territorial organization on the continent and to arrested mobility east of the iron curtain. Borders between the Soviet Union and other countries of the bloc were under strict control and generally not meant to be breached by regular citizens. The shaking off of Soviet control by socialist countries of East and Central Europe in 1989 and the subsequent collapse of the Soviet Union rendered the political rationale for maintaining rigid divides null and void. The simultaneous dawn of a free-for-all capitalism accelerated the breaking up of residual barriers. Postsocialist mobility changed Eastern European borderlands and interiors by enlivening local economies and injecting elements of diversity, cultural, linguistic, religious, and even racial, into mostly homogeneous societies. This was a novelty in countries that hitherto had experienced primarily the emigration of their own citizens, not the arrival of strangers. But as profound as these changes and challenges were, they were occurring in a broader context that needs accounting for. The shifts associated with the expansion of the EU cannot be reduced to a conflict between two different ideas of a border: on the one hand that of sharp divide between an inside and an outside, as in the Soviet model of borders; on the other, of a blurry zone of easy border crossings and connections, as between 1991 and 2003. The post-2004 external boundary of the EU contains elements of both. For some people, under specific conditions, the border remains quite permeable. For others, it is a gate that will open only after they jump through multiple legal and bureaucratic hoops. For yet another group, it is a wall that cannot be scaled.

In acceding to the EU, Poland and other countries of the region joined a bloc of Western European nations where the histories and realities of immigration followed their own trajectories, and where the discourses on migration and immigrants were of an altogether different caliber. The supranational system of bordering, which presupposes no physical borders between EU member states, but tight borders around the perimeter of the Union as well as stepped-up policing of the border-free territory, has a distinctly Western European genealogy. It is designed (in ways I discuss as this book progresses) to address and counter such issues and fears as the immigrant "mass invasion" of the West, the abuse of asylum procedures by "bogus asylum seekers," the access of potential and actual terrorists to EU territory, and the ostensible overrepresentation of Muslims among the foreigners living in Europe. These concerns, a tense fusion of the imaginary with the real, are products of the distinct history of colonialism, post–World War II economic development, and twentieth-century patterns of migrations in Western Europe. They originate in the old, not the new member states. But now, in becoming what might effectively be called an extension of the West, and adopting the EU approach to migrations, Eastern Europeans must embrace and act upon problems that are not of their own making.

The more time I spent in Poland and Ukraine on this project, and the more migrants, guards, and local people I talked to, the clearer it became that this produced jarring effects, on the borderland and beyond. Poles considered joining common European territory without checks on internal borders to be perhaps the greatest benefit of EU accession (see Chapter 4). But, as the following chapters will show, among both Poles and Ukrainians the tightening of the eastern border—the necessary price of Poland's EU and Schengen zone accession—generated ambivalent reactions and resistances aimed at preserving postsocialist mobility. The border between Poland and Ukraine thus became an awkward divide (Szmagalska-Follis 2011). On the one hand, it was redrawn as a sharp line with harsh new policies in place to enforce it. On the other, for many people it remained a key gateway to better economic opportunities. And, economics aside, for many Poles and Ukrainians it turned into a deeply contested emblem of EU's exclusionary politics.

Due to its history of competing nationalisms, subsequent Soviet isolation, and postsocialist mobility, the Polish-Ukrainian neighborhood already was a location rife with tension and unresolved problems, long before the EU expanded eastward. Questions of freedom of movement, enforcement, corruption, as well as the coexistence of historical trauma and expectations of a better future, predate Schengen regulations on the river Bug. But EU expansion (and here I mean the whole process of preparing for it, as well as the accession itself and the continuous refining of EU border policies) produced new vexations by implicating the Polish-Ukrainian border in the larger Western trends of controlling migration and other forms of human mobility.

Over the course of the post-9/11 decade, those trends, and the empirical and normative questions that they provoke, have been the subject of ample analysis and critique in the interdisciplinary social science literature. This huge body of work has dealt with issues such as immigrant and refugee rights (Smith 2011; Benhabib 2004; Bader 2005; Carens 2003, 2008), borderland economies between affluent and poor countries (Yúnez-Naude 2011; Bornstein 2002; Heyman 2004; Simon 2007), the securitization of migration policies (Inda 2006) and what Didier Bigo has called "the governmentality of unease" (Bigo 2002; Bigo and Guild 2005), the biopolitics of immigration control (Fassin 2001; Feldman 2008; Walters 2006) and the cultural politics of immigration (Bowen 2008; Hall 2002; Silverstein 2005; Stolcke 1995), to name a just a few of the most salient and controversy-inducing issues. This literature is generally informed by a form of ethical sensibility we might term cosmopolitan, in the broad sense that Pnina Werbner uses the term, that is, being "about reaching out across cultural differences through dialogue, aesthetic enjoyment, and respect; of living together with difference. It is also about the cosmopolitan right to abode and hospitality in strange lands and alongside that, the urgent need to devise ways of living together in the international community" (2008: 2). From this perspective, and in light of documented human rights abuses resulting from the functioning of the EU's border regime, contemporary trends in controlling the flow of new people to the developed West emerge as alarmingly repressive and retrograde. Not so, however, to those embracing xenophobic ideologies, and those seeking solace from the confusion of globalization in European integralisms (Holmes 2000). Those constituencies see the border regime as meek and vulnerable to breach by the purportedly ever-swelling masses of culturally alien and economically hostile people. Amid heated rhetoric, only most rarely is there any space for a discussion of what causes immigration in the first place, and of the legitimate concerns with its impact in democratic societies.

Meanwhile the repressive tools and techniques of rebordering are being sharpened and refined, following their own logic of techno- and bureaucratic involution. They are entering places, such the Polish-Ukrainian borderland, which until recently had no history of the kinds of problems the border regime is designed to address. Such places had, however, other experiences, which today, and no doubt in the future, will inform situated responses to the reality of the eastern boundary of the EU. These include local, rooted manifestations of the cosmopolitan sensibility, as well as discourses and practices that belong in the annals of the shameful history of racial and ethnic prejudice.

Chapter 3

I'm Not Really Here:
The Time-Space of Itinerant Lives

> Here in Warsaw we are seeing sort of a creeping borderland. Its
> first sign, a few years back, was the peaceful invasion of Russians,
> or newcomers thought to be Russian: the "Russian market" in
> front of the Palace of Culture, a head-on collision of the Eastern
> and Western markets. . . . This market made people realize the
> closeness of these distant neighbors in the East, the proximity of
> an authentic borderland, the transitory nature of every "center"
> and the imminent crumbling of its monolith. The [new market] at
> the crown of the Stadion brought a new scale and quality to this
> phenomenon, a palpable proximity of Asia. Unexpectedly, Warsaw
> found itself on the outskirts of a great borderland of the East and
> the West.
>
> —Piotr Lachmann, "Boundaries of the Borderland"

The images of the "creeping borderland" and a "peaceful invasion" moving in
the direction from east to west were an essayist's attempt to capture the 1990s
experience of the crumbling of the national homogeneity that had characterized life in Poland in the five postwar decades. The focal points that initially
attracted the flow of foreigners, and from which in turn many ventured into
the society at large, were the vast and unregulated marketplaces that provided the postsocialist population with access to all sorts of goods, at a time
shortly after the removal of trade barriers and before the establishment of
more permanent retail businesses. Consequently, these markets—which have

since shrunk as more people took their business to chain stores, retail parks, and malls—became also the first enclaves of cultural and racial diversity in postsocialist Poland.[1] Lachmann's images of a "collision of markets" and of "Asia in Warsaw" seem to be at odds with the neat divisions between Europe and non-Europe projected by the narrative and practice of rebordering. And yet the Stadion market, which I have mentioned in the previous chapter as the mother of all Polish markets, had been a fixture in the capital since 1989, and for nearly two decades it provided incalculable numbers of foreigners from the former Soviet Union and beyond with employment and livelihood, both directly, in transport, sales, and other commerce-related occupations, and by serving as an informal job fair for other types of employment.

Such sites are gray zones, part home, part abroad, dependent on the patronage of criminal gangs on the one hand, and on the willingness of local authorities to overlook the murkier aspects of their operation on the other. Gala, one of the women from Ukraine working in Poland as a cleaning lady, whom I met in early 2005, told me, "the best thing to do when you need anything, is to go to the Stadion. Anything you need, you can find there. Underwear. Purses. A phone card. A phone. A *bumaha* (colloquial word meaning paper, document). A passport too." Indeed, the Stadion, and its smaller clones in other towns, are places where one can shop or find a job or a place to live. One can also obtain a new identity by buying false or altered documents, purchase a rigged phone card, to call internationally for the price of a local connection, and conduct any other business necessary to immigrant survival.

These penumbral practices are ways of coping with unregulated status that underscore the half-shadowy, "hidden, yet known" nature of living in a foreign country without papers (Coutin 2005). Such acts are not criminal per se, but they teeter on the boundary between the licit and the illicit, and they may involve dealings with the criminal underworld. Migrant workers and entrepreneurs, who cannot rely on services and utilities ordinarily available to settled citizens, such as bank accounts, telephone landlines, protection of the law, official housing market, national health insurance, and all the other amenities that tether persons to places in the modern world, find ways to accomplish what they need by other means. Sometimes what is required is paying a premium, for example, for services such as Western Union to wire money, or private doctors to take care of health needs. Most often, however, migrant workers resort to alternative providers who operate in the shadows of the official economy and state services, and for whom places like the Stadion serve as hubs and grounds for recruiting customers. Unofficial couriers carry money, goods, and people to Ukraine. Athletic types involved with protection rackets help extract outstanding wages from tardy employers. Slumlords are keen to rent out decrepit quarters. Drawing on such resources, migrants enter unequal relationships with people and networks in the receiving country, while remaining connected with their own diaspora and their country of origin by murky routes that transcend borders. These resources, routes, and connections help navigate the time-space of their lives, the particular dimension of the social which is created by the European border regime on the one hand, and the political economy of postsocialist capitalism on the other.

Prior to EU enlargement, coming from Ukraine to Poland for work was facilitated by simple conditions of entry. Prospective workers did not have to resort to sneaking across the border like Latin Americans entering the United States. They crossed the border lawfully, but their legal situation in Poland was precarious and their employment unauthorized. The transformation of the border after EU accession in 2004 exacerbated this precariousness by complicating conditions of entry, imposing visas, and increasing the perils of illegality. It revalorized space on both sides of the border and introduced new temporal discontinuities. For most workers journeys between Poland and Ukraine became harder, costlier, and more fraught with risk than before. This chapter probes the specificities of dwelling in space and time across the Polish-Ukrainian border in the aftermath of EU enlargement by looking at the experience of women who live in Ukraine and work in Poland, in low-paid jobs on the outskirts of the official economy. To emphasize the transient and temporary nature of these work arrangements, I shall henceforth call them *itinerant* rather than *migrant* workers, which corresponds to the conceptual distinction between migration and "postsocialist mobility" discussed in the previous chapter.

An important caveat applies to the analysis that follows. It does not aspire to be a comprehensive account of the mobility from Ukraine to Poland, or of the situation of foreign women employed as domestic and other low-status workers.[2] What I seek to illuminate instead is a specific aspect of mobile life that often gets lost when the focus is on the political economy of cross-border movement. I look at how the participants in postsocialist mobility experience time and space, particularly as they adjust to changing borders. The notions of "time-space compression" (Harvey 1989) and high-speed modernity tend to be taken for granted in much of contemporary mobility studies (Urry 2007; Elliot and Urry 2010), but I find that a micro perspective and intimate portraits of particular individuals, sketched within the specific contexts of their lives, tend to shed a different light on the matter.

I focus here, therefore, on the existential condition of dwelling in bordered space, or on lives unfolding in what Peggy Levitt and Nina Glick Schiller have called "transnational social fields." They use this term to describe "a set of multiple interlocking networks of social relationships through which ideas, practices and resources are unequally organized, exchanged and transformed," and they assert that "transnational social fields" (as opposed to national ones) "connect actors through direct or indirect relations across borders" (2004: 1009). Levitt and Glick Schiller propose the concept of transnational social fields as a way out of the pitfalls of what they call "methodological nationalism," that is the "tendency to accept the nation state and its boundaries as a given in social analysis" (1007, see also Glick Schiller 2008). I too recognize the need to destabilize the primacy of the nation-state as an analytic category. But state borders divide not just states, whose hold over the lives of individuals and societies is indeed, all things considered, diminishing. They also separate spatial and temporal orders, which are partially constituted by states and state-like processes, and partially by global and transnational flows (Trouillot 2000). This is one of the reasons why borders hold persistent analytic relevance, or ought to, particularly within a transnational perspective.

"The globe shrinks for those who own it," Homi Bhabha observed, but "for the displaced or the dispossessed, the migrant or the refugee, no distance is more awesome than the few feet across borders or frontiers" (Bhabha, cited in Gregory 2006: 18). In the end my intention here is to flesh out, through a discussion of ethnographic evidence, a middle ground between transnational approaches that deemphasize the role of the state in the analysis of migration, and those that insist that "state-building (and state-destroying) activities should occupy a central role in the studies of human movement or its absence, alongside the more routine examination of states' immigration policies" (Torpey 2000: 6).

Transnationalism and Borders

Scholars of transnationalism have argued since the mid-1990s that the lives of increasing numbers of people—whether in networks, relationships, families, or workplaces—can no longer be understood just by looking at what goes on within national borders (Kearney 1995; Appadurai 1996; Levitt and Glick Schiller 2004; Glick Schiller 2008; Kaiser and Starie 2005; Hannerz 1996; Ong

1999; Favell 2008a). Nation-states, once conceptualized as essentially containers for society, ceased to define citizens' personal identities and histories. They
no longer have the monopoly on imposing economic orders, but rather they
are forced to adjust to global capital markets. Discussions of new transnational
phenomena, such as migration, commerce, activism and advocacy, crime and
terrorism, as well as transfer of knowledge, policy, and expertise, have focused
on new connectivities forged between people and places irrespective of national borders. Often the implicit or explicit assumption in these analyses has
been that it is the loosening or growing irrelevance of national boundaries
that has contributed to the emergence of transnational linkages (e.g., Lash and
Friedman 1992; Appadurai 1996).

On the other hand, much of the newer literature on borders coming out
across disciplines in response to international security preoccupations, resur-
gent anti-immigrant sentiments, and the rise of biopolitical border controls
offers a contrasting emphasis. From that perspective, state borders are understood to entail at once "concrete physical manifestations and more ethereal—
but no less present—metaphoric fixations" (Blank 2004: 354). This scholarship
points to the ways in which contemporary regimes of mobility and migration
produce individual and collective hardship and perpetuate various forms of
inequality, exclusion, and discrimination. It powerfully challenges the notion
that the global world is a world somehow unbounded (Andreas and Snyder
2000; Bigo 2002; Inda 2006; O'Dowd 2003; Walters 2002; Coutin 2003; Blank
2004; De Genova 2002; De Genova and Peutz 2010; Wang 2004; Dudziak and
Volpp 2006). Given this disjuncture, how can the insights of transnationalism scholarship and those of critical border studies be brought together as a
productive contribution to the study of rebordering? And more specifically,
what happens in a vibrant field of transnational traffic, exchange, and informal connections when a border that divides it is reaffirmed and reinforced
rather than abolished?

Gender and Migration

The questions just posed frame my interest in the stories of women who live
in Ukraine and work in Poland, and for whom straddling the new EU border
has become, all at once, a way of life, a burden, and a survival strategy. I write
of women to highlight the gendered nature of movement across the new EU
border. The feminist literature on migration provides a perspective that is

rarely adopted in the largely gender-blind discussion of Ukrainian workers in Poland.

Observers of contemporary mobilities have concertedly argued that global migration is a heavily gendered process, and that women today migrate in higher numbers than ever (Anderson 2000, 2001; Phizacklea 1983; Morokvasic-Müller et al. 2003, Morokvasic 2004; Ehrenreich and Hochshild 2004; Kofman 2000; Momsen 1999). This movement can be analyzed in class terms, as it involves a tense interdependence between the mobility of professional career women and that of their servants:

> Thanks to the process we loosely call "globalization" women are on the move as never before in history. Female executives jet about the world, phoning home from luxury hotels and reuniting with eager children at airports. But we hear much less about a far more prodigious flow of female labor and energy: the increasing migration from poor countries to rich ones, where they serve as nannies, maids and sometimes sex workers. In the absence of help from male partners, many women have succeeded in tough male world careers only by turning over the care of their children, elderly parents, and homes to women from the Third world. (Ehrenreich and Hochshild 2004: 2–3)

Ehrenreich and Hochshild write from and of the United States, although they imply that their observations apply across the global North. Like many accounts that take a broad-stroke approach to the inequalities between the global North and South, their discussion does not explicitly address the peculiar status of the postsocialist, or, as it was once called, the Second world. Meanwhile, the experience of women in general, and their trajectories as workers in particular, poignantly show that the process of postsocialist political and socioeconomic change has produced deeply divided, hybrid societies that unsettle the neat divisions between North and South, East and West. In Eastern Europe, some women's range of life options is only scarcely better than if they were born in one of the South's developing countries, while other women enjoy opportunities and material privileges no less than their counterparts in Paris or London. This is reflected particularly well in patterns of postsocialist mobility in and at the edges of the EU. Polish women, for example, have done the work of domestics abroad and have themselves employed foreign domestic workers.[3] It is not unusual to have experienced both situations at some point in one's lifetime.

Warsaw and other major urban centers in Poland, while not quite "global cities" in Sassen's sense ([1991] 2001, 1996), experience the same trends in female employment as those that stimulate the demand for migrant domestic workers in other developed capitalist economies. The investment of time and energy expected of women who want to hold a job and advance professionally is on the increase, as are the material rewards for doing so.[4] Care for children and the elderly is a private and privatized matter, creating prime conditions for the development of a shadow market of care and domestic services supplied by foreign women.

But the similarities between the experience of working Polish women and that of their sisters in much of Western Europe and North America should not overshadow their distinctive histories. State socialism ostensibly promoted equal rights between the sexes as part of its ideological doctrine.[5] Women gained access to professions previously closed to all but the very few upper-class females. The number of working-age women in full-time employment grew from 13 percent in 1950 to 69 percent in 1989 (Budrowska 2003: 36).[6] But, as Barbara Einhorn points out, despite these "advances," women still carried the burden of housework and state-enforced community participation in school and neighborhood committees and unions (1993: 117). Employment of domestic help under socialism was out of the question for most households, but when maids were hired they usually hailed from the countryside, not from abroad.

Elizabeth Dunn draws on compelling ethnographic evidence to argue that Polish women's identity centers on feeding and home creation, and that this is inherent to the Polish Catholic worldview (2004: 136–39). Indeed, such sincerely held beliefs for decades prevented women from questioning their responsibility for the "second shift" at home. The state helped somewhat in sustaining these commitments by subsidizing childcare and long maternity leaves, while ultimately doing nothing to draw men into household duties. Thus the combined burden of a full-time job, various forms of community service, and housework, all in conditions of material scarcity, explains why women felt no pride about the "right" to work, and instead perceived it as an obligation.[7]

This began to change with the collapse of the system, and with *reforma Balcerowicza*, named after finance minister, economics professor, and designer of the Polish "economic transition" Leszek Balcerowicz. The objective of this set of neoliberal reforms, rapidly implemented in the early 1990s as a "shock therapy" for the crisis-ridden postsocialist economy, was to set Poland on a straight path toward Western-style capitalism by opening to international competition, stringent control of inflation, privatization, and the curbing of social services (Balcerowicz 1995). As the reform began to bear its (for many unquestionably bitter) fruit, jobs in the "restructured" (or liquidated) state-owned enterprises started to disappear, leaving in the lurch women from small towns, those with little or no education, and those outside urban professional social networks.[8] At the same time employment opportunities began to open up in the ever stronger corporate sector. The ideal worker from the corporate viewpoint, however, was not the person who had just lost her job due to the closure of her textile plant or tire factory. In demand were the young and unencumbered, neither by family, nor by the baggage of socialist workplace experiences.

Thus many women who lost out in the process of the economic transition turned to low-wage employment opportunities abroad, initially particularly in Germany, and later also in other countries of the European Union. Meanwhile, the range of career paths and lifestyle choices available to educated urban women in Poland converged with those of their Western sisters. This included, particularly after 2004, also the path of the "Eurostar," as Adrian Favell calls the highly mobile professionals who work and settle in the increasingly diverse and cosmopolitan European capitals (Favell 2008). These women had little choice but to self-discipline and embrace the ethos of striving and competition, resignedly accepting the fact that in Poland state services designed to support working mothers all but vanished. As Hochshild observed,

> women who want to succeed in a professional or managerial job in the First World . . . face strong pressures at work. Most careers are still based on a well known (male) pattern: doing professional work, competing with fellow professionals, getting credit for work, building a reputation, doing it while you are young, hoarding scarce time, and minimizing family time by finding someone else to do it. (Hochschild 2004: 20)

That "someone else" is often a migrant domestic worker. A migrant domestic worker is a person, almost always a woman, who has left her country, and often family, to labor abroad in the home of another family, taking on, as Anderson argued, "the privatized responsibilities of the welfare state" (2000: 5).

In Poland, the privatized responsibilities of the socialist state became opportunities for Ukrainian *zarobitchany*, a Ukrainian word for economic migrants, from *zarobitky*, earnings or wages. Their work is part of a global labor circuit, one that Sassen describes as "an amalgamation of mostly informal flows (including both authorized and unauthorized workers), with perhaps the most visible circuits being those of the 'global care chains'" (2011: 57). Their experience is comparable to that of domestic workers from other countries elsewhere in Europe and beyond, particularly in terms of vulnerability, uncertainty, and subjection to the whims of the state and employer (Anderson 2000; Morokvasic 1991, 2004; Keough 2006; Parreñas 2004). But it is also distinctive, due to the patterns of women's work and Polish-Ukrainian politics and territorial proximity on the one hand, and the particular effects of rebordering on those two countries on the other.

Ukrainian women in Poland are often praised for being "good" migrants, hardworking, quiet and invisible, "not in anybody's way."[9] They are rarely harassed by border guards or police, and they seldom experience the public hostility, stares, or hate speech that frequently greet the more visibly different foreigners. Their labor is in demand, and the persistence of economic disparities between Poland and Ukraine has kept Ukrainian workers' wages down throughout twenty years of postsocialism. For all those reasons, their mobility and work can appear as a model of "desirable" migration, the kind that the European Union wants to promote and facilitate, as opposed to the flows of "undesirable" immigrants who are not seen as positively contributing to the EU economy, and who have no humanitarian claim to be in Europe. The 2005 Green Paper on an EU Approach to Managing Economic Migration stipulates that future harmonized EU-wide policies ought to be specialized and targeted to favor short-term over long-term labor migration. Migrations from third countries enjoying "special" relationships with EU countries might also be privileged.[10] The work of Ukrainian women in Poland already conforms to these specifications—they come for a short time and generally do not express the desire to settle permanently, and their journeys are facilitated by the relative leniency of the Polish government and law enforcement.

Mainstream political and media discourse in the West has a tendency to portray migrants as desperate individuals in search of better economic opportunities in richer countries.[11] But as Sassen pointed out in her history of migration processes in Europe in the nineteenth and twentieth centuries, if the flows of migrants were simply about an indiscriminate search for material advancement, then "the growing population and poverty in much of the world would have created truly massive numbers of poor invading highly developed countries, a great . . . flow of human beings from misery to wealth." This, she observes, has not been the case because in fact migrations are processes that are highly selective and structured by the relationships between the sending and the receiving countries (Sassen 1999: 2; see also Massey et al. 2003). Such mutual entanglements and commitments between Poland and Ukraine are often difficult to reconcile with the EU-driven imperative to build a tight eastern border. The state comes up with partial and confused responses to these contradictions, thus molding the time-space wherein the itinerant workers live their transnational lives.

The new border regime, with its restrictions on transit and length of legal stay, impels the Ukrainian women I met to move regularly across the border between the space where they live and the space where they work. This movement is a means to an end—an improved economic standing for themselves and their families. But it is not sufficient to reduce it to just that. Practiced over extended periods, it upsets expectations, forces adjustments of time horizons, and shapes and redirects life courses. It constrains agency, but it does not thoroughly negate it. In and of itself it becomes a way of life, and of being in the world.

Lena's *Korydor*

I met Lena in February 2005 in Warsaw. She was a twenty-five-year-old elementary school teacher. Someone I knew in turn knew someone at the Jewish Community where Lena, herself a member of a Pentecostal congregation in western Ukraine, had just started working as a live-in housekeeper.[12] Together with another young woman from Ukraine she was in charge of cleaning, cooking, and gardening. The Community was part of the recent gradual revival of Jewish life in Poland. In its large, two-story house in an upscale Warsaw neighborhood it hosts Shabbat and other holiday celebrations, lectures, and cultural events as well as Hebrew and conversion classes. The house features also a few guest rooms for the Community's foreign visitors. The upkeep of the vibrant center required hard work, but according to Lena it was an excellent job. She said she worked ten to twelve-hour days and often long past midnight on holidays. Her base pay was three hundred dollars per month, plus an extra hundred *złoty* (a little over thirty dollars) on Shabbat.[13] Foreign visitors often left what to her felt like generous tips. Lena was apparently well liked at her workplace for her extraordinary conscientiousness and pleasant personality.

So it chagrined her employers when in late April Lena's visa expired and she had to leave. She would have to return home for three months before she could apply for a new one. At the time, the most commonly granted visas were valid for only ninety days of effective stay in Poland. The passport was stamped upon entry and exit. If the total time in added up to more than ninety days, the holder would be ordered to pay a fine and would be barred from reentering for up to three years. The legal "in-time" had to be used up between the dates of issue and expiration, either as a continuous stay or over several visits. Visa holders had to wait out the remaining time back home before they were able to reapply. Only after a visa expired could its holder request a new one. My Ukrainian interlocutors called this period the *korydor*, the corridor. With this metaphor they evoked the double implication of the "out-time": like the corridor of an intimidating institution, the three months back home were the waiting room where they would idly await a new visa, an act of bureaucratic grace. At the same time, the *korydor* was the connection to home. It allowed them to see children, parents, relatives, and neighbors, in some measure creating an opportunity to address what Ehrenreich and Hochshild called the "care deficit" back home (2004: 8). It structured the schedule of such general business of living as going to doctors and dentists, paying bills, arranging for children's education, and caring for property.

Lena's employers told her they couldn't wait three months, especially because she was unable to promise a prompt return in July. She was from a small village, and her family had crops to tend. She was enrolled in an extramural degree program at the Pedagogical Institute in Rivne and had to pass her exams. On top of that, her fifty-two-year-old mother had serious health problems. Her older brother Bohdan was working as a bus driver in Moscow. His and Lena's income, combined with the modest returns from the farm and sale of berries picked in the forest, made up the family's budget. Lena's father had died from alcohol-related causes when she was little. Zhana, the sister-in-law who lived with the mother, was pregnant. She already had a three-year-old daughter, and besides she was practically in charge of the whole household. Lena's *korydor* this time could be longer than the usual three months. If it was up to her, she would not return to Poland at all, but she knew that without *polsky hroshy*, Polish money, life would be very hard.

Lena's home village of Markivka is in Rivnenska Oblast in Ukraine, about eighty kilometers northeast of Rivne. It is in the heart of a swampy rural region called Polissia, the butt of many jokes, as many Ukrainians consider it the most backward section of western Ukraine. It is at the same time one of the areas most affected by the Chernobyl disaster, that now experiences an exodus of the local population. Lena invited me there because she wanted me to meet her family and was also eager to show me the school where she was eventually hoping to get a job. Zhana, her sister-in-law, had been a physical education teacher before having her first child and had good contacts in the *raion*, the local administration. This gave Lena access to important knowledge about local bureaucrats—she would know whom to pay off and how much to give. Zhana, while she worked, was making 300 *hryvnia* (50 dollars), but Lena counted on the promises made to employees of the public sector during the Orange Revolution. The salaries were supposed to double. She said that if only she could make 600–800 *hryvnia* she'd much rather stay home and be a teacher than constantly go back and forth.

To get to Markivka one must first travel to Rivne, a city about two hundred kilometers east of the Polish border. With a population of 250,000, it is a regional administrative capital with a compact center, a broad main boulevard, blockhouse neighborhoods, and the vast Park of Culture and Recreation. The Park's now-crumbling attractions evoke the Soviet project of paternalistic oversight over the working people's well-being. The local economy is slow, so there is little new construction and significantly fewer cars than in Polish cities of comparable size. On the summer weekday when I got there, on my way to visit Lena while she was in the *korydor*, both the park and the center seemed empty, but the market just off the center was bustling with activity: people bought and sold groceries, clothing, and other goods. Most things appeared to be of Asian provenance and were more affordable at the market than they would be in a store. Opportunities for inexpensive shopping attracted people from nearby towns and villages to Rivne, a trade and transportation hub for the regions of Volhynia and Polissia.

The bus terminal had a connection with Warsaw, Lublin, and a few other Polish cities. It was crowded with people going abroad and returning from *zarobitky*, as well to and from local markets. There were Roma peddlers who got shooed from place to place, and unlicensed taxi drivers who vigorously solicited passengers. There was no direct connection to Markivka, but there was a *marshrutka* (minibus) to Dubne, a small town thirty kilometers from the village. This was the connection I took to visit Lena. After a two-hour ride from Rivne I arrived in the remarkably neat and quiet Dubne with another couple of hours to spare before the next *marshrutka* for Markivka was scheduled to depart. The town had a tiny bus station and an eating and drinking establishment with green plastic seating and umbrellas with local beer logos.

There was one grocery store, and one with a mishmash of toys, household items, toiletries, and other random objects. The local movie theater showed films once a week (the Hollywood blockbuster *Kingdom of Heaven* with Russian dubbing was announced for July 15).

"We have nice memorials in Dubne," Lena told me when she came to pick me up, "for the heroes of the Second World War." She uttered every word with a solemn inflection which made it easy to picture her as an elementary school teacher. I imagined that the tour she was giving me was similar to the school trips for local children. She showed me a brand new statue of Taras "Bulba" Borovets, a commander of Ukrainian Insurgent Army (UPA) units in Polissia, who before World War II was imprisoned in Poland for pro-Ukrainian activity and during the war was involved in the struggle with the Soviets, the Polish, and later the Nazis.[14] The statue was decorated with fresh flowers. We went also to see another monument, a modest slab of granite erected in 1992 near the local administrative building to commemorate the fiftieth anniversary of the UPA. It was engraved with an image of a woman in prayer and a rhymed dedication to Ukraine's "sons and victors." We ended our tour at a local cemetery featuring a sculpture of a heart pierced with a bullet, symbolizing the town's young men who had been killed in Afghanistan, in the Soviet Union's last war.

Lena traveled the arduous route between Markivka and Warsaw, via Rivne and Dubne, at least four times a year between 2000 and 2005 but less frequently afterward, for reasons I discuss in the Epilogue to this chapter. She was twenty years old when she went for the first time. Her jobs in Poland ranged from picking fruit at farms and selling merchandise at markets to babysitting, housecleaning, and taking care of older people. By the time I met her she spoke fluent Polish and felt thoroughly comfortable in Warsaw, though her mental map of the city was nothing like the tender sense of place she displayed at home.

In Warsaw, she knew the bus routes that connected Praga, the right bank of the city, to the city center. It was in Praga that most Ukrainians rented rooms. She knew the Stadion with its market and the nearby discount chain supermarket where she shopped. Most recently she lived at the Jewish Community where she worked, but before that she rented rooms she shared with female roommates. She had a tight network of Ukrainian girlfriends. Between themselves they would spread the word about new jobs. When one person was waiting in the *korydor*, she could always count on others to arrange a replacement to hold her current job. Such cyclical replacement arrangements between one Polish employer and two Ukrainian women were known as *ro-tacja*, rotation, and would sometimes last for years.[15] They kept each other informed about what was going on the border and at consulates. Did the lines improve or worsen? Did the guards let people through or get tough on controls? How much for jumping the checkpoint line?

They were all in their twenties and thirties, busy women moving about the city at all hours on public transportation, always clutching an extra bag with a change of work clothes and scheduling their next cleaning or babysitting stint on a prepaid cell phone. Nadia, one of Lena's friends, told me that on their rare nights off they liked to go to Plac Bankowy, a central plaza with a steel and glass skyscraper, to look at the cars and fantasize about the makes and models they would own one day. Or they would walk in the center in the evenings, window shopping after the stores were closed. This was only to keep up with the current fashions. They would not shop there, because the same things "you can get at the Stadion for one-third of the price."

These women, constrained as they were in their opportunities, were not passive victims of a repressive border regime and exploitive employers. Nor is it adequate to describe them simply as economic actors at the mercy of "push" and "pull" factors. While regularly taken advantage of and locked in their low status, they retained agency and often adroitly manipulated the regulations obstructing access to the labor market. But rebordering did reorganize their lives significantly, by amplifying discontinuities of the space they traversed and regimenting their time in specific ways.

By discontinuous space I mean a space where there is a significant and cumbersome physical boundary dividing the place of work (Warsaw) from the place defined as home (Markivka, or any other town or village in Ukraine). Neighboring Poland and Ukraine constitute a discontinuous space, where the first offers economic opportunity but scarce avenues toward legalization and integration, and the latter is a home in a legal and emotional sense but at the same time a place of economic hardship. The discontinuity is experienced as particularly acute not just because of the time-consuming border-crossing procedures, but also due to the haphazard nature of the transportation networks and infrastructure that connect Poland with its eastern neighbors. Despite the relative proximity of Ukrainian homes to Polish workplaces, the aging private buses, neglected bus terminals, bad roads, and scarce border crossings all contribute to making the "friction of distance," the time and cost it takes to get from place to place (Harvey 1989: 211), the key marker of spatial discontinuity and economic disparity. Regimented time corresponds to the experience of discontinuous space. Stretches of time spent on either side of the border are constrained by the duration of visas, lag times between obtaining documents, and costs in procuring them. The *korydor* is a spatiotemporal connection between home and abroad. It is a paradoxical bureaucratic artifact that helps straddle the divide, while at the same time deepening it. It undercuts the advantages of working in Poland. It interrupts the continuity of employment, stymies informal integration, and maintains itinerant women in a state of suspension between here and there, now and the future. The agency the women exercised during their travels across the reinforced border is therefore best understood in terms of their ability to navigate the timespace fragmented in this particular manner.

The *korydor* would interrupt the hectic Polish routine of Lena's and her friends' lives and transport them across the border. Time in Ukraine would have a different rhythm, organized not by the responsibilities of paid work, but by the demands of sustaining life at home. For Lena, that meant getting up even earlier than in Poland—at four in the morning to milk the cow rather than at six to start a day of urban housekeeping. But the Ukrainian women who came from town rather than country, like the twenty-two-year-old self-assured Vera from Ivano-Frankivsk who asserted she would not take a wage under ten *złoty* an hour, at a time when eight *złoty* was common, often complained that at home time is "slow" and there is "nothing to do." In that they expressed an existential predicament experienced by those who are made to wait: of, as Harold Schweizer put it, "having time without wanting it." While Schweizer observes that in modernity waiting can be valued as "temporary liberation from the economics of time-is-money" (2008: 2), the ability to savor such liberation depends on one's position in the socioeconomic hierarchy. These women want to use their time to sell their labor for money and cannot afford the luxury of idleness.

If the Warsaw Lena inhabited was a patchwork of public transportation routes and the hectic backspaces of her cleaning jobs, going back home was a shift that required her to reorient herself in space. She also had to adjust her perception of time, or to use Bourdieu's term, re-temporalize herself, that is, adjust herself to a different set of expectations and senses of possibility (2000: 213). In Poland she operated in the short-term present. At home she adjusted to a long-term anticipation of a better future. Even if she was there only for a short time, she immersed herself in a flow of time with an undetermined horizon. She did not know *when* she would be returning for good and living a better life, but she oriented herself toward that possibility, and this was reflected in her daily practices and emotional and financial investments.

Within the Schengen imaginary European borders are decisive divides. That is not the only way to represent them, however. In his Eastern European travelogue, writer Andrzej Stasiuk described the Polish border as a sort of unwinding of space: "Nothing was happening. You drive, and drive and all of a sudden the country ends, but it looks like this happens with no reason, as though it just got bored with itself" (2004: 259). Lena experienced the border as both abrupt and fluid. The transition into the other temporality occurs with passing the checkpoint. She described to me the nervous anticipation that accompanies approaching it. "When the bus gets across," she told me, "it looks the same but it *feels* different." Indeed, there is little that distinguishes the physical appearance of the Polish and Ukrainian sides of the border. Even roadside advertisements written in Cyrillic appear long before the Polish/EU territory ends. Border businesses—home furnishings, clothing wholesalers, eating establishments—cater to Ukrainians returning home with money. If it were not for the EU symbols and elements of the border infrastructure that communicate a decisive divide, it would be as though the two countries melted into each other. The ambiguity of difference between Poland and Ukraine only reinforces the subjective sense of disparate experiences:

Lena: It's like I had two lives. *Lena polska, Lena ukrainska* (Polish Lena, Ukrainian Lena).
Karolina: Is it the same Lena?
Lena: [silence]

It is possible that Lena did not answer my question because it missed the point. She had to have those two lives, precisely because it was not possible, within only one life, to reconcile what she had hoped for with the opportunities to achieve it. Lena Ukrainska showed me the school she had hoped to work in one day. The school is located in Balashivka, a village that neighbors Markivka. We rode bikes along the 11-kilometer brand new road that connects them. Lena explained that until two years before there was no asphalt, only dirt, and in bad weather it would have been impossible to pass. But this changed when President Leonid Kuchma decided Balashivka would become the site of one of the new schools he had vowed to open in rural areas all over Ukraine. This was part of a high-profile educational reform meant to improve the prospects of the new Ukrainian generation. The school had to be built on a tight schedule, and ready for a grand opening in fall 2003, when Kuchma himself would be the guest of honor at the inauguration.

Lena was not particularly interested in politics, but during the Orange Revolution she was firmly *za Yushchenka*, for Yushchenko. Over the year that followed, when the sense that the Revolution did not deliver on its promises was already widespread and palpable, she remained optimistic. She thought the country was such a mess that it would only be fair to give the new president some time. But this did not stop her from expressing a certain reverence for Kuchma, who cut a strong, Soviet-style paternal authority figure and had done good for her local community. At the same time she would declare that he was a thoroughly corrupt politician, but that hardly perturbed her, as "that's just how things are." She talked about how he arrived in Balashivka in a helicopter, and how the local authorities built roads and sidewalks to make a good impression.

Misha, Lena's childhood friend, was now the security guard at Kuchma's school. He would let us in, clandestinely, on a Sunday, and we would have to be quiet and careful. The school, I was told, had thousands of dollars' worth of valuable equipment, and strangers were not allowed in. Dima would turn off the anti-burglary alarm and watch the door while Lena gave me a tour. She was familiar with the building, because her sister-in-law had brought her along a couple of times, and since then Lena had often fantasized about teaching in the pristine classrooms.

The visibly new and modern bright two-story building with a light green roof looked surreal amid its modest surroundings, between wheat fields, about half a kilometer from the heart of the village composed of mostly wooden, and a few brick houses. The inside was clean and quiet. We made our way through the corridors to the Ukrainian language and geography classrooms. Each had a computer with a projector at the teacher's desk, and colorful maps, charts, and tables on the walls. The chairs were upholstered—a luxury Lena pointed out as something unheard of in Ukrainian schools. The foreign-language lab was wired for multimedia teaching. There were cubicles with small screens and headphones. This room was never used because the school did not have an English teacher; Lena herself hoped to learn English so she could teach it one day.[16] She did not know to what extent the computers in the computer lab and library were in use, but later Misha told us the students could use them after classes. The Internet connection did not work very well—there were some problems with the wiring.

We stood for a while in the cafeteria admiring a giant oil mural depicting

Mother Ukraine—a blond young woman in a blue gown with a braided crown, the traditional hairstyle adopted by the iconic leader of the Orange Revolution, Yulia Tymoshenko. She was holding a basket with a harvest cornucopia, an image suggesting that the children in the cafeteria would enjoy a plentiful supply of food—in a country scarred by the experience of famine, a particularly potent symbol of prosperity and wellbeing. But there was something else Lena thought I should see, and she went to confer with Misha about it. Finally she reappeared with a key and took me to a room near the principal's office. From her cautious moves it was clear that we were about to cross some boundary we *really* were not meant to cross.

We entered a large bright room which, as it turned out, was known in the school as the "Kuchma Museum." A variety of artifacts donated by Kuchma himself were displayed in glass cases along the walls and on a wooden island in the middle of the room. To the left was a framed "History of the Presidency of Leonid Danylovych Kuchma." Next were photographs of Kuchma and foreign leaders, Kuchma and Ukrainian children, Kuchma and factory workers, Kuchma and other politicians. There were an array of diplomas, awards, and documents and some pictures from the school's grand opening. There were gifts he was given during his presidency, such as an engraved saber from President Putin of Russia and a medal from President Kwaśniewski of Poland. There were vases and fine china adorned with the portraits of smiling Kuchma himself. Lena told me that the principal opens the Museum on special occasions for the children and parents to visit.

Our stealthy visit to the school revealed that Lena's hope and expectations for the future were anchored in a particular place, an oasis of the modern, not detached from her home like the relative conveniences of Warsaw, but an inherent part of it. The school was made special also by the fact that presidential patronage connected it to the larger Ukrainian statehood, thus ensuring continuity between the lessons of the local memorials to the "heroes of the Second World War" and objects contained in the school's museum. In that sense the specifics of Kuchma's political legacy were irrelevant—it was the generic presidential quality he bestowed that mattered to Lena, Misha, Zhana, and local parents.

Later that summer Lena found out that one of the teachers was going on maternity leave. She took 300 dollars of her Polish savings and went to Dubne to the local administration to "arrange" that she be given the position of a substitute teacher. She was thrilled when she found out that her temporary contract would start in the fall. In August she got a new visa and went back

Figure 3. Artifact in the Kuchma Museum, Balashivka, western Ukraine.
Author photo.

to Poland to work for a couple more weeks and close her bank account. Then she said goodbye to friends who were staying and returned home. When I visited again, her little room in the family's wooden house was cluttered with school books. There was supposed to be no more cleaning in Warsaw and no more *korydory*. However, it turned out a few months later, the economics of daily life at home again became unviable, and by the following year Lena was back in Poland.

Oksana's Passport

In November I met with Lena in Lviv, where she was on a weekend trip for a meeting of her church group. I was about to go back to Poland, so she gave me the phone number of her friend Oksana, who at the time was working in Warsaw. In early December, shortly after my return, I attempted to set up a time to meet with Oksana. She and Lena were the same age and went to school together. Oksana had been shuttling between Ukraine and Poland since she was eighteen; the first time her brother brought her along. She took temporary jobs ranging from picking fruit and cleaning in private homes to selling knock-off clothes and cosmetics at the Stadion.

I knew that Oksana was about to go home for the holidays, but she had no plans for a permanent return to Ukraine. Unlike Lena, she had no networks to fall back on. Her father was an alcoholic and had long ago abandoned the family. Her brother, like Lena's, now worked in Russia, and her mother had no skills or contacts she could mobilize for the benefit of her daughter. Oksana had gone to a vocational school and could work as a seamstress, but the enterprises in her region that could have employed her had collapsed over the initial few years of Ukraine's independence. As in other sites of postsocialist transformation, including Poland (where the nexus of work and kinship has been studied by Frances Pine), the kin-based networks that in the past would have helped place young women within the world of work had suffered a rupture (see Pine 2002a, 2006). Therefore, Oksana was content with her current job at the Stadion. She thought the pay of 40 *złoty* per day (about 13 dollars) was decent. In the winter she suffered frequent colds from standing outside all day. She also dreaded the constant tension involved in the sale of counterfeit merchandise. Despite these inconveniences she did not intend to quit. But when we finally met, the first thing she told me was how much she'd been missing home, and how badly she needed a break.

Oksana knew I would call her, because Lena had sent a text message to tell her about me. I tried calling but no one answered, nor was there a voice messaging system. Ukrainian itinerants rely strongly on cellular telephones. They usually have one phone and two SIM cards—one for the Polish, one for the Ukrainian network. When they cross the border they switch the cards. But they use the cheapest available prepaid systems, that at the time offered no advanced features such as voice mail. I followed up with a text message asking when would be a good time to call. The message I received read: *Not now, I'm at the police busy with passport.* I was alarmed—it did not seem a good thing for an illegally working Ukrainian to be anywhere near the police, whatever the reason. The Stadion as a known hub of illegality was a particularly perilous place. Oksana could have been in trouble.

As a general rule, immigrants with unregulated status avoid law enforcement—and that is true everywhere, from Arizona to Kyiv, and from Dubai to Moscow. Not being able to resort to police protection, they often become victims of organized crime, trafficking, abuse, and exploitation at the workplace, discrimination in the housing market, theft, and many forms of harassment. Even in such cases, they hardly ever report to the police. But before I had time to imagine a worst-case scenario, Oksana called me back and in a cheery voice apologized for not answering the phone. The situation was instantly clarified: "I couldn't talk, I was there to say I lost my passport. There were so many people there, I thought I was never going to get out. You know, the holidays are coming, *everyone* is losing their passports."

Oksana was not in trouble. She was merely resorting to one of the many tactics that allowed itinerants like her to manipulate their immigration status, and thus exercise more control over her time than the border regime afforded her. She did not really lose her passport, and neither did most of the people with whom she stood in line at the precinct. She was simply pretending that this was the case, because being temporarily passportless freed her of the confines of the *korydor*, and gave her a clean slate in dealings with border guards and consular authorities.

Oksana's visa was issued on January 2, 2005, and lapsed on June 30. She had entered Poland on January 2, but should have left by March 30, as this was the end of the ninety days she could legally spend in Poland during a six-month period. However, since her visa did not expire until June 30, she could not have applied for a new one until July 1. If she had acted in accordance with the law and left on March 30, she would have lost her job and three months of income, not to mention jeopardizing her relationship with her Armenian boyfriend Samuel. She decided that leaving Poland and waiting out the *korydor* this time was not an option.

She stayed, but the original visa in her passport with its lapsed expiration date was proof of her illegal status. "Losing" the passport erased that history. With no passport, there would be no Oksana who stayed in Poland for nine months longer than the authorities were prepared to tolerate. There was only an undocumented Oksana who would be issued a one-way pass allowing her to leave. Border authorities would not harass her because they would not see the invalid visa on her departure. The official note she got from the police confirmed she had reported a loss of her passport. On that basis, the Ukrainian consulate would issue a temporary travel document that she would use to return home.

Oksana and I met shortly after our phone conversation. She had taken the day off to deal with the passport formalities. She instructed me to wait for her at a small mall in her unglamorous neighborhood in Praga.[17] She arrived slightly late. She was tall and slender, but her serious face, marked by vertical lines on her forehead and by the sides of her lips, gave an impression of someone much older than twenty-five. The day we met was cold. Sidewalks were icy, but she appeared to be accustomed to wearing high-heeled boots with her outfit of tight jeans and waist-length jacket. Later she would tell me that this was how she was expected to show up for work: "dressed like a woman." While I accompanied Oksana on her shopping errands (she bought mostly snacks, supermarket brand coffee, and sweets to take back home), she told me about the local police precinct. She remarked that the police were rather accustomed to issuing "lost passport" notes. "They were asking," she said, "if we all have to come in at the same time. They ware a little annoyed . . . I understand this. They were asking if we just sell our passports to the Arabs."

The idea of "selling the passports to the Arabs" seemed comical to Oksana. She said she would not sell hers to anyone. But in fact trafficking in documents is one of the Stadion's more profitable activities. A Ukrainian passport, hardly a prestigious item when we consider the hierarchy of citizenship at the EU borders, may be of tremendous value to persons who appear racially different or come from countries which figure on terrorism watch lists. Oksana, aware of that, told me she knew that she had it better than her boyfriend Sam, who sometimes experienced harassment because of his dark complexion.

While we shopped, Sam called to say he was on his way home, and a few minutes later he joined us at the supermarket. His soft voice did not seem to fit with his muscular frame. He was 29 and had been in Poland slightly longer than Oksana. He was less confident with the Polish language than she was. At first she spoke Polish to me, interspersed with some Ukrainian words. After he arrived the conversation among the three of us shifted to a mixture of Polish, Ukrainian, and Russian, with the two of them communicating in Russian. Sam remarked that in this neighborhood people were accustomed to hearing *ruski*, but that elsewhere in Warsaw they got stared at when speaking Russian in public.

After shopping we went over to their place. For the past couple of months Oksana and Sam had been renting one room from an elderly man. The building was dilapidated inside and out, like most in the area, but they got along well with their landlord and the arrangement was affordable. Their room held a sofa bed, an armchair, and a shiny set of shelves and cabinets of the type that in the 1980s was associated with high living standards. Oksana pulled out a small folding table where she served cookies and potato chips. Beer and tea were offered, and we spent the afternoon and evening chatting and watching pirated music videos from the Stadion.

Sam and Oksana's days were organized by the rhythms of the Stadion. It was the hub of their social networks and the gravitational center of their Warsaw. This former sports stadium, originally built in 1955 to commemorate the tenth anniversary of the establishment of the People's Republic of Poland and defunct since the eighties, was encircled by the so-called "crown" (*korona*), the embankment that used to support the tribunes, which had crumbled over the years. Trade activity spread from the top of the crown to the adjacent area and spilled over to a nearby square and bus station, which had several daily connections to cities in Western Ukraine and Belarus. After 2008, when the market ceased to operate to make space for construction of the new National Stadium, to be finished for the 2012 Euro Cup soccer championship, the market at the bus station remained the only vestige of the old Stadion. The market covered a huge area and had its own spatial hierarchy. According to Oksana, the more profitable the business, the closer to the crown:

> The most important ones are at the crown. Disks, computers, guns. Let me tell you, I haven't been everywhere myself. There's all sorts of people at the crown. There is Poland, Ukraine, and Russia and various strange nationalities. And I've seen these Georgians and Indians, and Lithuania, and Russia, and Poles. . . . And who else? And Indians. They all want to be there. . . . And Blacks. It's *international*, no? [says

the word in English, laughs] Here, where I am with the shirts it's just our people and Armenians.

Oksana talked about the wholesalers who bring the merchandise at night, and the early hours that she must work to help with unloading the clothes. She described how she and Sam had met:

> We met there [at the shirt stand]. The boss is Armenian. You see, my aunt worked there first. She went home. It was time for her to go, [because of] visa. She recommended me, I got in for her. Now she is in Italy. He [Sam] was bringing stuff to the boss. We met. I like Armenian people. They are more like our people.

She recalled the sensation of alienation and confusion which marked her first times in Poland; "In the beginning I cried all the time." She was happy to break it up every three months to go home for the *korydor*. But, unlike Lena, she made no long-term plans connected to Ukraine. Until she found work at the Stadion, her time, like Lena's, was regimented by visa-mandated sequence of "ins" and "outs." By choosing to ignore what the documents told her to do, she eschewed the *korydor*. In doing so she gained continuity of employment and some measure of day-to-day stability, but at the same time she became a deportable illegal immigrant.

Finally I asked her what did she really do with her passport. "Nothing. It's here." She pulled out the document in a plastic cover from a cabinet in the room and showed me the picture of her significantly younger-looking face. "You know," she said, "I'm not *really* here. I live here, work, pay rent, but the passport says something else. I'm not here." The now officially vanished passport was evidence of her awkward position in relation to time, space, and the law.

The next day she'd have to cope with another long wait for the Ukrainian consulate to issue her temporary travel document. On the following day she would be ready to board the bus to Rivne. It would take her across the border in Rawa Ruska to her destination, where it would arrive at two or three in the morning, after a sixteen-hour ride. From there, via Dubne she would get home to Markivka. Back in Ukraine, Oksana would apply for a new passport. After it was issued, she would take it to the Polish consulate in Lutsk, where a consular officer would stamp a new visa into it. Getting a new passport would take a few weeks, but visas at the time were issued practically on the spot. The time to process the documents would let Oksana take a break and reconnect with her mother, with whom, unlike Lena with her mother, she didn't have a very strong relationship, and whom she didn't regularly support with her Polish earnings.

With a new visa she would legally reenter Poland and return to work at the Stadion. At the time, in the winter of 2005 and 2006, the Schengen database called VIS, storing information on everyone who was issued an EU visa, was still in the realm of distant plans. The consulates claimed they did keep records of visas issued, but mainly for statistical purposes. Barring any unforeseen circumstance that would arouse suspicion and prompt the consular officer to run a check, operation "lost passport" was virtually risk-free. She would probably stay another year or so, unless a better opportunity presented itself. But what that could be, she did not know. In the past she used to entertain vague thoughts of going to Italy one day, to join her aunt, but now, because of Sam, she no longer did so.

Oksana's border-crossing is not just a record of circumventing formal regulations. Rather, her account of work, home, and managing the logistics of tricking the state is a narrative that speaks to the ways of inhabiting the discontinuous space of borders and experiencing regimented time. Oksana was "not *really* here," because she was neither home nor abroad, physically present, legally absent, socially a dweller in the "creeping borderland," a space imbued with contingent opportunities and an ever-present possibility of violence and exploitation, primarily at the hands of shady employers, coworkers, and criminal gangs. Looking at what occurs in the spaces that open up when the law is circumvented helps us appreciate the cunning of manipulating official documents. Itinerants creatively harness such devices as passports and visas to their needs. Without quite entering the risky territory of theft and forgery, but clearly using them in ways other than the state intended, they undercut what John Torpey has called, in a Weberian vein, "the state's monopoly over the means of movement" (2000). Rather then being instruments of control, identity documents are appropriated as means of resistance, and instead of restricting, they enable and facilitate the ongoing, politically and emotionally charged exchange between the two sides of the new Euro-border.

Visa Politics

The itinerant lives of Lena and Oksana are characterized by what Diana R. Blank aptly called the "condition of contingent mobility" (2004: 350)—an ability to leave one's country without really having a viable and certain destination. Much of postsocialist mobility is contingent in this sense—postsocialist citizens in the former Soviet Union, after decades of isolation, were granted the freedom to move at the same time as most Western countries closed their borders to them.[18] The particular stories of Lena and Oksana demonstrate some of the ways in which such outsiders within the new EU borders cope with the contingency. Looking at the details of their lives helps us appreciate the intense labor of negotiating their limited opportunities, as well as the resourcefulness they demonstrate in responding to such constraints as lack of paths to legalization, absence of protection, and limited control over their time and spatial location. The experience of Lena and Oksana is not exceptional—most Ukrainians in Poland never completely arrive or ever fully leave Ukraine. They live simultaneously on both sides of the border. Visas, seemingly banal bureaucratic devices, to them are coveted objects that can open up a new dimension of social space: neither home nor abroad, a semi-accessible approximation of "Europe," not quite Western, but also not as intimidating and not too different from home.

In the context of the intense, two-directional flows of people and things across the border in the aftermath of the border's reopening, it became apparent that setting up a visa requirement on the eastern border would develop into a tense issue. Visas were one of the key measures designed to exercise better control over the future external boundary of the EU.[19] Due to the special relationship between Poland and Ukraine, the Polish authorities, in a highly publicized move, declared that although the visa regime was necessary, all efforts would be made to make it as painless, hassle-free, and inexpensive for Ukrainians as possible.

Visas, like passports and other travel documents, are an expression of the state's monopoly over the legitimate means of movement (Torpey 2000: 53). They are key elements in what Aristide Zolberg (1999) calls "remote control" immigration policy, a system of checks of prospective visitors exercised well before they even approach the border. They are advance permits to enter a country temporarily, for which one applies at a consulate, the local administrative outpost of the receiving country. They are also a powerful political symbol. First World countries rarely require them of their citizens. For others they symbolize an obstacle to movement and reinforce perceptions of inequality and marginality. (See, for example, Bekus-Goncharova 2008; Miklósi 2008; and, for another geopolitical context, Wang 2004.)

Standard visas in the European Union are granted for short visits, not exceeding ninety days, and do not stipulate the right to work, which is subject to other regulations.[20] In Poland the lack of any significant modern history of immigration explained why there was no preexisting policy concerning the presence and employment of foreigners. In its absence, visas became the de facto instrument of quasi-regulation.

As the Polish government prepared the new visa policy, many commentators on both sides of the border protested, sensing the emergence of a new iron curtain (Boratyński 2002; Fediv 2003; Wagstyl 2002).[21] To be sure, the objections they expressed were futile. The visa policy was simply part of the whole package known as the European *acquis* which Poland had to adopt prior to joining the EU. It was one of integration's many take-it-or-leave-it propositions, subject to no public debate. There was, however, a margin of choice as to *how* exactly the new policy would operate. Instead of immediately rolling out a harsh Schengen-ready system, the government introduced a more lenient transitional solution. For an initially unspecified time, visas for Ukrainians were to be free of charge, based on a simple application, valid for 90 days of stay in a six-month period. In this way the government simulated change: it "tightened" the border as it was required to, without significantly restricting traffic. To justify the new policy, some analysts represented visas as "user friendly" devices for promoting higher civilizational standards. One expert expressed the governmental agenda as follows:

> For the negative view on visas we have to substitute a positive one: of the new rules as a means of introducing to Eastern Europe urgently needed elements of order, legality and predictability applied to the movement of people. . . . Given the painfully wide civilization gap between the EU and the three countries in question [Ukraine, Belarus, and Russia], consulates ought to serve also as exhibition windows and places of breaking fresh ground. (Najder 2003: 5)

This rhetoric of a "friendly border" and a "civilization gap" went hand in hand with assurances of cultural and economic "partnership." Labor migration went unmentioned, although a few observers remarked that visas were going to make the lives of Ukrainian workers more difficult (Batory Foundation 2004;

Boratyński 2002).[22] Rather than simply crossing the border, prospective travelers now had to make additional trips to one of the four Polish consulates in Ukraine and endure the chaos of lines of a hundred to two hundred people.[23]

A petty industry of "facilitators" quickly started to exploit the determination of visa applicants. Gangs took control over the good spots in the queues and the paid services of filling out forms. Once, on a fall day in 2005, as I chatted with visa applicants in front of the consulate in Lviv, a woman came up to me and offered to arrange a visa for 300 *hryvnia* (60 dollars). The service would cover the application process and pick-up. A hustler for the illegal visa procurers, she was so eager to make the deal that despite my telltale accent she did not even notice I was Polish, and therefore hardly in the market for a Polish visa. Regardless, 300 *hryvnia* was a steep price, considering that at the time, for example, the monthly salary of a teacher was about 360. But many applicants who could write only in Cyrillic felt compelled to pay at least 60–100 *hryvnia* (12–20 dollars) just to have the document filled out in *latynka*, the Roman alphabet, as the consulate required.[24]

Meanwhile, between 2003 and 2005 registered unemployment in Poland hovered around 18 percent.[25] Thus, regulating migrant work had not reached the governmental agenda, especially since the low-wage and low-status jobs available to Ukrainians in the shadows of the official economy were in vast supply. Farmers offered seasonal employment. There was no shortage of construction and housekeeping jobs. Think tanks and NGOs estimated that the number of Ukrainians working illegally in Poland oscillated between 300,000 and 500,000 per year (IOM 2004; Herm 2008). Regulation advocates called for clear procedures for recruiting and legalizing workers (Frelak 2005; Kaźmierkiewicz 2005), but to no effect.[26] A Polish visa with the *korydor* was all one needed to access these work opportunities.

The results were mixed. Some itinerants, like Lena, complied with the *korydor*. Others, like Oksana, circumvented it. The choices they made depended on their relative investment in both spaces they occupied (the space of work and the space of home) and on the temporal projections they made for their lives. For example, among my other interviewees were Zina and Luba, who as mothers took the obligation of the *korydor* as a kind of forced blessing. "It's not so bad," Luba told me. "Three months there, three months home. At least my sons remember what I look like."[27] Lena did not have children at the time, but she had long-term plans firmly grounded in Ukraine. Those plans provided the overarching framework for her life, thus reducing her time in Poland to a succession of finite shifts.

In spite of the relative inconveniences of the *korydor*, the visas were a valuable resource. Considering that about the same time Western European consulates restricted the number of visas they issued, for many potential migrants Poland became one of the few viable destinations (Riabchuk 2005).[28] One popular way to travel to the West was to enter Poland legally and from there arrange for clandestine transit westward. There was no shortage of locally operating trafficking networks involved in the transfer of Ukrainian and other workers to Western Europe (see Hughes 2000; Hughes and Denisova 2003). Maria, a former factory worker in her early forties whom I met in Ukraine as she was waiting out her *korydor*, told me a story of her cousin and the cousin's friend, who were taken from the Polish-Ukrainian border to Spain rolled up in carpets stacked in the back of a van. The trip was not completed because the *ruskie mafiozy* (Russian mobsters) who drove them demanded more money than the women could pay. They were kicked off in France and have since made their way to Italy. Many such deals, however, have had worse endings. Women, of course, are particularly vulnerable to trafficking that lands them in indentured servitude or sexual slavery either abroad or without leaving Poland.[29]

But overall, going to Poland for three months and returning after the period of legal stay expires was and remains a low-risk proposition. The trip, though long and hardly comfortable, required no hiding and was relatively cheap. The languages are close enough, and everyday practices translate well between the Polish and Ukrainian cultural contexts. In most cases home can be reached within twenty-four hours.[30] The disadvantage is the lower wages paid in *złoty*, not euros. Either way, adjusting to the discontinuities of space and the regimentation of time appeared to be an acceptable price to pay for the opportunity to go *na zarobitky* to Poland.

Anxieties of Mobility

The fact that Ukrainians undertake journeys to Poland is the result of economic disparity, but the particular form these journeys take is a product of the simultaneous dismantling of internal EU borders and the erecting of external ones. The media noticed the difficult lives of Ukrainian doctors, teachers, and music professors who were forced out of their home country by a deep economic crisis and ended up in Poland sweeping floors. A typical passage in one women's magazine read as follows:

Masha, 30, graduated from medicine in Kiev. Next year she plans to get married and needs money. As a pediatrician in a hospital she was making 64 dollars [per month]. She was recommended as a cleaning lady to a Polish family. This family recommended her further. "Now every day of my week is busy," Masha smiles contently. "I clean in wealthy homes. Journalists, bankers, radio reporters. I even have one minister!"—she says with pride.[31]

Such accounts were symptomatic of a particular politics of sympathy. Pity for the downtrodden migrant worker was mixed with pride that Poland had finally transcended its perennial condition of being a country of emigration, and become the kind of place where others immigrate. While Poles continued to leave, in large numbers and with a renewed purpose, given that since 2004 they can legally work in the "old" EU, the ability to attract and employ Ukrainian domestics was seen as sign of economic and civilizational progress. As studies of domestic migrant work have shown, hiring a domestic worker raises the status of the employer (Anderson 2007: 7). Ukrainians not only literally "filled in" for the Poles working outside Poland, but as a group they also provided a symbolic counterpoint to the historically pathetic figure of the underpaid and exploited Polish guest worker in the West. A satisfaction that these are no longer "our people" who often despite higher education, are reduced to lowly tasks was intertwined with compassion and the commonly expressed moral imperative to give work to "our neighbors" who need it for survival. These sentiments were validated by casting the Ukrainian workers as grateful recipients and as an embodiment of the virtues of self-discipline and self-reliance, which rank high in the neoliberal value system that became hegemonic with the advent of capitalism (Keough 2006).

Exploitation often masquerades as kindness and charity.[32] Ukrainians came to be stereotyped as poor, hard-working, humble people fit for various forms of service work. Their modest pay expectations were welcomed as a matter of course. A justification familiar from other immigrant-employing societies would be brought up: the meager incomes they could make were a boon anyway, in light of the dire economic situation in Ukraine. "True, it's not much what I pay her," admitted to me one employer of Ukrainian domestic workers, who insisted in 2005 that an hour of cleaning work was worth eight *złoty*, when the wage of a Polish cleaning lady could be as high as fifteen. "But with what she makes here, she and her family will live for the next three months."[33]

While thousands of Ukrainians were finding jobs in Poland, the UK, Ireland, Sweden, and later Spain and Portugal opened their labor markets—as part of expanding the shared EU economic space—to immigrants from Poland. The scale of the departures exceeded all expectations. By the end of 2006 it was estimated that approximately two million Poles had found work abroad (Herm 2008). This number started to dwindle in 2008 as the crisis hit Western Europe.

In December 2005 the British ambassador to Poland wrote an informal memo to Tony Blair that was leaked to the press and provided a window on the ambivalence attached to this wave of labor migrations. The diplomatic scandal occurred during the tense negotiations in Brussels over a new EU budget. The British official ridiculed the "selfish" Polish position regarding the Union's finances. He quipped in his email note to the prime minister that by opening its labor market, "Her Majesty's government did more to fight unemployment in Poland than the Poles did themselves." This "help" was provided in spite of their "rudeness and ingratitude." The letter, first cited in a Sunday *Times* article tellingly titled "Crikey! FO speaks truth about Europe" (Cracknell 2005), offended many in Poland, prompting calls for an apology, forcing the ambassador's resignation, and in the process highlighting the uglier side of borderless Europe. In one radio show, callers were saying that if it wasn't for Polish nannies, there would be no one to care for "the Brits' obnoxious children," and, alluding to the ostensibly "excessive" tolerance displayed toward Muslims in Britain, one man ironically wondered if the British would really "prefer terrorists to pretty Polish waitresses."[34]

The outrage quickly blew over. But the week-long flurry of radio call-ins and Internet commentaries by Polish readers brought out the unease over the new population movements. Is emigration a good thing or a bad thing? Are today's emigrants going to come back? What if they are not? Are Poles abroad valued as solid honest workers, or are they despised as the most recent wave of unwanted foreigners? Are "our women" respected? These were some of the unanswered questions that came into sharp relief during the row.[35] They echoed the questions Ukrainians asked themselves about their emigrants. As one of my interlocutors in Ukraine, the editor-in-chief of a Lviv daily, told me, "we keep waiting for the *zarobitchany* to come back and invest their money in Ukraine." Without going into a fullblown critique of capitalism, he wryly observed that instead their wages are spent on consumption ("expensive cell phones for the children" that are supposed to "make up for the absent mothers"), and Ukrainian women end up marrying foreign men.

In the end, Eastern European *Gastarbeiter* in both the "old" and the "new" Europe remind us that there is more to their journeys than economic desperation and powerlessness. Women in particular are simultaneously, in Poland as in Ukraine, objects of harsh moral judgment ("loose women" or "bad mothers") and protagonists of heroic narratives about industriousness, diligence, and selfless sacrifice which are stimulated by and resonate within the capitalist value system. Experts and politicians might lament the national disintegration caused by mass departures, but, following the neoliberal logic that values personal industriousness over governmental intervention, they also emphasize the positive impact of migrant remittances on national economies. Neighbors might exchange malicious gossip about migrant women's conduct abroad, but they are also often in awe of what their labor can accomplish. The itinerants themselves craft their trajectories amid these conflicting attitudes and sentiments, both in spite and because of them.

Epilogue

In early 2006 Lena decided to take out a loan to buy a place for herself in Dubne. She found a little one-room apartment (twenty-nine square meters, about three hundred square feet) that cost ten thousand dollars. She had almost three thousand in savings, but her position as a substitute teacher was not secure, and it did not qualify her for a bank loan. Following the recommendation of a neighbor, she borrowed money from a private lender. She had to meet her monthly payments and the high interest rate or lose the apartment. Securing steady income became very urgent. Lena was gradually coming to terms with the fact that she could not afford to be a teacher any more, especially since there were no signs that she would be offered a permanent position.

In summer 2006 she was working in Poland again. She wanted to come again during the winter break, but in January 2007, even though school was in recess and she was not missing any classes, she was supposed be around for administrative duties. To get around it and be able to leave, she showed the principal a hospital statement saying that she was in treatment for chronic throat problems (she had paid a forty-dollar bribe to obtain it). After her short-term work stint she went back to finish the school year, and in June 2007 she was back in Warsaw. In the meantime, as part of the impending Schengen expansion, Polish visas became harder to obtain. This time Lena would not be returning home for the *korydor* after three months of work. She wanted to return to her old job at the Jewish Community, but the position was no longer available. However, thanks to excellent recommendations from this employer, she landed a full-time job in the home of a wealthy man who had recently returned to Warsaw after several decades overseas.

The job combined housekeeping with caring for the man's wife, who had begun a slow slide into dementia. It came with amazing perks—Lena was given her own, fully equipped one-bedroom apartment on the same gated estate as her employer's home, and she had generous time off to compensate for the taxing nature of caring for the wife, who would occasionally become abusive. (Rather than relaxing in her independent quarters, she used that time on small cleaning jobs solicited through her extensive network of previous satisfied employers.) All those benefits came on top of the whopping 3,000 *złoty* basic monthly pay, almost $1,000 at the time. Moreover, the employer offered to arrange a work visa, which would make her legal—by the time I visited her in her place in August 2008 she had been in Poland without a valid visa for more than a year, and hadn't gone home at all during that time. In the meantime Poland became a full member of Schengen, and visas for Ukrainians were no longer automatically granted. Many of those who previously practiced the *korydor* now preferred to stay put in Poland for fear of losing the opportunity to leave Ukraine altogether. However, for reasons Lena could not explain, her employer's efforts to legalize her fell through, and she continued to live in fear of being apprehended (her employer wouldn't talk to me).

Besides bus rides to her other jobs she rarely left her gated estate, watching TV in her apartment any time she had an hour to spare. By the end of that summer she had paid off her place in Dubne, which she was able to rent out. She was also planning to use her considerable savings to buy land in her village, and eventually build a house there for her future family. Her wedding to a fellow member of the Pentecostal church from another village in Polissia, whom she had met in 2007 and stayed in touch with mostly via text messages and Skype, was planned for 2009 in Ukraine.[36] She would change her last name to her husband's and apply for a new passport as a new person. That way she would be able to return to Poland for as long as it took to complete her construction project, and save up enough to pursue her dream of teaching and, eventually, having her own children. By then she would be close to thirty—an alarmingly advanced age, by rural Ukrainian standards, to start a family. But those were no longer the standards by which she judged herself. In Warsaw she had cleaned for plenty of childless women in their thirties, and she had come to see her own lack of children as natural for a working young woman who must first establish herself and then think of having a family.

Oksana, as far as I know, hasn't been home since her holiday trip in the winter of 2006. She has since had a new passport, but the visa she entered on had long expired. She continued to work at the Stadion for another year. Meanwhile, the Ukrainian government has been upgrading its passport issuing system as well. It introduced anti-forgery measures and a computerized system of ID numbers that will make it difficult to keep asking the authorities for new passports. Moreover, it wasn't clear how much longer Oksana would be able to keep her Stadion job. In spring 2007 Poland and Ukraine together won the competition to organize the Euro 2012 soccer cup. Since then word had spread that the Stadion would be razed to the ground and a new modern soccer stadium built in its place. Rumors became reality in 2008 when the market finally shut down, with only remnants remaining in operation in the vicinity of the bus station. By then Oksana had apparently left Poland and, according to a mutual acquaintance, had gone to Germany with Sam, sometime in early 2008. After her Polish phone number ceased to work, I lost track of her.

In 2007 the Polish government took steps to solidify the status quo. It had become easier to legalize citizens of Ukraine and Belarus for seasonal employment in Poland.[37] They were allowed to enter the country on a regular visa and work legally for 90 days. They could repeat it once in the same year, provided that 90 days passed between their first departure and second arrival. Thus the *korydor* across the EU border was sanctioned and normalized.

While it is to be expected that promoting future efforts to regulate labor migrations from "third countries" will draw on the familiar rhetoric of ordering, reforming, and civilizing, it is important to note that this will also introduce further categories of persons into the existing border regime. The subjectivity of the short-term labor migrants, where the self is indelibly marked by the border, will become a regularized existential condition in the European Union. Endowed with variable rights and devoid of political representation, they will inhabit the fragmented time-space of borders, which—in Balibar's words—"becomes almost a home—a home in which to live a life which is a waiting-to-live" (2002: 83). This waiting, which, Schweizer remarks, is "assigned to the poor and powerless so as to ritualistically enforce social and political demarcations" (2008: 6), may well last to no end.

Chapter 4

Seeing like a Border Guard:
Strategies of Surveillance

> The Union shall set itself the following objectives: . . . to maintain
> and develop the Union as an area of freedom, security and justice,
> in which the free movement of persons is assured in conjunction
> with appropriate measures with respect to external border controls,
> asylum, immigration and the prevention and combating of crime.
> —Treaty of Amsterdam, 1997

The abandoned watchtowers and empty checkpoint booths, such as
those that line the Franco-German or Dutch-Belgian borders, have become
symbols of European integration and freedom of movement in the post-
Schengen era. Could the once barbed-wired borders of postsocialist countries soon look the same? In 2005, one year after Poland had been formally
accepted as an EU member, its western and southern borders seemed to be
losing the ominous feel of rigid international divides. Fewer guards on duty
and no customs officers signaled a new organization of space in a region
once located east of the iron curtain. Meanwhile, the opposite was happening at the eastern border. There the density of patrols and the sophistication
of surveillance technology were increasing. Seen up close and traveled by
bus, by train, and on foot, it appeared at once as a formidable obstacle to
human mobility and a chaotic site of an ongoing struggle for livelihood.
Besides becoming a symbol of a new line of division in Eastern Europe, it
emerged as a precarious location of trafficking in living bodies, time, labor,
and goods.

In Poland and other new EU countries, free travel within EU boundaries was presented by integration proponents as one of the main benefits of enlargement.[1] In December 2002, while the government negotiated the accession treaty and public support for joining the Community was at a moderate 52 percent (Eurobarometer 2002), the Polish daily *Gazeta Wyborcza* listed the "end of border controls" as the first among its three main reasons to support Poland's membership (the other two were "stable law" and "billions of euros in aid to local governments and enterprises," December 13, 2002). The article voiced the widespread notion that the absence of internal frontiers denotes a higher civilizational standing, and that this constitutes an antithesis to the Cold War-era restrictions on movement.

To the inhabitants of the former Soviet bloc, the ability to cross borders without enduring long lines, presenting passports and other documents, or explaining the purpose of travel would be a new and powerful experience. It would be a manifest change in status, a collective promotion to a higher order of political membership. This was the case especially for postsocialist citizens who remembered the pre-1989 era, as well as for those who traveled abroad in the early nineties, when Eastern Europeans, who at the time had just begun to explore their post-Communist freedoms, were still regarded with suspicion in the West of the continent.[2] In 1995 Croatian writer Slavenka Drakulić thus captured the fear of borders that she and her fellow citizens experienced:

> I no longer live in communist Yugoslavia, but in democratic Croatia. Similar is the case of Romanians, Poles and Bulgarians, for that matter. Why, then, has my fear of borders not gone? Why do I feel as nervous going west as ever before? . . . We believed that after 1989 we would be welcomed to an undivided Europe, that we would somehow officially become what we always knew we were —that is, Europeans. . . . But we were wrong in nourishing that illusion. Today the proof of our status in Europe is easy to find. It awaits us at every western border crossing in the stern face of a police officer looking down upon us, even if he doesn't say a word. (Drakulić 1997: 15)

The authoritative gaze of the border official was internalized. In an act of self-discipline, holders of Eastern European passports would walk straight to the *Other Passports* line at airports, and assume, regardless of the purpose of their journey, that they could be questioned, searched, and harassed.

This look has not changed. I know it by heart. I remember it from before—police officers at crossings have always looked at us that in that way. They know perfectly well that this look would make us nervous, because we always had to disguise the amount of money that we possessed, or lie about the dying aunt that we were supposedly visiting or just about the hidden bottle of home made plum brandy. Then there was look number two: the screening, X-ray officer's look, suspecting everyone of wanting to get illegally employed in his country, if not—God forbid!—asking for asylum. Once you have felt that look of suspicion, you don't ever forget it and you can recognize it from miles away. (Drakulić 1997: 15)

Such hierarchical encounters made the boundaries between the two parts of the continent palpable and acutely real, long after the actual barbed wire was taken down. The eastward shift of EU borders reorganized traffic at border checkpoints, adjusted the hierarchy of citizens and their passports, and sorted people anew into those who wait in designated lines, and those who are swiftly ushered across. This reorganization of space and traffic produced new senses of spatial belonging and entitlement in citizens of the included nations, while reinforcing the experience of marginality in those who were not.

On October 1, 2003, in anticipation of EU accession planned for the following year, the Polish government deprived Ukrainians, Belarusians, and Russians of the privilege of visa-free travel to Poland.[3] As the EU domain crept up to their national frontiers, their access to a country which in the past they could enter freely was restricted. A few months later, on May 1, 2004, in return for tightening their eastern boundaries, the citizens of the newly admitted member states acquired the right to use their national ID cards in place of passports when traveling within the EU. In Poland, the borders with Germany, the Czech Republic, and Slovakia became internal EU ones. For a few years (May 2004 to December 2007), controls remained in place while Poland and other new members continued to upgrade technology and infrastructure to meet the Schengen standards (Schwell 2006). However, customs inspection was abolished right away, the guards no longer checked all traffic, and drivers could pass through without stopping unless flagged. These adjustments in the regulation of movement, while seemingly small, locally represented a radical change. Before, when Poland's border with Germany was the external EU boundary, hours-long waits at the checkpoints, disrespectful treatment, and harsh controls constituted its daily reality (Freudenstein

2000: 174).[4] Introducing new standards of civility, clearing up the burdensome traffic congestion, modernizing the crossings and bridges on the Oder and Niesse rivers, and establishing joint Polish-German border patrols were the most visible and striking signs of Europeanization in the western border region.

Meanwhile, the eastern borderland was Europeanizing as well, although there this entailed an opposite set of legal, administrative, and practical changes. The mandatory visa for non-EU aliens and fast-track lanes for EU citizens became the most visible signs of the new. The transformation was comprehensive and did not happen overnight. "We must clarify this right away," Colonel Władysław Szymanek (not the real name) of the Border Guard headquarters said to me during our first conversation in the summer of 2004.[5]

It was not that May 1 (2004) came and hurray, we are in Europe, but on April 28 we didn't know what was going on. In reality it was in 1997 that we adopted a plan of reinforcing the eastern border. Since then we have been developing our facilities in the east, adding new checkpoints, watchtowers and young personnel. . . . Meanwhile, operations in the west were being gradually reduced.

As described by this and other officials, recasting Poland's eastern and western borders has been a multi-tiered, time and resource consuming, and ultimately unfinished process. From the point of view of these practitioners, the daily business of enlarging Europe consisted of such mundane activities as beefing up patrols, training personnel, introducing high-tech equipment, reorganizing bureaucracy in response to new laws and regulations, commissioning contractors, and receiving EU visitors on monitoring missions. As my Border Guard interlocutors would often emphasize, their responsibilities have been the practical, not theoretical or—God forbid!—political aspects of border-making. "We are concerned with practice (*praktyka*). We deal with what's going on in the field," an information coordinator for a regional Border Guard unit explained to me one time. "Guarding the border happens right here, on the river banks and in these shrubs, not at an office desk in Warsaw or Brussels." In this he pointed to the ultimately situated nature of border policing, where decisions are made on the spot and guards put their practical knowledge before the imperatives of Europeanization.

Agents of Surveillance

The introduction of new modes of surveillance is a salient element of rebordering, a source of a renewed sense of agency for border services, whose redirected and newly enhanced ability to watch and see is at the heart of new strategies of border control. The new responsibility of the Polish authorities to guard the external boundary of EU territory is the responsibility to look out for anyone and anything that can threaten the whole "area of freedom, security and justice." The EU border regime contains within it a particular vision of a secure future, and of a shared territory rendered governable through the application of high technology for the ordering of mobility and migration. In this chapter I describe the intrigues and intricacies of the quotidian practice of surveillance which emerge on the frontier between Poland and Ukraine in the context of adjusting to Schengen.[6]

Bringing the maintenance of the Polish eastern border up to the capacity required by the EU should not be seen merely as a technocratic process of upgrading laws and state services. It is rather an inherent part of the complex cultural and technological shift that I call rebordering. It is a material and discursive adjustment which reinforces the narrative of belonging to Europe through an emphasis on civilizational advancement within a secure, prosperous, and bounded space. New regulations and technologies on the Polish-Ukrainian border are not only and not simply a means for an unconditional fight against illegal immigration on behalf of united Europe. They are deployed with a twofold objective. On the one hand, agents of rebordering must convey their civilizational aptitude and competence in "European standards." To this end they must show efficacy in combating and preventing the influx of "undesirable aliens." On the other hand, however, they must ensure that the protecting of the border does not stifle the commerce and flow of labor that are vital to the local and national economy. In the years 2004–2008 this involved ensuring that the Polish labor market, affected by the flight of roughly two million Polish citizens to other EU countries, would receive a supply of workers from Ukraine.[7] Thus the daily work of rebordering entails performing a fraught task: keeping at bay immigrants thought to be headed via Poland for Western Europe, and who might otherwise be "suspicious," while continually admitting a steady flow of those believed to be bound just for Poland. In this sense, Poland's external border is no new "Iron Curtain," that, like the old one, would block the mobility of everyone but the highly privileged few. It is rather a fine mesh, a site for making complex and discretionary distinctions.

It is a place where well calibrated political calculations determine the openings and closures experienced by the people who cross it.

Critical to the functioning of such a border is the eye of the border guard, together with the binoculars, cameras, and myriad other technological enhancements of vision. I therefore suggest that one way of understanding the rebordering of Europe is to recognize it as an effort to reorient the way authorities see, in terms of both direction (east instead of west) and techniques of looking and seeing. The administrative ordering of society must no longer be guided by the perspective of the nation-state, but rather by that of a supranational community (Scott 1998: 4). This entails potential conflicts and contradictions, even as it promotes greater flexibility and the ability to navigate complex agendas. The challenges are amplified by the underdefined nature of EU supranationality. In this context, the work of sorting performed by individual agents requires more skill, as the new paradigm of territory and population posits more kinds of people who appear at borders and must be admitted or rejected.

Imagining Europe Through Schengen

It is through its most ambitious policies, such as the common currency and the development of Schengen, that European integration takes shape and palpably transforms the experience of daily life for people inside and outside it. Rebordering is the European Union at its most concrete. Timothy Snyder has argued that "more than other projects of European integration, the creation of an external frontier directly requires the EU to take on state-like functions, assume state-like roles, and acquire state-like capacities" (2000: 222). But following Cris Shore and Susan Wright's argument about policy as an anthropological field, I propose that such projects are not accurately described as mere instruments of government for the top-down regulation of populations. "Policy is the ghost in the machine—the force which breathes life and purpose into the machinery of government and animates the otherwise dead hand of bureaucracy" (1997: 5). Grand governmental schemes contain and supply a language, a form of cultural agency, and a political technology for the active remaking of societies and envisioning their future (19–29).

Long before champagne corks popped to celebrate Poland's accession to the European Union, the word "Schengen" became shorthand for the new organization of space on the continent. Newspaper articles as well as expert reports emphasized that the enacting of new rules for admission and exclusion of foreigners goes hand in hand with increased security and the spread of new freedoms associated with EU citizenship (see, e.g., Pawlicki 2005; Niklewicz 2005; Kaźmierkiewicz 2005; Najder 2003). Even a popular TV show that aired on Poland's biggest private network, TVN, in 2003 and 2004 was wholly devoted to showcasing the work of the upgraded border services. Entitled *Granica* ("The Border"), it depicted, in the style of the American show *Cops*, the spectacular law enforcement actions of the guards.[8] There was tracking and capturing of illegal immigrants on the Polish-Ukrainian and Polish-German borders and intercepting of small and large contraband. There were examples of the use of such technology as x-rays of cargo containers and thermal cameras. One episode showed Polish guards collaborating with the German *Grenzschutz* in the pursuit of drug traffickers and smugglers. Another explained how adjustment to Schengen will make it virtually impossible for suspected terrorists to enter EU territory. Through this show, as well as through countless newspaper articles and other media communiqués, Schengen was cast not only as a promise of freedom to move about Europe, but also, in the age of fears concerning terror and excessive immigration it became a reassuring narrative of safe space within secure boundaries. As such, it emerged as such an unquestioned social good that it was rare for anyone in the Polish mediascape to dwell on the philosophical or political foundations that underpin "the area of freedom, security and justice." The notions "illegal migrant," "refugee," and "asylum seeker," previously absent from postsocialist public discourse, which was largely unaccustomed to immigration issues, now became matter-of-fact designations for people who are, quite unquestionably, strangers. This contributed to the emergence of what one might call a banality of exclusion—banality in the Arendtian sense of an uncritical acceptance of the premises of the state (Arendt 1963; see further discussion in the Conclusion).

Schengen helped normalize and provided irrefutable justification for the myriad institutionalized ways in which foreign persons are segregated from the native society as a result of their noncitizen status. Balibar speaks in this context of a European apartheid. Cognizant of the polemical nature of this comparison, he emphasizes that (for the time being) it is not the suffering created by one or the other of the two systems that he finds similar, but rather the structures.[9] He finds two key reasons to pursue this juxtaposition:

> One is that the position of the important group of workers who "reproduce" their lives on one side of the border and "produce" on the

other side, and thus more precisely are *neither insiders nor outsiders* . . . produces a steady increase in the amount and the violence of "security" controls which spread everywhere in the society and ramify the borderline throughout the "European" territory, combining modern techniques of identification and recording with good old "racial profiling." This in particular is what the Schengen agreement was about. The second reason is that the existence of migrant *families* . . . has become a true obsession for migration policies and public opinion. Should the alien families be separated or united? If so, *on which side of the border* . . . with what kind of rights? (Balibar 2004: 123, emphasis original)

Whether Schengen is about segregation or about splendid freedom of movement is a key question when evaluating the democratic credentials of the project of European unification, and I shall return to it (see Conclusion). But as Poland was becoming folded into the new border regime, emphasis on the new freedoms thoroughly overshadowed any public worry about Schengen's apartheid-like effects. As I have shown in the previous chapter, yes, the imposition of visas for Ukrainians was decried, but when it became apparent that such restrictions were here to stay, the state and migrants tacitly colluded to defang them. Against this background, an implicit consensus emerged: to leave one's country and seek better fortune elsewhere might be an act of desperation, but it is still a personal choice. To be caught, detained, and deported is bad luck. Those are banal facts of life, not the kind of structural problems that would require a systemic (or political) solution.

On the professionals involved in retooling borders, Schengen bestowed a new form of agency and responsibility. In their circles, the term was not just a metonym for intra-European freedom of movement, but it indexed a cluster of rather specific requirements and stipulations. The project of turning the national border into a Schengen one entailed the adjustment of border-policing capacities to norms already practiced in "old" EU member states. It involved, among other things, the synchronization of national immigration databases with the Eurodac system for the fingerprinting of asylum seekers, and with the megaservers of the Schengen Information System.[10] Both databases contain and process information concerning "third-country nationals" entering the shared territory. They consist of central units located in the heart of the EU, and of thousands of terminals distributed along its perimeter and at airport entry points.

These databases, together with the expanding legal provisions for read-mission, help border guards in their key task of ordering traffic. Readmission agreements between neighboring states allow for immediately sending illegal entrants back to the country they came from. Poland has had one with Ukraine since the mid-1990s. The Schengen databases further facilitated the practice of prompt removals. This record-keeping machinery establishes the migrants' trajectories and determines, based on their citizenship and past migration history, whether they do or do not have the right to be inside the EU. In this way, these specific technologies and administrative procedures have become key instruments for the fighting of unauthorized migration at territorial borders. They are tools whose ultimate purpose is rendering every immigrant attempting to enter the shared European territory known and traceable. As such, they are firmly inscribed in the genealogy of borders as sites of biopolitics, that is, places where authorities can gather vital knowledge about the health, economic status, and movement of populations. William Walters described the biopolitical aspect of borders as "an assortment of technologies, simple and complex, old and new. These include passports, visas, health certificates, invitation papers, transit papers, identity cards, watchtowers, disembarkation areas, holding zones, laws, regulations, customs and excise officials, medical and immigration authorities" (2002: 572). The deployment of these technologies requires of course the involvement of not just the border services, but other state agencies and professionals in locations on the frontier and beyond. The biopolitical border is a dislocated and ubiquitous one.

The Eurodac and SIS databases thus belong to an evolving biopolitical assemblage whose beginnings date back to at least to the late nineteenth century, when modern states began to regulate immigration.[11] To be sure, they serve repressive purposes, in the sense that they make possible the collecting, storing, and retrieving of information which can incriminate foreigners and lead to their detention and deportation. But this effect is in a sense secondary to their key role, which is helping make the mobile populations of the European Union knowable and governable in the first place. The fact that border and other internal security agencies *throughout the Schengen area* have access to such data vastly expands the scope of possible interventions into human flows.[12] When an asylum seeker crosses an external EU border, the record of his or her doing so becomes instantly available to law enforcement agencies throughout the EU.

Integrating Poland and other new member states into these data circuits implies a shift in thinking about, and acting upon, populations and territory.

The task is no longer to patrol *national* borders, and prevent unwanted intruders from encroaching on *national* territory. It is now the whole of the EU, cast and reimagined as eminently penetrable by undesirable persons and groups, that demands protection. When a unit commander who once served in the socialist Border Protection Forces said to me, "We had to learn to think differently," he signaled not just new ways of doing things, but a whole paradigm shift in border protection. The shift was not simply about introducing new concepts and tools of policing. It was also about reorganizing allegiances and identifying with new constellations of power. For the border guards, the remaking of Poland's eastern borders into the external boundary of the EU meant, for all practical intents and purposes, assuming control over the unambiguous external border of the West. Over the course of a few years, they found themselves on the frontlines of the EU's evolving and intensifying struggle against unwanted immigration.

Remaking Border Service After Socialism

The Polish Border Guard is headquartered in a modernist building in the leafy Warsaw neighborhood of Mokotów, south of the city center. A district of elegant villas and apartment buildings inhabited in the 1920s and 1930s by Warsaw's intelligentsia and middle class, Mokotów was seized during the Nazi occupation. It was colonized by Hitler's plenipotentiaries and bureaucrats dispatched to oversee the affairs of Generalgouvernement, as occupied Poland was called. This is why the area was largely spared in the wholesale destruction of Warsaw in 1944.

The Border Guard building was constructed in the 1920s as one of the military edifices of the then just-reborn Polish state to house the Borderland Protection Corps (Korpus Ochrony Pogranicza). The Borderland Protection Corps was the military unit that defended Polish eastern borders from Ukrainian diversion and a possible Soviet attack in the interwar period. World War II put an end to its existence. After the war the Mokotów headquarters became the command center of the Borderland Protection Forces (Wojska Ochrony Pogranicza, WOP), that is, the professional division of socialist Poland's army delegated to border tasks. But in 1945 the borders to be guarded had a different outline from those before 1939, and the mode of protecting them followed a decidedly different logic.

After asserting its rule over postwar Poland, the new Soviet-dependent government was compelled to organize the protection of its fully redrawn borders following the model practiced in the Soviet Union. Army units returning from the front were renamed Borderland Protection Forces (Wojska Ochrony Pogranicza, colloquially referred to as *pogranicznicy* or *wopki*), and delegated to the task. Like their prewar predecessors, between 1945 and 1949 they were also clashing with Ukrainian independence fighters, this time on behalf of the Communist government. The struggles in the eastern borderland, especially the Bieszczady mountains, ended with Akcja Wisła, the large-scale resettlement of the remaining Ukrainian population (see Chapter 7).

The role of WOP was the "military-political" protection of the border (Dominiczak 1985). While the *military* responsibilities were fairly self-explanatory (be prepared for a possible attack, especially from the West), the mandate of *political* protection required tight cooperation with other institutions of the socialist state, such as passport bureaus, local Party committees, and workplaces, all of which were thoroughly infiltrated by agents of the security apparatus. Political protection involved far more than preventing the entry of spies and saboteurs. It entailed investigating shipments of banned literature in both directions, and stopping cash, printed materials, printing equipment, and other aid smuggled into Poland, as well as *samizdat* going abroad. Above all, *pogranicznicy* had to prevent and combat clandestine escapes and intensely scrutinize those who were granted the scarce benefit of travel.

The Polish People's Republic differed from the GDR or Czechoslovakia in that it was territorially enclosed within the Eastern bloc. Unless we count the Baltic Coast separating it from Scandinavia, it shared no borders with any Western states. This somewhat reduced the everyday drama of both the political and the military aspects of border protection. Even though the Federal Republic of Germany did not officially recognize Poland's postwar borders until 1970, the GDR provided a buffer against any potential retribution. The Borderland Protection troops were only sporadically involved in foiling the kinds of ingenious escapes in self-made vehicles and flying objects that happened on a regular basis on the East-West German border.[13] Persons who fled socialist Poland usually did so after they actually got permission to leave or, as for Polish Jews in 1968, were forced to leave after being handed a one-way passport out of the country.

Immigration into Eastern bloc countries was practically nonexistent. The rare exceptions were students from socialist developing countries who were invited to Poland and other People's Republics to study at universities and polytechnics, and occasionally stayed. Also, in 1949 the Communist Polish government accepted in a gesture of solidarity approximately fifteen thousand Greek refugees who fled Greece after the failure of the Communist insurgency. (Most of them subsequently left back for Greece or Germany; today the Polish-Greek community, according to the Greek Embassy in Warsaw, is estimated at approximately 4,300.) But in the end, not control over incoming foreigners but ensuring the immobility of socialist citizens was the key state concern. This helped minimize the seeping of capitalist discourses and practices into the socialist domain.

The Decree on the Protection of Borders issued by the Communist authorities in 1953 specified that WOP was responsible for controlling cross-border traffic and protecting state borders from military attack and individual acts of violation. In reality, however, the borders of states remaining within the Soviet Union's orbit were part of a larger security scheme covering the entire Warsaw Pact (Dominiczak 1985: 224).[14] The main efforts of soldiers on duty were focused on preventing westward escapes, infiltration by foreign agents, and the import of banned literature, as well as defections from within their own ranks. Handling nonpolitical trespasses (for example, of fugitive criminals illegally crossing borders) was exclusively in the competence of the Milicja, the socialist police force. From the political point of view, the western, not eastern borders that required the most intense vigilance on behalf of WOP. In the words of Władysław Szymanek, the jovial Border Guard colonel who was my liaison at headquarters, and who recounted for me the basic outline of his organization's history, this became a "serious shortcoming" after the system changed:

> You know, the system of border protection in that other political-legal order was more or less such that everyone minded their western border. The Russians had this whole so-called *systiema* that came up to our eastern border. They had barbed wire, strips of plowed ground, signaling equipment. . . . We on the other hand had a dense line of watchtowers on the Odra so that people wouldn't escape, and unwanted individuals [spies] couldn't get in. Signalization and other equipment that was sophisticated for the time.

The imperatives guiding this mode of border protection changed with the collapse of the Berlin Wall. Szymanek continued:

And then the system changed, and it turned out that what we have in the east was basically like Swiss cheese. And so we had to turn the protection around. What immigration in the east? [Before] nobody thought that anybody might want to cross our eastern borders. Nothing was happening there. Sometimes someone wandered across in the mountains without realizing it, but that was extremely rare. That you could run into Nigerians, Vietnamese, Chinese, or people from Angola at our border, nobody dreamed about it. . . . This is why since the establishment of the Border Guard we have opened forty new units on the eastern border.

Summing up, in the Cold War decades, border protection was governed by the imperial interest of the Soviet Union to preserve the integrity of the bloc. By and large, people's ability to move, travel, and associate freely across borders undermined the strategic goals of socialist states and of the Soviet bloc as a whole. If Katherine Verdery is right that what ultimately killed socialism was the "collision of two differently constituted social orders, together with the notions of person and activity proper to them" (1996: 37), then it is hardly surprising that the socialist ruling class sensed a great danger at their western borders. Thus the Borderland Protection Forces, along with other security organs, took part in a concerted effort to curb, contain, and control human mobility as part of their political mandate. The practices associated with accomplishing this goal were rarely openly violent. They did, however, involve various forms of repression, from flat-out refusals to issue passports, to drawn-out procedures and pervasive bureaucratic harassment involving encounters with security forces.[15]

All WOP's material assets and human resources were transferred to the newly formed Border Guard in 1990. Building on that, the postsocialist administration had to establish a modern European border force that would emulate Western rather than Soviet models. It had to deploy a system geared to the post-Cold War reality that was just beginning to unfold. But at the Warsaw main office, initially little changed inside and outside the building, other than the plaques at the entrance and the selection of portraits and national symbols inside. Little appeared different, until the push to begin adjusting to the EU and Schengen led to a complex upgrade and refurbishing that would render the place an appropriate site to house the reformed and reorganized Border Guard, receive European visitors, and convey adherence to European standards and norms.

In 2005, the year of my first visit, the Border Guard building was undergoing extensive interior and exterior renovation. Rugs, worn-out armchairs, and metal ashtray stands from the 1970s disappeared from reception areas and hallways, replaced with modern upholstered chairs and end tables strewn with glossy pamphlets. While the corridors leading to the offices of high-ranking commanders were being painted and recarpeted, office staff would meet for cigarette breaks in back staircases still awaiting their turn to be remodeled. Secretaries who escorted me in and out of the building apologized for the unsightliness of those rear spaces. But they offered an opportunity to catch a last glimpse of the disappearing material and visual culture of a socialist institution. In the back, oil-painted walls still carried framed black-and-white photographs of border soldiers on duty. Two men with rifles and a dog in the snow. A patrol in a motor boat on a border river smiling into the camera. Some of the pictures were missing the glass that once covered them; in others the frames were warped. Once, I asked a young officer whom I accompanied on his cigarette break what was going to happen with the photos. "They'll just dump them, I guess," he answered, "Too bad, they are cool. Our guys don't look like that any more. "

Throughout months of research, all my contacts and encounters with guards who were directly involved in patrolling the border had to be cleared through headquarters in Mokotów. I went through the routine of leaving my documents and going through security in the building's vast foyer many times before I was allowed to meet with anyone "in the field," *w terenie*. Colonel Szymanek took charge of guiding me through the clearance process. He was also the one to introduce me to his organization's official views and reasoning in the context of EU integration and the ongoing adjustment to Schengen. He would always emphasize that coordinating the work of border services of 25 countries was an uneasy task, but that any delays in getting Poland "ready" would not be the fault of his organization. By 2006, the Border Guard building in Mokotów reflected this institutional sense of preparedness. The façade, once grayish and worn, had been refinished in two chirpy shades of green. The EU flag was flown next to the Polish one.

In the Field: The Eyes of the Guard

There are twelve border crossings in nine towns along the Polish-Ukrainian border, of which six are rail crossings serving cargo and passenger trains and six cater to road traffic. During my fieldwork I visited seven of the twelve and additionally one with Belarus. After a protracted process of reviewing my request and institutional accreditations, the Bureau for the Protection of Undisclosed Information at Border Guard headquarters: Warsaw granted permission to visit the divisions in charge of the Polish-Ukrainian frontier. The following sections draw on my observations at two crossings, each in the purview of one of the divisions: Dorohusk in the northern section, and Medyka in the southern. Medyka, which connects to the Ukrainian village of Shehyni, 70 kilometers east of Lviv, is a particularly heavily traveled checkpoint, which in addition to serving passenger and cargo vehicles features the only pedestrian crossing along the Polish-Ukrainian border. Dorohusk links to the Volhynian town of Ustilug and has some of the most modern facilities at its passenger and cargo crossing.

I discuss also my observations beyond checkpoints, where the frontier consists of the so-called *zielona granica*, "green border," the terrain where the borderline is demarcated across fields, forests, and meadows and along the river. The green border is marked by poles, plowed ground, and—in some places—barbed-wire fencing. In 2005–2006 the installation of electromagnetic motion sensors, radar, and other technologically advanced surveillance equipment was in progress. These investments were made to ensure the impermeability of the green border in preparation for joining Schengen. I was allowed to visit one of the approximately 50 green border units. In every instance I was accompanied by a senior officer who determined the extent of my access to other personnel and their activities.[16]

The legally enshrined tasks of the Border Guard are manifold. Besides controlling traffic and preventing and combating illegal immigration, they include fighting such cross-border crimes as trafficking in persons, smuggling, and unauthorized import of weapons and dangerous substances, especially drugs and radioactive materials. They must also cooperate with the Customs Service in preventing unauthorized export of cultural artifacts and the influx of objects, animals, and persons that might present an epidemiological or phytosanitary threat.[17] In my interactions with the officers, I was interested in how they described all these realms of activity. I let them guide me toward issues that they considered most pressing. "Illegal migration," *nielegalna migracja*, uniformly received the most attention and, as I show below, it was most decisively constructed as a "problem" and a "challenge" (*wyzwanie*).

When considered from Brussels, or Warsaw's Border Guard headquarters and other central institutions, "illegal migration" appears mostly as a theoretical problem, an object of specialized knowledge and intervention. Not so at the land border. There all aspects of "prevention and combating" overlap in the daily practices of uniformed guards and civilian personnel, meshing in the surveillance, categorizing, sorting, and disposing of foreigners.

There are many ways of keeping the border impervious to breach. Shielding the territory of the state from illegitimate movement is a serious and costly project that involves carefully written laws and cutting-edge technology.[18] I arranged to visit sites "in the field" to see these methods at work. Anyone can travel through a crossing or wander along the boundary line, although when approaching it at a distance of less than 500 meters one must be prepared to be stopped for questioning and ID checking. But these sites take on particular characteristics when seen through the eyes of uniformed functionaries. I was conscious of the constraints that would be placed on my visits (my clearance did not include access to "undisclosed" information). But still, I wanted— even if only for a moment—to gain access to the guards' perspective, to grasp the practicalities of surveillance at modern European borders.

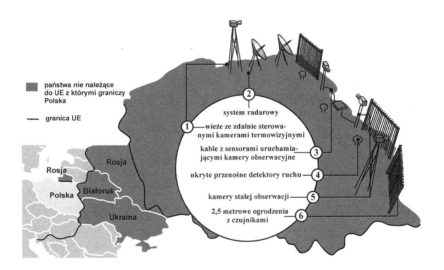

Figure 4. Media representation of border surveillance, extolling cutting edge technology. Dark gray: non-EU states. Symbols: (1) radar system; (2) towers with remotely operated thermal cameras; (3) cables with camera triggers; (4) portable motion sensors; (5) surveillance cameras; (6) 2.5 meter fence with sensors. Zbigniew Lentowicz, "Warownia nad Bugiem: Od Wschodu oddzieli nas system elektonicznych zabezpieczeń" (Fortress on the Bug: System of Electronic Safety Devices Will Separate Us from the East), *Rzeczpospolita*, May 20, 2005.

My designated chaperon at the division I visited was Colonel Janusz Wró-bel, a military type with upright posture and an old-fashioned mustache. On my first visit, he welcomed me in his office with kindness, though not without distanced bemusement. Subsequently, over the course of our in-person and phone conversations he loosened up, and by the second time I came he insisted we drop the formal address and go by first names.

One day in summer 2005, Janusz arranged for a service vehicle and a driver. We were going for a day trip. We approached the borderline along one of the regional roads heavily marked by commercial traffic. Before arriving at the crossing, we saw plain black-and-white road signs first announcing "Border Zone" (Strefa Przygraniczna) and then "State Border" (Granica Państwa). Once we got to the crossing, symbols appeared corresponding to the border's dual status: the white and red flag of Poland was flown next to the blue EU one, with a circle of twelve yellow stars. The territory of the nation-state and the territory of the European Union were thus marked as one, but the EU flag was not *like* the Polish flag. Shore and Abélès have observed that "the EU suffers from a paucity of rituals and symbols when compared to European nation-states. However, this lack of symbols underlies a more fundamental problem: the EU's chronic lack of cultural legitimacy and popular consent. Despite enormous advances toward economic and legal integration, there is still little tangible sense of belonging or shared identity among the putative citizens of Europe" (2004: 10). Indeed, at the border the EU flag is a symbol of a status, not a *demos*. It is clear that it signifies not statehood but rather something like membership in a club with rules and privileges. My interlocutors left no doubt that the border was Polish, and that Polish, not European, guards were patrolling it.

Administrative buildings that house customs and border guard authorities were marked with Polish national symbols. Inside, beyond EU stickers on electronic equipment that said "purchased from European Union funds," little indicated the presence of a supranational authority. The course of the borderline was marked by approximately one-meter-tall pyramid-shaped concrete blocks. Five meters into the territory of each country were poles painted in national colors (white and red for Poland, blue and yellow for Ukraine). The uniforms of border personnel were also Polish, following the traditional pattern for state services (dark blue for customs, military green for border guards). There is no such a thing as an EU border uniform, just as there is no single EU border authority. "There isn't one, and there won't be one," Janusz explained, referring to the now-abandoned idea for a shared border service floated in Brussels about the year 2000. The idea was ultimately reframed and materialized as an "agency for operational cooperation" known as Frontex, established in 2005 and headquartered in Warsaw.[19] He was emphatic about the reasons such patrols would be senseless:

> What does a Portuguese, or a German border guard know about pa-trolling Polish borders? With all due respect, nothing! They know their shores and their shrubs. But these are ours, our river [Bug] and our mountains [Bieszczady]. We know every bit of land here, and there is no way that an EU border guard would do a better job than we do.

Asserting in this way his own and his fellow servicemen and -women's authority over the physical features of the border terrain, he pointed to the experiential nature of the knowledge required to perform the ultimately hands-on job of a border guard. Like his colleagues at the Warsaw headquar-ters, he spoke with impatience of the foreign "experts," that is, security spe-cialists and border servicemen from EU countries, who come on behalf of EU institutions to train Polish officers in the art of patrolling the border.

The single instance when he had good things to say about foreign visitors was when he was recalling a field training with Native Americans. According to his story, which I ended up hearing many times from different people, a couple of years earlier, a group of Native American specialists in traceology (a branch of forensics concerned with interpreting traces and marks) who nor-mally work at the U.S.-Mexico border had been sent to Poland as part of an international cooperation program. The "Indians," Janusz said, did teach the guards a thing or two about how to read human presence from broken sticks and fractures in the mud. After all, he thought, for them reading traces in the wilderness is surely an innate, natural skill—no wonder they would be mas-terful at it. Janusz's retelling evoked an image of young boys "playing Indians" in a pretend Wild West, rather than grown men learning modern policing skills. The training was fun; everyone got to spend a few days in the woods. The "Indians" were apparently impressed with the Polish guards' compe-tence and equipment. "They were envious of our boots," Janusz laughed as he proudly described the impermeable footwear used in swampy terrain. "They came from America to Poland, and yet they never saw boots like this." Sym-bolically, the superior boots put an end to an Eastern European inferiority complex toward anything Western. Overall the Poles got along well with the "Indians." This was because they too understood that patrolling the border is an art that, according to Janusz, Polish guards have "in their blood." It is not a technicality that can be taught by detached and overly formal EU experts.

Policing the border is a combination of two tasks. First is overseeing passenger and cargo traffic at crossings. The vast majority of foreigners who come through passenger checkpoints are Ukrainian citizens who carry Polish tourist visas, but who on reaching Poland take up low-paying seasonal or medium-term jobs.[20] The guards check their documents, "financial means" (which in practice means asking to see cash), and occasionally belongings. The second task is patrolling the green border. There, the unauthorized entrants who are most likely to attempt a crossing on foot or by boat are citizens of former Soviet republics in Central Asia, Pakistan, Afghanistan, Vietnam, India, and China. The majority are headed for Western Europe, where they can take advantage of strong immigrant networks and better standards of living. All guards, regardless of rank, must be competent to carry out controls at the crossings and patrol the green border. Anyone, any day, can be assigned to sit in the control booth and check passports, or go with a rifle, on foot, or on a motorcycle, with or without a dog, to patrol a particular section. "Do you know what is the most precious equipment we have?"—Janusz asked me when we were talking about the new binoculars and cameras acquired by the division. "It is the eyes of the guard."

There are a number of things at the border crossing that the eyes of the guard must be trained to spot, for example, suspicious behavior suggesting that a person is carrying concealed objects, or signs that something, or someone, might be hidden inside or under a vehicle.[21] Guards must also watch for signs in a person's behavior that suggest that "the purpose of entry is other than declared." This arbitrary clause is written into the Aliens Act (Art. 21, par. 4). It provides authorities an opportunity to turn away people who cannot be turned away for any other reason. Their documents are in order. They are able to produce passport, visa, and requisite "financial means." Still, if the "circumstances of entry indicate" that they are up to something other than what they say, they can receive a refusal of entry.

"How do you decide who gets a refusal?"—I asked one of the guards I was introduced to when visiting my first border crossing. He explained that experienced guards "just know" when someone is lying.

> We have all these Ukrainian women here. They often say that they are going shopping, or to visit relatives. "When are you going back?" [we ask]. She says "Monday." We open the trunk, and there's a bag of

clothes, enough for 3 months, not for 3 days. In the bag some aprons, gloves, all this kind of stuff for cleaning. And she wants me to believe that she will be cleaning for her relatives?

The vast majority of persons crossing the border could qualify under this clause as ineligible to enter. Predictably, the guards do not acknowledge any arbitrariness and show no interest whatsoever in discussing, on the record or off, whether and when issuing refusals is "fair." But the point is not really to stop the influx of Ukrainians intending to work in Poland. The discretion clause asserts the right of the guards to exercise their own judgment of who, when, and how does not meet the criteria to cross the border.

Refusal decisions are made and delivered in a publicly visible manner. Others awaiting entry always see the process of turning their fellow passenger away. The guard takes the passport, searches the vehicle or luggage, asks questions, disappears, returns with the documents, sends the person away. In making a spectacle of denying entry to a selected few, the officers strategically distribute fear and intimidation among the majority who are admitted. It is a disciplining practice that reinforces the perception that the tacit acknowledgment of illegal labor is tentative, contingent on the evolving needs of the state, and subject to withdrawal at any moment. It renders the migrant population docile and adaptable to the shifting demands of the unregulated labor market.[22]

The people who are more than willing to discuss refusals, their implications, and ways to get around them are the passengers of cross-border buses, especially while they are stuck in long lines awaiting admittance. There, the communal setting is conducive to telling stories, trading fears, and sharing warnings. The passengers are convinced that the guards use quotas and deny entry to an average of five people on each bus (the guards deny this). "So-and-so got a refusal because she didn't say *dzień dobry*" (a polite greeting). "So-and-so's daughter was sent back because the guard didn't like her face." "Don't say anything if they don't ask you." "Say you are going to visit somebody." I witnessed the process of turning people away as a passenger too. Inside the hot and stuffy bus full of frightened and intimidated people it doesn't matter *why* the guards deny entry. Each time a name is called and someone is thrown off, it sends a current of panic through the bus, which, after the control is over, turns into relief for those who once again made it across.

This strategic management of the local (that is, as far as the guards can see, Poland-bound) traffic is a pragmatic response to the imperatives of controlling the national border. However, when EU territorial integrity and security are at stake, practical knowledge and the naked eye appear to be insufficient. In the process of Schengen adjustment, the discretion, experience, and working intuition of the guards are cast aside as unreliable resources. Policing the supranational boundary requires a higher order of intervention and expertise as well as new technologies of seeing. For example, the naked eye can spot visual and tactile signs of primitive forgery in documents and currency. But the kind of counterfeiting that threatens "Europe" is a sophisticated art that requires equal sophistication in detecting it. Identifying forged documents is high on the priority list; the eye needs enhancement. Microscopes developed specifically for this purpose are among the equipment introduced on the Polish-Ukrainian border as part of the Schengen upgrade. At the crossing I visited with Janusz, I could watch an officer on duty operate one. He happened to be examining a forged Lithuanian passport confiscated during a routine control. He explained the telltale signs of tampering with a document by pointing out the tiny bubbles of air trapped under the passport's lamination and the protruding rough edges of the photograph—a sure sign it was not the original. A Moldovan man attempted to use the passport to enter Poland. Lithuania is in the EU, and successful passing as a Lithuanian would have enabled him not only to enter Poland, but also to continue his trip farther into Europe. But the extra-careful scrutiny delivered expected results. The man was now arrested; a prospective illegal immigrant headed for the EU had been stopped.

The ubiquitous cameras likewise augment the naked eye. Hardly any public institution in the developed world today eschews the panoptic power of closed-circuit TV (Lyon 2002). A border crossing is no different. Once, during a checkpoint visit, one of the deputy commanders asked me if I would like to see the "true Big Brother." It wasn't clear whether his reference was Orwellian or the reality TV show. It is likely that, in line with Zygmunt Bauman's observation that "both Big Brothers—old and new—sit next to each other in the passport control booths" (2004: 132), he did not distinguish between the two. The point was that all is seen, at all times. I was admitted to a room equipped with a wall of TV screens that constantly stream the picture captured by over a hundred still and rotational cameras installed directly at, and in the vicinity of, the facility. The signal they stream allows for an anticipatory monitoring of traffic and helps spot troublesome individuals and fights and scuffles between people stuck in lines. It provides the operator with data that help determine where and when to send reinforcements.

The men explained to me also which other types of equipment were supposed to be introduced on the border in the near future. I learned, for example, about the heartbeat detector, which without opening the car or truck can detect a heartbeat of a person or animal hidden inside. The device, resembling a giant stethoscope, is placed on the external surface of the object to be tested, and results are displayed on a hospital-like monitor. International security firms submitted bids for providing the equipment, and my hosts were looking forward to using the machine, already in use in Dover and other European ports.[23] It would vastly speed up the search for "illegals," as the signals emitted by their live bodies would provide all the signs needed to apprehend them. It was to be delivered in a matter of weeks, initially only for testing, later as permanent equipment.[24] Another planned innovation was the forthcoming installation of a virtual fence along the border. It would be a combination of towers with remotely operated thermal cameras, radar, motion detectors, and cables embedded in the soil with sensors that could trigger the cameras.

"Our equipment is up to the highest European standards." Janusz repeated that many times, echoing not only others at his own organization, but also the Polish media, which at the time of my research frequently ran stories on the advances in border-keeping. But one thing worried Janusz. "Make sure," he said to me, "that you don't write that the European Union bought this stuff for us. Reporters write this all the time, but that's wrong. *We bought it*, not the European Union. They only gave us the money." It was important to affirm his own and his fellow guards' autonomy and technological competence, in spite of economic dependence.

Thus the agency of the Polish border guard—and, by extension, of the Polish state—was reasserted toward the powerful but abstract body of the European Union. *Our boys* bought the machinery, and they know what to do with it. To appreciate the pinnacle of modern surveillance technology, I was to be taken on a nighttime patrol, to watch the guards watch the border through the lens of the unit's most expensive night vision thermal cameras. In an apologetic tone, Janusz said he couldn't promise we would catch any illegal migrants. But he expressed hope that seeing the camera operated by young functionaries at the moonlit Polish border would be attractive in itself. In that area the patrols usually apprehend one group of illegals every week. The total apprehended in 2005 and 2006 on the external border was about fifteen hundred per year, of whom close to one thousand were crossing from Ukraine.

That evening, a driver took us through the open space, empty of people or settlements. We were supposed to meet up with the crew of a thermal vision vehicle, a van equipped with a thermal camera mounted on an expanding external pole. The lights of our car had to be off in order not to expose our or, more important, the van's location. Inside the vehicle the guards are forbidden even to light a cigarette. This section of the border had a history of numerous illegal crossings. There were individuals and, more often, organized groups of "illegals." The river around this area is shallow and does not present a life-threatening obstacle. The shrubs along it are dense. Nonetheless, there are also vast empty fields on both sides, where anything that moves is clearly visible to the naked eye during the day, and to the thermal camera at night.

We approached the vehicle and got out of our car. There were two young guards on duty, both junior rank. The older one opened the door on the passenger side for me. I entered the van with Janusz. To the side of the steering wheel, it was outfitted with a console and two screens. The screen to the left showed a detailed interactive map of the area with our position in the center. On the screen to the right was an image of our surroundings. The view was captured in the darkness by a special lens equipped with a device that detects radiation in the infrared range. In contrast to older models of infrared cameras, which delivered images by registering the otherwise invisible moon and starlight reflected off objects, thermography records an object's own infrared radiation.

On the screen, shades of gray formed the shapes of plants, trees, buildings, and electric poles in the range of three kilometers in all directions. All objects emit radiation; its intensity depends on temperature. Cool waters of the river show as almost white. As the temperature increases, the image becomes darker. Janusz instructed the older guard to find a "live object" in order to demonstrate the camera's capacity.

Monochromatic thermography makes living bodies visible as black shapes. Humans and animals appear as blurry silhouettes against a much lighter background. Their shapes are clearly discernible, but their contours are soft. "This is really cool, you will be surprised." The boyish bragging about "our" technology seems for my hosts to be an important part of showing me around. The older of the two guards operating the machinery zooms in on a black dot in motion. "A hare," he states authoritatively, "about 800 meters away." Indeed, that's what the leaps of a small rounded black figure across the screen suggest. As the camera rotates and zooms in and out, we look at birds in the bushes, which appear as black specks against the background of bright gray leaves, and at a group of deer at the edge of a grove. The guards don't hide their enthusiasm at using thermography for detecting "illegals" on their way across the borders. The process of staking out the trespassers is about introducing the subjectifying gaze into a hitherto indifferent space. Janusz remarked that

> our guys are never bored here. . . . Sometimes they just sit here and watch the fauna [laughter]. But when it comes to action, this is a tool that they couldn't even dream about before. The group is coming, happy they made the crossing, they might even think they are already in Germany, and there's a surprise. Our people are waiting for them right here, with handcuffs and everything else.

In Jeremy Bentham's original Panopticon, back lighting deprived inmates of the privacy of shadows and exposed them to constant surveillance. As Majid Yar observed, even though contemporary forms of panopticism encompass new techniques and seize on new subjects, the Foucaultian logic of visibility-vulnerability-subjectification is still a viable analysis of the specular dimension of social life (Yar 2003: 258). With thermal vision, the darkness of night and the shadows cast by trees no longer provide protection. Visibility, once again, is a trap (Foucault 1977: 200). Janusz explains that there is extensive collaboration with patrols on the Ukrainian side. He marvels at how well it is working out, while at the same time emphasizing the superiority of the Polish Guard in terms of training and technological advancement. For example, the range of the thermal cameras allows for capturing the image of the Ukrainian side of the border. Polish functionaries, when they spot "illegals" on the other side, alert their Ukrainian counterparts, who are then obliged to intervene. This, for the Polish guards, is a favored turn of events: "Ukrainians catch them, they're a problem of the Ukrainians."

That night the patrol didn't catch any illegal immigrants. But it was clear that thermal vision is a remarkable tool, geared directly toward the kind of priorities that inform the policing of external EU borders. The entire Schengen-related transformation of the border guard culminates in this refined act of seeing: to be an agent in charge of the security of European borders is to have enhanced specular agency, to see into pitch-black darkness and beyond the limits of state territory. Seeing persons approaching the border *before* they even get there absolves the state of the responsibility and expense of handling their cases, whatever those might be. The would-be entrants might seek asylum, or they might "only" be "economic migrants." Whatever the case, it is not Poland, or any other member state, that has to process their refugee status applications or arrange for costly and often logistically complicated re-moval. Their journey instead will end in Ukraine—a country where services designed for citizens are hardly functional, to say nothing of its systemic ca-pacity to maintain an extensive border regime which could handle foreigners who bounced off the walls of Europe.

Life Scanning

Convenient handing over of the problem to Ukrainians isn't always possi-ble, however. Some people do successfully make the trek across. The messy business of disposing of them was first described to me at another regional division by Milena Nagórna, a perky information coordinator assigned to oversee my visit. As we were having coffee in her cozy office furnished with a 70s-style desk and cabinets, she described to me one of the division's latest coups:

> Not so long ago, we caught I guess five groups of illegal immigrants from Vietnam. These are small groups, sometimes five, sometimes six Vietnamese, sometimes just women. There's always someone to look after them, Ukrainian guides. Recently, there were seven, seven Viet-namese, guided by two Ukrainians. The transfer technically looks like this, that they lead them on foot, across the green border. Here a Pole waits for them to take them farther.

She hesitated briefly when describing the participation of local people in human smuggling networks. She chose not to dwell on it.

> M.P.: You know, it varies with the local people. . . . Sometimes people come all the way from Podlasie [a region 200 km. to the north] to re-ceive a group here. They come down in luxury cars. . . . Now of course the Border Guard is already sensitive to that, a luxury car and inside 11 or 12 Vietnamese. Squeezed on the seats, under the seats, in the trunk. They lie there like herrings. They are little people so the [or-ganizers] can arrange them like this [she makes a motion suggesting stacking. Uses the verb *poukładają* normally applied to things]. And they think that if the car is fancy, the Border Guard will not know that they are shuttling a group.

The narrative is meant to assert that the Border Guard can outsmart any such naïve plot.

> *Milena*: So, these are the cars that they use. But all the group is trying to do is escape from here as soon as they can. Get lost in traffic. . . . [If we didn't get them] they would go to Rzeszów or to Warsaw. . . . And usually from there they have an organized transfer to Germany.
> *Karolina*: Is this where most of them want to go?
> *Milena*: Yes. Yes. But I personally think, and this is my opinion, that these Vietnamese [people] should be very happy to stay here in Poland.

It is a matter of pride. New, Europeanized Poland ought to be no less an immigration destination than Germany. When the plot is foiled, however, as in the case Milena described, the guides (the "two Ukrainians") are arrested and await further handling by local organs of criminal justice. As for the "illegals," there is a range of possible scenarios. If they are not caught in the act and therefore cannot be immediately handed over to Ukrainian border authorities based on the readmission agreement, or if the Ukrainian border authorities refuse to accept them on procedural grounds (which happens, according to Milena), they become the responsibility of the Polish state. If any of them happen to file an application for refugee status, their cases will be processed according to the dedicated procedure whose purpose is to check whether they match the legal criteria to be considered refugees (more on that in the following chapter).

Immigrants who do not formally seek asylum are channeled into a different legal pipeline from those who do. The former are uniformly headed for removal procedures, the latter for the bureaucratic quagmire of the refugee status application process. Both categories of persons are subject to fingerprinting, although their biometric data are filed under different headings. Here another machine is central to the proper organization of movement. It is called a *lifescanner*, and in the division I visited it was in a criminology lab in one of the buildings of the post-military complex.

The lab is a bright room with windows facing a construction site. Outside, Schengen adjustment funds are being spent on a new, state-of-the-art detention facility. The lifescanner, in spite of its ominous name, resembles nothing more than a regular copy machine connected to a computer. It is hooked up to the servers of the EU-wide Eurodac system, which stores the fingerprints of all persons who have requested asylum in any EU country, as well as those of all illegal entrants and foreign nationals found illegally present in the territory of any member state.

Next to biometric passports and airport security checks, Eurodac is another of the recent expressions of how efforts to control populations increasingly come to rely on biometric data. As the EU official portal explains:

> The Eurodac system enables Member States to identify asylum applicants and persons who have been apprehended while unlawfully crossing an external frontier of the Community. By comparing fingerprints, Member States can determine whether an asylum applicant or a foreign national found illegally present within a Member State has previously claimed asylum in another Member State or whether an asylum applicant entered the Union territory unlawfully.[25]

Calling the operation of collecting biometric data "fingerprinting"—a word that evokes dipping suspected criminals' fingers in ink—is somewhat misleading. In fact, the digital device scans the entire hand, five fingers and the palm, and then separately the thumb and index finger. There are no black inky traces that stigmatize the suspect for at least as long as it takes to scrub them off. Lifescanning leaves no marks on the hand of the person, but the digitized prints have a durability and infinite reproducibility that no ink and paper can match. The image is encoded with other personal data and sent electronically to Brussels, where all the information is stored. There, the computer compares the image against existing data and returns results within a few hours (the processing time depends on the workload of the servers).

If the scan produces a "hit"—as the criminology technician called it—this could mean that the person had already been admitted to, or requested asylum in, one of the other EU member states. Based on the Dublin Regulation, the state that permitted the asylum applicant to enter or reside is responsible for conducting the asylum procedure.[26] For example, someone who clandestinely enters Germany after being admitted to Polish territory will not be permitted to submit an asylum application there, but will be sent to Poland. But in the case of Poland's eastern border "hits" indicating a previous history of application for asylum are a rare occurrence. The technician explained that this is because Poland is the first EU country on most migrants' route. Thus, for most apprehended migrants fingerprinting there constitutes their first record in Eurodac. When that is the case, he or she may be transferred directly into the custody of Ukrainian border authorities, based on the readmission agreement, or detained in Poland for the purpose of eventual deportation.

The fingerprints are stored for the next ten years in the case of asylum seekers and for two years for illegal entrants, retrievable anywhere in the EU. The technology makes it possible for all immigration authorities to check where and how this person first entered the common territory and thus who is to be responsible for the eventual "processing" or removal. According to Brussels press releases, in 2004 Eurodac processed 232,205 fingerprints of asylum seekers, 16,183 fingerprints of people crossing the borders irregularly, and 39,550 fingerprints of people apprehended while illegally on the territory of a member state. In 2006 those numbers were respectively 165,968, 41,312, and 63,341; the shift might be attributed to a growing emphasis on policing irregular migration within states' territories.[27] In this way persons of unregulated legal status, who for various reasons, willfully or otherwise, found themselves in legal limbo, are being "seen," and their whereabouts controlled as never before through the application of networked digital information systems. This isn't to say that the system is perfectly Orwellian. It remains possible to escape the gaze of the state, to fall off its radar and through the cracks of complex immigration or asylum bureaucracy, as indeed thousands of immigrants do. But the point is that as more and more Eurodac terminals will be installed throughout the territories of all member states, reappearing—by an instant electronic "hit"—emerges as a perennial practical possibility, a manifestation of Balibar's "ubiquity of borders" (2002).

Between the Nation-State and Europe

The precision of Schengen adjustment protocols notwithstanding, ethnography shows that new regulations and technologies on the Polish-Ukrainian border emerge as something other than simply means for an unconditional fight, on behalf of united Europe, against illegal immigration, smuggling, and security threats. Instead, they are deployed strategically in pursuit of two objectives that don't necessarily overlap. On the one hand, the agents of rebordering must embrace their EU mandate and protect the boundaries of the larger, albeit underdefined, community. On the other hand, they remain in service and in charge of the nation-state's interests. Constantly negotiating between these dual roles, they engage in ongoing reconciling, prioritizing, and choosing between the kinds of inclusions and exclusions they produce.

Notwithstanding the political debate about the future and the boundaries of Europe, rebordering unfolds at its own swift pace, and—to a large extent—independently from the periodic slowdowns of the grand project of EU integration. It draws on vast monetary, technological, and human resources to preempt the imagined intrusion of unwanted multitudes. It relies on the constructions of the "illegal immigrant" to promote continental integrity and uses restrictive immigration policy orientation as one of the instruments of building cohesion.

The Polish-Ukrainian border is one of the newer sites of supranational governmentality and cutting edge surveillance. Polish officers embrace new technologies, laws, and approaches, but only insofar as they help them recast their service and professional status as "European" and civilized. They resist the authority of international experts and of the abstract EU bureaucracy, perceiving them as disregarding and underestimating their own embodied and practical knowledge of the border. Polish agents of rebordering end up circumventing the EU blueprint for thick borders by exercising their own situated judgment over who gets in and who doesn't. They know, as one Border Guard expert put it, that an aggressive pursuit of Ukrainian workers would mean rotten apples in local orchards, and thus trouble for Polish farmers and local economies (Dąbrowski 2007: 1). By tacitly accepting the cross-border movements of itinerant workers, they address the political and economic impracticality of the rigid boundary. At the same time they remain structurally locked into a position of indifference toward the inequalities and individual hardships perpetuated by the border regime. The guards' practical local knowledge, combined with forbearance at higher levels of state administration, averts the stalling of cross-border traffic that would have resulted from rigid implementation of EU laws and regulations. That might well help the cause of EU integration—James Scott argued that that those formal orders that do not allow for nonconforming practice, or that attempt to stamp it out, are the ones that fail (1998: 352). On the other hand, the pragmatics of seeing like a border guard help sustain an inequitable arrangement. Unregulated labor migrations between Poland and Ukraine remain a known and thoroughly normalized fact of postsocialist life and political economy. As a result of this type of strategic Europeanization, the "actually existing EU" represents a political model that is considerably less hopeful and fair than the framers of its key legal documents would have us believe.

Chapter 5

Economic Migrants Beyond Demand:
Asylum and the Politics of Classification

> I understand, NGOs, they do human rights. But I, besides human
> rights, I have this border and my job is to watch this border.
> —interview with a unit director, Border Guard

Although the border guards at Poland's eastern border stand prepared for every conceivable attempt to breach the boundary without authorization, and millions of euros have been poured into that preparedness, it merits emphasizing that the sheer fact of Poland's entry into the EU did not result in any sharp increase in the number of migrants coming into the country.[1] As previously noted, since 2000 this has oscillated between 300,000 and 500,000, depending on who is counting and how (see, for example, IOM 2004; Fundacja Inicjatyw Społeczno Ekonomicznych 2008). But, as I began to demonstrate in the previous chapters, what did change is how migrants entering Poland are classified, assigned legal status, and represented in the public discourse. Here I unpack the tensions and entanglements between managing economic migration and protecting refugees. Since the mid-1990s Western Europe has seen a rise of public perception that "bogus asylum seekers" routinely abuse asylum systems designed to grant protection to persons fleeing persecution abroad (see, for example, Bohmer and Schuman 2008; Good 2006). The efforts to curtail such abuses have converged with the rebordering of Europe, particularly with the EU's policy of streamlining and harmonizing asylum systems across old and new member states (Da Lomba 2004; Lavenex 2001; Bunyan 1999; Human Rights Watch 2003). One of the ostensible goals of these reforms is a more efficient sorting of "bona fide asylum seekers" from "economic migrants" who have no claim to international protection. The figure of the "bogus asylum seeker" is indispensable in these efforts, as a rhetorical justification for excluding large groups of people from the benefits and opportunities of asylum. But what is important to point out is that the "bogus asylum seeker" cannot be simply dismissed as a media construct, or a figment of the xenophobic imagination. Rather, this unjustly demonized category of migrants—those who see asylum systems as their only chance to enter the host society—is a direct product of laws that ignore the ambiguities of need-driven migration.

As I signaled in the preceding chapter, those asylum seekers who arrive by land begin their asylum application processes at the land border. Their petitions are adjudicated in the first instance by the Aliens Bureau, a central (Warsaw-based) immigration agency of the Polish government.[2] So, in this chapter we move from the checkpoints, the green border, and border patrols to Warsaw, following, so to speak, the paper trail. Based on fieldwork among officials of various ranks, I discuss the assumptions and implications of migration regulations and practice that inform the sorting of persons into asylum seekers, refugees, and economic migrants.

Who are economic migrants in the "new" Europe? Which economic opportunities can they take advantage of? Which are foreclosed and for whom? These questions are made particularly urgent by the fact that the once sharp categorical distinction between economic migrants and refugees is growing increasingly blurred. For most of postwar European history, and especially in the aftermath of the 1951 Geneva Convention Relating to the Status of Refugees, persons fleeing political crises and seeking protection abroad were defined as refugees, while those migrating voluntarily in pursuit of better earnings were characterized as economic migrants (Sassen 1999). Today, besides wars, among the most formidable hardships that trigger refugee flows are poverty, natural and man-made disasters, and prolonged low-intensity conflict. The experience of persons displaced under such conditions increasingly defies the distinction between economic migration and seeking political refuge. Their legal status is also ambiguous. But the restrictive asylum reforms of the past decade that seek to reduce to the minimum the numbers of refugees admitted to EU territory lead to the practical and legal narrowing of the definition of the refugee and the dismissal of the majority of asylum seekers precisely as "economic migrants," who in practice are persons at the mercy of the state, ineligible for international protection.[3]

If "third country nationals" arriving from conflict-ridden and impover-ished regions like the Caucasus and parts of Central Asia are increasingly unlikely to be legally recognized as refugees, can they take advantage of any alternative paths? Or will they be permanently excluded and barred from ac-cess to European territories and resources, as the EU as a whole and member states individually develop selective immigration policies that privilege some sending countries over others? It is through such legislative and policy trends and their attendant security discourse that "fortress Europe" materializes and evolves. As Sandra Lavenex observed,

> At the national level, the claims for restrictive asylum reforms and in-ternal security are linked through a fear of welfare losses and a spread of racism and xenophobia. Within the European Union, the need to cooperate in asylum matters has been presented from the outset as a necessary compensation for the abolition of internal border controls in the single market with its associated "dangers" for internal security. (Lavenex 1999: 163)

Thus claims of internal and international security converge on the figures of the immigrant and refugee, and lend legitimacy to the classificatory system that distributes categories of migrant legality (Bigo 2002: 63). These claims proved immensely versatile, responding to the fears of European constituen-cies over international crime, terrorism, drug trafficking, and job and welfare losses, particularly in the aftermath of opening internal borders.

It was in this context that asylum reform became an issue of border con-trol, rather than—as asylum was for most of the twentieth century—a matter of human rights. With the imperative to "fix" the system of admitting foreign-ers by, among other efforts, curtailing the "abuse of asylum" that was decried in Europe in the 1990s, the issue of refugees receded as a humanitarian con-cern and resurfaced as a matter of national and EU security. This new, secu-rity-driven approach to asylum not only obfuscates complex and ambiguous realities of human mobility, where persecution, victimhood, suffering, and voluntary versus forced departure are all relative and contested matters.[4] It is also a harbinger of a new politics of segregation, especially in places like Poland, where state authorities are cobbling together a modern immigration policy for the first time in the history of a nation that for centuries experi-enced mostly emigration.

In fact, refugee rights were the first immigration-related policy area that was tackled by the postsocialist state. The signing of the Convention and Protocol Relating to the Status of Refugees (usually referred to as the Geneva Convention and the New York Protocol) by Poland's first post-1989 president, Lech Wałęsa, in 1991 was an act of significance in international politics, part of establishing the country's credibility in the aftermath of the collapse of socialism. Shortly thereafter the conflict in the former Yugoslavia brought the first groups of contemporary refugees into Poland.[5] When in 2006 I was sitting in the tiny reading room of the Aliens Bureau and perusing documents and publications on the beginnings of postsocialist Poland's engagement with the arrivals and presence of foreigners, I was struck by the ubiquity of references to "modern" approaches and "civilized" or "European" standards in the treatment of foreigners (Łodziński 1998; Hryniewicz 2005). It is difficult to resist the impression that the launching of the first governmental agencies dedicated to aiding foreign refugees was motivated not just by need, but also by the desire of the newly minted political elite to legitimate and strengthen the self-representation of the state as both modern and European. About the same time the UN High Commissioner for Refugees established an office in Warsaw, further drawing Poland into the circuit of refugee-receiving countries. With time, the initially minuscule asylum-handling operations expanded into a powerful legal-bureaucratic network wherein individual pleas for asylum are received, negotiated, and adjudicated.

European Union accession forced further changes in the system. Poland's evolving asylum and immigration policy must at once conform to EU security standards, respect the state's human rights commitments, and respond to national economic needs, affected, especially in 2004–2007, by massive departures of Poles seeking employment elsewhere in the EU. Driven by these conflicting imperatives, the emerging approach to foreigners in Poland tends toward the lowest common denominator, that is, the connected assumptions that (a) asylum seekers are a suspect group of whom the majority are seeking to exploit the system while only the slim minority are the "truly" suffering deserving of political recognition, extended through the granting of asylum; (b) economic migrants are needed on the local market, but they ought not to present security or integration challenges or drain the scarce resources of the state.

These assumptions are reinforced on the one hand by anti-Muslim sentiments radiating through the media and the internet from countries of the "old" European Union, and on the other by the contemporary and historical representations within Poland of Poles abroad as "the good immigrants," self-reliant, hard-working, often victimized, but minimally burdensome to their hosts. At the same time the numbers of asylum seekers coming to Poland remained small enough largely to stay off the radar of the general public. The issue has not, at least as of the parliamentary campaign of 2007, been drawn into electoral politics, or become a populist cause in quite the way it has in the West of Europe or in the United States. Open anti-immigrant statements have appeared mostly in the texts of fringe neofascist groups and in the un-moderated and anonymous online comment threads. In the local election campaign of 2006 there were also some signs that the nationalist-Catholic movement, closer to the mainstream than the neofascists, was beginning to experiment with anti-immigrant rhetoric. A local newspaper in Lublin, in-formally connected to the far-right League of Polish Families, stated in an editorial opinion:

> If we don't want the [immigration] problem of France to soon concern us too, we must limit immigration to Poland to the minimum. . . . Po-land ought to admit people close to our own culture, nations of Slavic roots. Europe has bred a viper which regards the holy war as more im-portant than the values of the continent that gave them a new home.[6]

But between 2003 and 2008 examples of such discourse were rather iso-lated, indicating that these were merely exploratory steps in a new territory, not a coherent political agenda.[7] But according to some policymakers and media, there is indeed a lesson to be learned from "old" Europe's immigra-tion woes, or from what one Interior Ministry official responsible for im-migration policy described as the "French mistakes with the Arabs and the German mistakes with the Turks."[8] Judging from this official's rather typical comments on Muslims' "inability to assimilate," that lesson seems to be "don't admit too many, avoid the 'culturally different,' and make sure that in the end they leave."

Against this background, the bureaucracy of legal status and the funnel-ing of people into respective legal and administrative pipelines emerge not as neutral efforts to order human flows, but as inherently political interventions that actively shape the contested landscape of immigration in Europe. Zyg-munt Bauman notes that the sole existential mode of the ubiquitous boundar-ies which divide our world into the included and the rejected is the "incessant *activity* of separation" (2004: 84). In this vein, I am concerned here with the practices and tools for sorting out migrant persons, and with the precarious condition of people who are "classified out."

The sorting unfolds in institutional contexts that form the interconnected nodes of the border regime. One such node is the Warsaw Aliens Bureau, that is, the governmental authority coordinating the legalization of foreign citizens in Poland and representing the first instance in asylum procedures. When I met with the head of the Bureau in the fall of 2005, he defended the high rate of asylum claim rejections on the grounds that "we cannot accept every economic migrant who just wants a better life and just waits for the opportunity to go further west, to Germany or elsewhere in Europe." He said further,

> Poland recognizes as many refugees, as many persons, in the course of the administrative procedure we conduct, convince us that they fulfill the requirements stemming from the Geneva Convention. That they are individually persecuted because of race, religion, nationality, or political views. This is the first thing. The second thing is that indeed we receive many, compared to other European Union countries, Russian-speaking candidates for refugees, but in great majority these people are *classic economic migrants* (*klasyczni migranci ekonomiczni*). This means that they left their own country primarily because of the economic situation in that part, where they . . . [hesitation] for example in the Russian Federation from where they originate.

This official's use of the notion "classic economic migrants" deserves a closer look. In applying it to persons who have been denied recognition as victims of persecution, he symbolically displaces them from the community of refugees and characterizes their journey across borders as an act of choice rather than necessity. He delegitimizes them as potential beneficiaries of the asylum system, which in theory is animated primarily by human rights concerns.[9] Instead the "Russian-speaking candidates for refugees" (and, indeed, non-Russian speaking as well) are recast as voluntary migrants, and as such subject to the policies and politics of border security and economic immigration, rather than asylum. Rhetoric corresponds to practice—failed asylum seekers lose the right to accommodation in refugee centers, and in some circumstances can be detained and deported even while their appeals are pending.[10] No longer assumed to be victims in need of protection, these "third country nationals" instantly become undesirable and thus deportable. Even if what pushed them to leave home were indeed primarily economic and not personal safety needs, they are not the people who would be given the chance to meet the sizeable demand for immigrant labor in Poland. For them, the asylum pipeline is the only chance to be legally admitted into Polish/EU territory, but when it fails, it is supposed to shoot them right back out (a perverse effect indeed, when we note that one role of the sorting machinery is to guard against the abuse of human rights provisions). Meanwhile, economic migrants from Ukraine, and to a lesser extent Belarus, are in the ideal structural position to meet the labor market's demand for immigrant workers.

Asylum in the "Area of Freedom, Security, and Justice"

Opening internal borders to flows of goods, people, and capital went hand in hand with what Peter Andreas called the EU-wide "pooling of sovereignty" (2000a: 5) in matters of internal security. Asylum and immigration were key areas affected by these developments. Freedom of movement within Europe had been designed for Europeans. But with internal borders open, "third country nationals" admitted to one EU country could travel to another just as easily as citizens. This, as I mentioned in previous chapters, caused a great deal of anxiety in Western Europe on the eve of expanding the Union eastward. Politicians, the media, and especially representatives of immigration-weary constituencies were asking if the new members were fit to defend and protect the external boundaries of Europe.[11] Or would they be the weak link, allowing an uncontrolled influx of criminals, illegal immigrants, and asylum seekers into EU territory? Among the laws and technologies designed to prevent this, and to alleviate such fears in the context of EU enlargement, the European Commission, especially the Directorate-General for Justice, Freedom and Security, with input from national governments and a number of other bodies such as Frontex and Europol, developed a framework for the Common European Asylum System. This system, which is continuously refined and upgraded by EU officials and experts in an ongoing stream of conferences, summits, policy papers, directives, and regulations, entails tight collaboration and coordination in matters of asylum between member states, so as to reduce the overall numbers of asylum seekers in Europe by ensuring that only the genuinely persecuted have the chance to enter and reside in EU territory, and that the burden of hosting them is distributed among all member states.[12]

The Common European Asylum System, with its reliance on electronic databases, new surveillance technologies, and distribution of responsibility across a cluster of interlinked nation-state administrations, is a key case in point for rethinking what borders are and how they work. They are no longer the clearly locatable political artifacts that enclosed the Westphalian state; no longer simply territorial markers of sovereignty or privileged locations for the articulation of difference. They are rather, as Chandran Kukathas has argued, "complex systems of machinery" (2011: 327), where the degrees of openness and the extent of permeability are determined along multiple axes.

> Policy can . . . make borders more open and yet, at the same time, more closed. This is because policy can change the terms of entry in a number of different respects. It can vary the terms by specifying i) what kinds of people may enter and what status they may hold on entering; ii) how long they may stay; iii) what qualifications or characteristics they must possess to enter; and iv) what procedures they must follow to remain within a territory. Policy can also specify v) the number of people admitted in various categories. (327)

If this selective and variable permeability is a key feature of contemporary borders, then this insight must also guide ethnography; hence the need to examine the places, agents, and practices whose quotidian tasks involve precisely this sorting of people. Where and how are "third country nationals" arriving at the external gates of the EU assigned different rights and legal status? How does it transpire that some end up with no legal status at all, and therefore no sanctioned way to be present within EU borders?

Flexible Asylum

Efforts to construct a common asylum system in the European Union date back to the original Schengen Accord (1985). But the European Council Summit in Tampere, Finland, in 1999 can be counted as the beginning of the most vigorous phase of harmonizing Europe's outlook on refugees. In Tampere, the Council for the first time ever met to debate exclusively the issues of justice and home affairs (Dinan 2005: 572). The "area of freedom, security and justice" was officially elevated as one of the primary EU objectives, though critics observed that of the three, "security" received by far the most attention (Bunyan 1999).[13] The need for an approach to asylum that would be common to all EU member states was reiterated as one of the key ambitions laid out in the 2005 Hague Programme, the document that determined Community priorities with respect to "freedom, security and justice" until 2010. At the core of this objective is the notion that the unified community should "share the burden" of providing protection to refugees. For that purpose it subjects asylum practices to regulations transcending the nation-state. The key regulatory instruments to this end are the Dublin Convention (signed 1990, first enacted 1997) and the subsequent Dublin Regulation (2003). Together they set out the terms for determining the responsibility of member states toward asylum applicants, and for enforcing the principle of first asylum, which holds that the applicant's claim ought to be adjudicated in the first safe country he or she entered on leaving the area of danger.[14]

In principle, since each member state has made an equal commitment to observing the right to asylum, and human rights in general, protection granted in one EU country should be equivalent to that in another.[15] With EU enlargement, this idea was of course extended to Eastern European states, which for historical reasons have received comparatively small numbers of applications for international protection. Now, in the framework of "burden-sharing" and with the help of biometrics and digital surveillance technology, newly admitted postsocialist states are obliged to take over some of the claims that otherwise would be lodged in Western Europe. The Dublin agreements, with the mandate to detain, remove, and resettle people to enforce the principle of first asylum, are a technical means to achieve that. They are also a flashpoint for much of the criticism of "fortress Europe." Many refugee advocates see them as an emblem of the inhumane nature of state logic, which in the name of utilitarian goals brutally deprives asylum seekers of agency and choice, and condemns them to the limbo of unregulated status.[16]

The work-in-progress on common asylum standards is one of the realms of EU activity that most aptly substantiate John Borneman's and Nicholas Fowler's point that united Europe is a "political unit of a novel order" (1997: 510)—not a nation-state, not *like* a nation-state, but something altogether different. A prospective asylum seeker cannot request asylum *in the European Union*. He or she however ought to be able to expect (again, in theory) that whichever country's authorities hear the case, the verdict would be delivered with the same fairness and efficiency. Therefore the effort of bureaucratic and police coordination must somehow reconcile the often inert and idiosyncratic workings of national systems within the Union-level design. The Union-level design, on the other hand, envisions asylum procedure as a sophisticated precision tool. It aims at efficient, emotionless, and error-free decisions which result in adequate protection for those who are deemed to need it, and orderly and delay-free removal for those who are not.

It is worth noting that relevant EU documents prefer to talk of "instruments of protection" rather than "refugee status."[17] This reflects the fact that, like other facets of governmentality in the global world, asylum policy is being remade into a flexible set of tools that allow for customizing protection to particular cases and changing conditions. It absolves national agencies of commitment to long-term assistance to refugees and helps cut down on governmental investment in integration programs. As Nancy Fraser observed in her analysis of globalized governmentality, "the hallmarks of flexibilization are fluidity, provisionality and a temporal horizon of no long term" (2003: 169). In this context, this means that national authorities have the EU-encouraged option to provide asylum seekers with renewable residence permits and other forms of subsidiary (read temporary) protection instead of long-term rights based on the 1951 Convention. Moreover, the EU agenda embraces what might be called the "dogma of return," that is, the idea that in principle repatriation is the most desirable outcome of refugee policy.[18] It envisions a comprehensive return policy, that is, solutions that will allow for withdrawing protection and sending asylees back home when their lives are deemed to be no longer in danger.[19] In short, flexible asylum imbues the already precarious condition of seeking refuge with temporal uncertainty, effectively foreclosing the possibility of anchoring the self in a new and coherent life-world. As for itinerant workers (Chapter 2), the lived consequences of illegal status manifest themselves as spatial and temporal discontinuities—particularly as exclusions from the "time-space compression" that ostensibly defines our current phase of modernity.

One-Stop Shop

Making internationally recognized refugee status, and the right to a Geneva Travel Document (a passport issued to a refugee by the host country), an ever scarcer resource to the worldwide population of the displaced is being justified by the need to curtail "abuse of asylum" by persons who do not meet the criteria. The Geneva Convention defines a refugee as someone who,

> owing to well founded fear of being persecuted for reasons of race, religion, nationality, membership of a particular social group or

political opinion, is outside the country of his nationality and is unable or, owing to such fear, is unwilling to avail himself of the protection of that country; or who, not having a nationality and being outside the country of his former habitual residence as a result of such events, is unable or, owing to such fear, is unwilling to return to it.[20]

Of the approximately eight thousand people every year who file asylum claims with the Warsaw's Aliens Bureau, only about 5 percent are found to meet the Geneva criteria. Of the remaining applicants, approximately 40 percent receive, often as a result of an appeal, so called "tolerated status," a form of subsidiary protection that protects them from deportation, but grants no social benefits and no right to travel in the EU.[21] The remaining ones become "failed asylum seekers," whom the officials describe as "economic migrants" who are "simply searching for a better life." Having no access to legalization, they are either detained and deported to their countries of origin or—if they succeed in avoiding apprehension—disappear off the official radar and sink into a life of legal nonexistence in Poland or elsewhere in the EU.

These numbers are the outcome of a number of steps in the asylum procedure. The first one is eliminating disorder caused by people referred to as "asylum shoppers." This informal term describes seekers who try to defy the principle of first asylum by filing applications in multiple countries, or who attempt to reach a particular destination, rather than filing their request in the first country where they set foot. The Eurodac machinery for storing and retrieving the fingerprints of all asylum seekers (described in Chapter 3) is designed precisely to curtail this unwelcome practice.

Marek Piekarz, the matter-of-fact lawyer who was in a managerial position at the Aliens Bureau at the time of my research, and whom I met on my first visit, described what an asylum seeker ought, and ought not, to do:

The way it works is that nobody prevents this foreigner from picking the country where they would like to have protection. Nobody prevents a Cameroonian before he leaves Cameroon [to say]: I will go to Germany and I will apply there. But if so, then he ought to go to Germany right away. But he cannot roam just so [*tak sobie jeździć*], and say: I'm here, I don't like it here, houses are bad, streets are too dirty, it's better and nicer there, I'll go there. For the way it works is that he must de facto apply for protection as soon as he leaves the area of danger.

In other words, a person leaving the area of danger and finding him- or herself in a "safe third country" rather than the EU ought to remain there. Similarly, if the person is fleeing a place considered by the authorities to be a "safe country of origin," the application will be rejected.

The EU, Piekarz explained, in its endeavor to create the Common European Asylum system, developed a single asylum procedure. "They call it," he used the English phrase, "*one-stop shop*. This means you can buy everything in one place." The approach is to conduct the procedure in a "cascading manner." First, the applicant is considered for refugee status. If status is denied, the next step is to check if there are grounds for subsidiary protection, the so-called "tolerated stay" (*pobyt tolerowany*; a direct translation of German *Duldung*). This form of protection has been so named with brutal honesty—"tolerated stay" is just that—a bare-bones right not to be removed.

> But if we determine that we are not granting tolerated stay, that is, he can return [to the country of origin], and nothing [bad] will happen to him, then we move to step 3: "I oblige you to leave the territory of the Polish Republic." This de facto means removal. If he does not oblige, we will remove him under duress. Forcibly. And this is the single asylum procedure. All the way from the first form of protection to removal.

With the metaphor of shopping, asylum emerges as a commodity in a strange market. The currency is suffering, and the bargain goes to those who in the course of a bureaucratic procedure, involving a hearing, verification of testimony, and a background check, are deemed to suffer correctly, authentically, and according to standards. To make sure there is no trespassing or shoplifting, bouncers at the gates are equipped with a whole arsenal of background check and surveillance devices.

In our conversation, my informant's tactic was to offer exaggerated examples to illustrate his points. It was as though he assumed that if only the picture he painted was vivid and commonsensically convincing, this in itself would void further questions. He used this tactic when telling me about applications for asylum which the Bureau considered "manifestly unfounded," *oczywiście bezzasadne*. In such cases the procedure is accelerated to reach a decision without the burden of a full investigation into the case. What is a "manifestly unfounded" application?

This is how it is. A foreigner comes to Poland, asks for asylum and says: please give me refugee status because I have a sick aunt. One could say, what kind of a reason, or basis having to do with persecution is this: the sickness of a relative. None, right? . . . So, to make it short, [this is] a manifestly unfounded application.

He dismissed my objection that surely there must be more ambiguous situations. He averred that the Bureau's staff have the necessary resources, professional experience, and good judgment to manage ambiguity and tell truth from lies.[22] He also avoided confronting gray areas when asked which countries his Bureau considers "safe"—he offered the basically noncontroversial examples of the U.S. and Germany. What interested me, however, was not so much the general idea of "safety," but rather which countries outside the EU are considered "safe" in the context of "burden-sharing." The question led into politically charged terrain.

You are asking what is a safe country? There are two approaches to this problem. Poland takes the first one, which I consider the better one. The first approach is to create a definition in the legislation [stipulating] the conditions for a country to be a "safe country of origin" or a "safe third country." The second approach is not to create a definition, but rather a list of [those] countries. Here in Poland we believe, that this second thing, which is nota bene what the EU wants, the list of safe countries, that this is bad.

Piekarz explained that a list would be "too political" and might upset some governments ("And Russia? Should it be on it, or not? You see. We've got a conflict"). The definition, which he read out loud from the 2003 Act on Granting Protection to Aliens, was "better" because it was less rigid.[23] And, one might add, quite convenient at the same time, in that it allows for more discretionary decision-making.

From the point of view of managing the eastern external border of the European Union, the key question is whether Ukraine is a "safe third country" or not.

Ukraine ratified the Convention [Relating to the Status of Refugees]. I don't know to what extent Ukraine applies it. We do not send foreigners, Russians, that is, Chechens, that is, Russians, to Ukraine. We do not consider Ukraine to be a safe country for Russians of Chechen nationality. Nor do we send them back to Belarus. . . . We will however send back Afghanis, Iraqis, Pakistanis. We know that they won't be in danger, that they will find protection.

This variable practice is a strategic response to the challenge of squaring Poland's Geneva Convention-based commitment to *non-refoulement* with a tight working partnership with Ukraine. In light of human rights organizations reports that Ukrainian authorities have a record of sending Chechen refugees back to Russia (as Russian citizens), Polish officials must make sure that they are not accused of contributing to this practice (Human Rights Watch 2005).[24] At the same time, with the delimitation of the EU border, Ukraine's capacity to receive and process rejected asylum applicants and "illegal migrants" thrown out of Poland/EU becomes critical to the functioning of the border regime. "Burden-sharing" is not limited to member states, but it draws also on the presumable ability of non-EU countries to provide protection, and other capacities collectively referred to as "migration management." An open designation of Ukraine as an unsafe country would be politically damaging to the EU project of reforming asylum.

Hence the practical solution, where the Polish state grants very few Geneva statuses and more temporary residence permits, as subsidiary protection. This is in keeping with the broader European trend. Temporary asylum—a sort of mid-point on the spectrum of the "instruments of protection"—is ultimately a pragmatic response to some, but by no means all, of the ambiguous situations that emerge in asylum practice. But there is also, as Table 1 illustrates, a very high proportion of applications categorized as "discontinued/left unacknowledged." Officially, these are the ones where the claimants never turned up for their hearings, or to receive a decision. But the border guards I spoke to said that these are people who subsequently illegally cross the border to Germany and who, if they get apprehended, will be detained and possibly sent back to Poland. In practice, these numbers correspond to the condition of sinking into in the cracks of the border regime, without rights, protection, or recognition.

The Sorting Machine

To help me appreciate the sophistication and purported objectivity of the asylum decisions reached at the Bureau, the manager gave me permission to

Table 1. Summary Results of Asylum Procedures, 2005 and 2007

	Total no. of apps.	Geneva Convention status	Tolerated stay	Negative (app. rejected)	Discontinued/left unacknowledged
2005					
Russian citizens	6248	285	1768	1862	4158
Total (Russian citizens + all other applicants)	6860	312	1832	2284	4413
2007					
Russian citizens	9239	104	2824	1194	965
Total (Russian citizens + all other applicants)	10048	116	2866	1732	1103

Source: Bureau of Repatriation and Aliens, Poland. Total numbers of applications are greater than the sum of resolved cases due to applications pending or being appealed in a given year.

meet with Jarek Łukowski, one of his subordinates, who works for the country of origin research division. Jarek's looks were far from the stereotype of a square bureaucrat. On a spring day in 2005, when he greeted me at the guarded entrance of the Aliens Bureau, he was sporting a ponytail, jeans, and a T-shirt, and only the ID with a magnetic stripe he was wearing around his neck served as a reminder of the fact that he was actually working here, employed by the Polish state to facilitate sorting "true refugees" from those who apparently only pretended to be such. Jarek agreed to meet with me to explain how the Aliens Bureau, or more precisely its Asylum Department, protects itself from bogus asylum claims and how it sorts truth from lies in the testimonies of asylum seekers who explain to the Bureau's caseworkers the specific conditions that had forced them to flee their home countries in the Caucasus, Central and Southeast Asia, the Middle East, and Africa.

After greeting me at the door, Jarek took me upstairs to the smallish office where he and his team of five equally casually dressed colleagues, three men and two women, conduct their daily research on the situation in the non-European countries that generate refugees. They use vast resources of international Internet-based information services to answer detailed queries from caseworkers who interview asylum seekers whose applications are pending with the Bureau. Everyone in the office holds an advanced university degree. There are three MAs in linguistics, one in ethnology, one in political science, and one in theology. All the employees are well traveled and seem passionate about the countries they research. Languages spoken in the office include Russian, English, Ukrainian, Arabic, Spanish, French, and Georgian. At the time of my research their main object of interest was the situation in Chechnya, as approximately 90 percent of all persons seeking asylum in Poland came from there.[25] From their desks at the office the team could compile detailed and up-to-date information on places and events in Grozny and vicinity, as well as in other places in Central Asia, the Caucasus, the Middle East, or Africa.[26] Their work yielded responses, Jarek said, "that are precise down to the smallest detail, including local sports clubs, neighborhood stores and what one could buy there, restaurants, radio stations, neighbors, circumstances of particular raids, who was the chief of the village, and what is the name of the street a person claims they lived on."

These data are then used to verify such details of asylum seeker testimonies as geographical locations, timelines of particular conflicts, armed attacks, kidnappings, and relations between different political factions or kinship groups. It helps establish that claimants are who they say they are, and that the events leading up to their departure have indeed taken place. Ultimately, it serves the cause of sifting what the officials regard as credible cases of individual persecution from those that will be dismissed as unfounded. "We know from experience," Jarek said, "that very many testimonies are simply made up." He explained that if someone claims to be fleeing persecution, that person should be able to provide verifiable information concerning who has been a threat, when, and under what circumstances.[27] Fleeing a situation that is not life-threatening but merely difficult, whether on account of war, political instability, or poverty, does not, he said, warrant international protection under the Geneva Convention. Moreover, echoing many of my other informants, Jarek added that Poland is not a wealthy country and does not have the resources to support refugees other than those who truly *had to*, not just *wanted to* leave. ("There are 5 million Polish citizens who live in poverty," another Bureau official said to me, "they are the ones deserving the state's care and interest before we extend it to foreigners.")[28]

The work of Jarek's office and the rationales behind it are emblematic of the larger conceptual basis that underpins contemporary approaches to "third country nationals" in the expanded EU. The discourses and practices of regulating immigration at the outer edges of Europe today are not about blind exclusion. Instead, they depend on construction, maintenance, and legitimation of a sharp distinction between voluntary and forced migration. Economic migrations are assumed to be voluntary, driven by desire for a better life; only migrants directly and verifiably forced to leave their home countries can count on the privilege of asylum and the associated financial assistance that eases their entry into the new society.

The stakes of maintaining this distinction are high: Poland and other new member states located at EU's eastern edges must square their declared commitment to the protection of human rights with the imperative to guard the borders of the entire community against an "uncontrolled" influx of immigrants. To use Didier Fassin's terms, they must reconcile institutional compassion for the few recognized as legitimate victims of persecution with repression of the many assumed to be "merely" seeking an improved material standing.[29] National authorities do so in ways specific to local economic, social, and political contexts. But, notwithstanding such particularities, they are all involved in policing the boundary between "genuine refugees" who will be offered the opportunity of legal inclusion, and the presumably voluntary "economic migrants" who will not. Maintaining this boundary requires the production and sophisticated application of specialized knowledge, the task with which Jarek's team was charged. It is no accident that his unit is the youngest and the best educated one in the entire Aliens Bureau. The Asylum Department director told me, "The foreigners don't like them. But they the avant garde of the modern and truly European state administration."

Selective Permeability

As the case of Poland's eastern borders amply demonstrates, the refashioning of the national border into a supranational boundary does not happen seamlessly. As I have argued in earlier parts of this text, it produces puzzling contradictions and dilemmas for those in charge of protecting and enforcing borders. The new external boundary of the European Union is administered by the Polish government and patrolled by Polish Border Guards who conceive of themselves first and foremost as keepers of the national territory. Yet the new policing protocols that govern their work emphasize impermeability and firm restrictions on the entry of non-EU citizens. These protocols are grounded primarily in EU internal security concerns, especially in the imperative to curb and prevent illegal immigration. The need to embrace the larger EU border agenda created an awkward dilemma for Polish authorities: how to fulfill Polish commitment to maintaining a tight boundary, without stifling ongoing traffic between Poland and Ukraine.

This dilemma pushed the Polish authorities at once to embrace and to resist the rigid border agenda. As EU border administrators and enforcers, governmental bureaucrats and rank-and-file border personnel must show efficacy maintaining strict control over human traffic and preventing the influx of "undesirable aliens." As the previous chapter has shown, they rely on cutting edge surveillance technology and new legal categories in the relentless practice of watching, sorting, admitting, and disposing of foreigners. In so doing, they convey and perform their civilizational aptitude and competence in "European standards."

However, notwithstanding their role as protectors of shared EU territory, the guards are simultaneously in charge of administering and enforcing the national border. With this task, the priorities change. While the image of invincible external boundaries serves the political demands of integration and is an essential element of the sense of supranational cohesion carefully crafted by agents of integration in Warsaw and Brussels, on the ground it can be politically problematic and economically impractical. Politically problematic, because maintaining good relations with Ukraine has been on the agenda of all Poland's post-1989 governments, and closing off the border undermines this effort. Economically impractical, because overall economic growth and the exodus of two million Polish workers to Western Europe—after EU borders and labor markets were opened and before the financial crisis reached Western Europe in 2008—increased the demand for cheap labor that was not matched by local supply. Opening up to migrant workers from outside the EU would have required a political decision—the beginning, at the very least, of an immigration policy—that no one was eager to risk. Politicians on the left and on the right, whatever those imprecise terms mean in Poland, worried that creating favorable conditions for the legal employment of foreigners would have been politically perilous, but also technically challenging.[30] It would involve officially sanctioning the presence of "third-country nationals" and convincing the rest of the European community that these workers would not subsequently move further west, taking advantage of the Schengen openness.

Therefore, as Chapter 3 has shown, access to low-paid jobs without the right to legal residence or social protections is the opening available in Poland to economic migrants from neighboring countries, especially Ukraine. They participate in a highly structured migration circuit, following well-traveled routes and tapping into existing immigrant networks to find employment on farms, in construction, and as participants in what Saskia Sassen calls "the return of the serving class" (2011). The presence of these workers is well known, accepted, and even desired, even though their work has not been legalized and therefore their rights as laborers are not subject to state protection.[31] Poland's EU accession increased the demand for their work, and its December 2007 admission into the Schengen zone without checks on internal borders forced the first serious attempts to regulate it.

These same jobs remain largely unavailable to economic migrants from farther away, notably those who attempt to enter the EU as asylum seekers and fail.[32] Based on the assumption that they will not stay in Poland, but migrate farther west, undermining Poland's reputation as a capable protector of the EU border, they are prevented from crossing the border in the first place. Chechens, Afghanis, Pakistanis, and others are excluded from legal means of entry. Unlike Ukrainians, they face often insurmountable expenses and intense scrutiny in their visa applications, and even if they manage to obtain a visa, they are often returned from the border on the grounds that they lack the means to finance their stay. The asylum process is their only opportunity to enter, save for being smuggled or otherwise crossing the green border illegally. Yet, due to the extra scrutiny and tremendous resources devoted to sorting "true refugees" from "economic migrants," few are allowed to stay. As for those who clandestinely sneak across the border, as with all illegal crossings it is impossible to say how many people actually pursue this option, given that—as Peter Andreas has shown in his analysis of the use of statistics by the U.S. Border Patrol—official statistics capture only those who attempted to cross and failed (2000b: 106–12). As I indicated in the previous chapter, currently in Poland this number oscillates around fifteen hundred people annually and does not capture those immigrants who were apprehended by the Ukrainian patrols.[33] Either way, failed asylum seekers and failed clandestine crossers meet in the same detention centers, maintained by border authorities in Poland and Ukraine, where they await deportation or the results of appeals.

As Verena Stolcke noted in her prescient analysis of the rhetoric of inclusion and exclusion that has arisen in Europe since the 1970s, it is not quite accurate to describe anti-immigrant constituencies as racists. Their contribution to the shameful history of prejudice and discrimination is a cultural essentialism that postulates "a propensity in human nature to reject strangers" (1995: 1). Stolcke shows that the construction of a radical opposition between nationals and foreign migrants relies on "a reified notion of bounded and distinct localized national-cultural identity and heritage that is employed to rationalize the call for restrictive immigration policies" (1). And not just restrictive immigration policies, one might add. This nationalization of culture and identity, seminally analyzed by Anderson (1991), Hobsbawm (1990), and others, legitimates the "national order of things" (Malkki 1995) itself, with institutions such as national citizenship, welfare rights, and territorial belonging.

In post-EU accession Poland curious things are happening to this form of essentialism. An adherence to it is reflected, for example, in the remark by the head of the Aliens Bureau, who expressed to me the view that "that there are things in the culture and psyche of the Chechen nation that just make it impossible for them to adapt to life in European society." But, at the same time, the collective Polish experience of emigration to more affluent countries of Europe and to the United States, with its ethos of hard work and pathos of underdog endurance, mobilizes compassion, and makes wholesale anti-immigrant arguments generally (so far) unpalatable and unpopular.[34] Nonetheless, the restrictive asylum practices and maintenance of a tight border trigger no protests and appear wholly reasonable. Representing them as security devices partly accounts for their appeal. But equally important is the fact the border regime was implemented in ways that by and large didn't block traffic between Poland and Ukraine. This made it possible to view it not as directed against all migrants in general, but rather as a tool for defending Europe from specifically those foreigners considered irredeemably other, possibly troublesome, and therefore undesirable. It is a particularly pernicious effect of the EU's new border that those who are most energetically kept from entering are the ones whose human rights are often in the most dire need of protection.

As for the fact that economic migrants are needed west of the border, it appears that in the ongoing battle of contradictory imperatives the immigration conundrum presents, one way out has been to agree that some foreigners are less foreign than others. "Those who easily adapt and whose culture is similar to ours will always be welcome," according to the same Ministry official whose warnings against the French and German mistakes I cited in the opening of this chapter.[35] Ukrainians, as well as Belarusians and, to a lesser extent, Russians, are the ones who fit the bill as white, Christian, "culturally similar," and by and large nonthreatening non-EU Europeans. Another way to think of them, following Svetlana Boym, is as "Europeans without the euros" (2002: 221), persistently constructed as inferior to those from the European "core." Chechens, Afghanis, Pakistanis, and others from beyond the continental boundaries do not meet the criterion of cultural proximity. Therefore, unless they must be admitted under international law as human rights subjects and legalized as refugees, they will be excluded as a residual and disposable category, economic migrants beyond demand.

Epilogue: Speechlessness and Politics

It is this group of people—the undesirable migrants, those who leave their ruined homelands but have no place that would welcome and accept them— who today embody what Lydia Morris has called "Arendt's paradox." She uses this term to capture the historical relationship between citizenship and human rights discussed by Hannah Arendt in *Origins of Totalitarianism* (Morris 2010: 1–2). Writing in the direct aftermath of World War II, at a time of mass population displacements, Arendt observed that people without meaningful citizenship, understood as full membership in a functioning national polity, had no means of claiming their human rights (1951; see also Chapter 7). Today "Arendt's paradox" manifests itself as the tension between sovereign territoriality and observance of universal human rights (Benhabib 2004). At a time when so many people migrate in search of personal and economic safety and security, conflicts are bound to arise between the economic and political needs of states and the needs of people on the move. But, as Morris writes,

> The issue of who has what claim to which rights is not . . . determined once and for all by the question of membership but is revisited in the context of a global competition for skilled labor, of family members wishing to rejoin their migrant kin, and of civil wars and oppressive regimes generating large numbers of asylum seekers. While modern democracies . . . have undertaken commitments which govern these and other situations . . . many of the rights at issue remain subject to qualification, limitation and interpretation. Some of the so called universal human rights can be qualified with reference to national

security, public safety or economic well-being of the country, while even those rights which are absolute raise difficult questions of interpretation and application. (2010: 5)

European integration makes these "difficult questions" even more perplexing, bringing "Arendt's paradox" to a new, supranational level. Prior to EU asylum cooperation, nation-states defended themselves individually from what they saw as excessive numbers of needy foreigners. To this end they drew on the figure of the "bogus asylum seeker" to justify restrictions on the basic human right to asylum. Today, in the context of the Common European Asylum System, the Dublin Convention, and the notion of "burden sharing," the scope of possibilities for avoiding responsibility, denying legal status, and justifying detention and removal is vastly expanded. Indeed, the new flexible asylum is not so much about "burden sharing" as it is about burden shifting, preferably onto "safe third countries" and beyond EU boundaries altogether.

But just as no rights are in practice absolute, neither is the state's power over the life and death of noncitizens who do enter their territory as unauthorized migrants. One Border Guard official who collaborates with the Aliens Bureau on the deportation of undesirable migrants told me the following story:

We had this situation once, that we had no contact whatsoever with the foreigner. [We had to establish his identity to proceed with the removal but] the foreigner did not react to anything. We tried with various interpreters, various languages . . . nothing. We tried to see if he would react at all.

I asked whether the guards knew anything about this person, which country he came from at the very least, how he got to Poland, or whether perhaps he suffered from trauma.

We did not know anything. He did not react to anything at all. He was being spoken to but he did not react to any language. At all. He was doing it on purpose, of course. This happens sometimes.
Q: And what happened then?
We had to file for the inability to remove. We had to give him a name for the paperwork. Kowalski it was, or something like that. And that's it. He was free.

Thus "Kowalski," a modern day stateless person, presumably owing solely to his own reticence, had to be reluctantly taken on by the Polish state, based on the international legal commitments that Poland had signed. Prior to being released, he spent the prescribed one year in predeportation detention as a nameless, voiceless human being—a condition which yields a strong temptation to see in him the embodiment of the modern *homo sacer* (Agamben 1998). I bracket that interpretive route, however. I do so on the grounds that calling on grand categories such as statelessness and bare life as analytic models for understanding exclusion shifts the emphasis toward the inevitability of the fact of exclusion itself, and away from the ongoing evolution of national and international legal systems and enforcement practices. As Sally Merry points out, "international law is changing and developing at the same time as its enforcement mechanisms are ambiguous and dependent on a complex set of social processes" (2006: 101). Asylum seekers and migrants today are subjects of both national and international laws and it is within this transnational landscape of evolving legal norms, policing practices, and their social contexts that the discarded refugees-cum-economic migrants exercise their agency and subvert the mechanisms of legal exclusion.

"Kowalski" (the irony of the border guards baptizing him with the most stereotypically Polish last name should not be lost) acquired "tolerated" status, and while basically left to his own devices, he was granted the rudimentary protection of the law. This would have ended after one year, whereupon he would need to continue his silent protest to have the status extended.[36] He might have done that, but he may have also sunk into the legal limbo of unregulated status, as a *sans papiers* in Poland or farther west. What helped him accomplish his presumed goal of not being thrown out beyond the borders of Europe was not a testimony of an ordeal. It was the determination to remain silent that proved most effective. While it was not an asylum claim in any formal sense, we can interpret it as one. "Kowalski" lodged a *mute claim*, in effect a new way of exacting the right to be where he didn't legally belong. It was a form of resistance to flexible asylum and the realities of the border regime. If he were to be apprehended, for example, in Germany or France, he could not be detained indefinitely, or deported outside the EU. Instead he would have to be sent back to Poland, where, still as the mute "Kowalski," he would most likely be granted tolerated status again.[37] This act of letting him stay, unwillingly and for some time only, would be another of the partial and tentative responses to the conundrum presented by contemporary human mobility.[38]

For as long as nation-states and capitalism exist, and European integration progresses along its established path, there will be no clear solutions to the plight of people like "Kowalski." There is of course always the possibility of embracing a radical anti-statist and anti-capitalist perspective and from this standpoint advocating the abolition of borders altogether (Alldred 2003; No Border 2004). While nothing short of undoing the national order of things would accomplish that goal, and while it remains an open question whether this would constitute a general improvement of human affairs, this mode of critique and activism is vitally important to the democratic debates on migration. It identifies and calls public attention to the unjust and inhumane outcomes of "migration management" and their broader contexts:

> Anti-capitalist perspectives refuse the distinction between economic and political refugees that allows the tabloid newspapers their pious moral distinction between the deserving and undeserving. The condemnation of refugees and migrants is seen as the scapegoating of those who suffer the worst effects of the new capitalist world order and individualization of the problem that serves to distract from the broader economic relations at play. (Alldred 2003: 153)

But in Europe today such claims on behalf of the disenfranchised migrants and asylum seekers compete in the public sphere with the ever more powerful calls for a retrenchment of the cosmopolitan ideal, and for a "renewal" of national communities through the purging of otherness. While many partisans of that cause welcome the more repressive features of the EU border regime, and lobby for hardening them further, it is important to point out that its present shape is less the result of the ideological zeal of the opponents of immigration than the outcome of technocratic logic, bureaucratic involution, and the modern international legal responses to Arendt's paradox.

EU borders, in short, are anything but democratic, that is to say, their legal form and means of policing are not a true reflection of popular will regarding who and on which terms ought to be admitted into European territories and societies. However, as European integralists (Holmes 2000) in various countries build support for identity-based politics and gain influence through electoral means, and as labor markets shrink and expand to the rhythm of economic cycles, the pressure on national governments and EU bodies to "do something" about "excessive" numbers of foreigners will continue to mount. This pressure translates into laws and policies, but the details of what exactly is being done remain obscure to all but those who most vigorously pursue them. It is this knowledge of the precise human cost of maintain the border regime, however, and the study of the causes and dynamics of human mobility today, that I see as the only potential source of a politics geared toward preserving and nurturing the idea of shared humanity and human rights for all, not just for those more or less arbitrarily deemed to deserve them. Whether such politics is capable of resolving Arendt's paradox, or only mitigating its most harmful effects, is a matter for another discussion, but without it undemocratic borders will encircle ever more closed polities.

Chapter 6

Capacity Building and Other Technicalities: Ukraine as a Buffer Zone

The Common European Asylum System the European Union has been developing, to spread the burden of receiving asylum seekers, to increase the efficiency of national asylum infrastructures, and to clear them of "bogus asylum seekers," is a prime example of how rebordering engages people, places, and institutions across national and EU territories. But it is far from the only element of the border regime that instantiates these tendencies. The creation of a secure, prosperous, and bounded space within the European Union demands extensive cooperation and technological coordination between governments and law enforcement agencies of the EU member states. This chapter zooms in on the day-to-day realities of the "partnership" between Poland and Ukraine to discuss how the border regime penetrates outward and how it draws in the union's neighbors.

One of the key innovations introduced to Eastern Europe in the course of rebordering is the externalization of undesirable migrants, that is, ensuring that as many of them as possible (a) never enter European territory in the first place; and (b) can be legally removed to a neighboring third country if apprehended within EU territory. This requires neighboring states such as Ukraine to cooperate in the endeavor of securing EU borders, in effect serving as flexible "buffer zones" (Lahav and Guiraudon 2000: 59) between the Union and migrant-generating regions farther east.

As discussed previously, one aspect of being a buffer zone is cooperating in matters of asylum as a "safe third country." But collaboration must cover also other facets of border protection, that is, migration as well as border control and policing. In an article published in 2000, when Poland was not yet a member, but only a candidate for EU membership, Leszek Jesień, a negotiator of Poland's accession to the EU, noted that

> certain EU member states, notably Germany, Austria, Sweden and Finland . . . would like to have the new EU members as a buffer zone filtering all unwanted elements of the flux of people and goods between East and West. . . . Here is where an enlarged EU area of "freedom, security and justice" will be tested. Here is where freedom will weigh less than security. (Jesień 2000: 189)

A few years later the new eastern external EU border was set up. It was organized and equipped according to the wishes of the affluent old members. But requiring construction of a tight border before ceding the responsibility for the EU's eastern frontier to Poland and other postsocialist states was in itself not enough to preserve Western Europe's sense of internal security. The postenlargement design had to involve setting up a new buffer zone. Or, to be more precise, a new layer of buffering integrated with that already provided by the new members.

Externalization: The Larger Picture

In June 2003, at the European Council Meeting in Thessaloniki, representatives of EU governments met to debate a proposal prepared in the UK concerning a "new vision" for global management of refugees, asylum seekers, and other migrants. The proposal stipulated the establishment of "processing centers" outside EU boundaries, where persons seeking asylum in European territory would be required to submit their claims and await admission or rejection decisions. The British Ministry of Interior touted the proposal on the grounds that it would sharply reduce the number of asylum seekers lodging their applications in the EU. It kept the pretense of caring for their interests, too, by emphasizing that the proposal would help grant protection to refugees "in countries that are geographically closer to their homes" (HRW 2003: 2). Among the states where protection would thus be outsourced were Albania, Iran, Morocco, Turkey, Russia, and Ukraine.

The British proposal was sharply criticized by Human Rights Watch (2003) and other refugee advocacy organizations (see also Betts 2005; Agier 2008).[1] In a position paper "An Unjust Vision for Europe's Refugees," published shortly after the Thessaloniki Summit, Human Rights Watch pointed out that "The British proposal attempts to circumvent its legal obligations to refugees," and that it is "a means of pandering to xenophobic sentiments at the expense of human rights" (HRW 2003: 2). Further, the document listed specific ways in which the idea of "processing centers" violates human rights and refugee principles. The authors argued that forcible confinement in outside facilities constitutes a breach of the right to seek asylum and the right to *non-refoulement*, that is, the right not to be removed to an area where the person's life would be threatened "on account of his race, religion, nationality, membership of a particular social group or political opinion" (4; see 1951 Convention, Art. 33). They were also concerned about lack of procedural safeguards that would protect asylum seekers from abuse and discrimination during processing (7). Moreover, current human rights records and handling of refugee matters in the countries in question indicated that those governments would not be able to ensure adequate conditions in the "processing centers." These factors combined would lead to ineffective protection and significant risks to physical security and human rights of persons covered by the proposal (14).

Despite criticism, a new version of the proposal was back on the European table the following year. This time, the German and Italian interior ministers promoted establishing "processing centers" in North Africa to curtail the "uncontrolled" flow of migrants and asylum seekers from the South. At an EU Justice and Home Affairs summit in the Netherlands (September 2004), the idea created a controversy and was subsequently rejected by France, Belgium, and Sweden. In the following months it continued to circulate at policy meetings and expert discussions, with German interior minister Otto Schily a most prominent backer. However, at the time transit countries like Libya rejected assuming responsibility for European asylum seekers.[2] According to Human Rights Watch, this was because they were not offered sufficient payoff guarantees. The human rights watchdog summed up the controversy by concluding, "this resistance, coupled with legal and moral objections from refugee advocates, the media and other EU governments, finally scrapped the idea" (HRW 2006: 91).

But was the idea really abandoned? While the blatancy of the straightforward outsourcing proposals might have left some of the EU human rights faithful with a bad taste in their mouths, the externalization of immigrants and asylum seekers is nevertheless very much on the union's agenda (Da Lomba 2004; Lahav and Guirardon 2000; HRW 2005, 2006). Conducted under the innocuous-sounding guise of "partnership with third countries" (Hague Programme 2004: 20) as of 2009, when the Stockholm Programme replacing the Hague Programme was drafted, it was not about establishing "processing centers" per se, although the future may very well bring this postulate back, under this or another name. Nonetheless, externalization is an ongoing practice premised on the interconnected concepts of *safe third country*, *readmission*, and *capacity building*.

A *safe third country* is a designation that pertains to non-EU states that have been presumed to comply with international human rights law and thus to be safe for asylum seekers (HRW 2006: 91).[3] *Readmission* is the practice of transferring persons lacking legal status in the EU to a neighboring non-EU country. *Capacity building*, in the context of the European border regime, is the commitment to channel development aid into third countries to create the infrastructure for receiving, detaining, and removing migrants (92). In other words, in theory the EU has committed itself to building the capacity to warehouse its own rejected, before actually transferring them beyond its boundaries. In reality, a network of bilateral agreements countries concluded between themselves outside the EU framework allowed for the ongoing practicing of readmission long before any semblance of "capacity" was reached.

The Ice Castle

Poland and Ukraine have had an active readmission agreement since 1994. For example, in 2004, 4,013 people were readmitted from Poland to Ukraine. The majority (3,397) were Ukrainian citizens.[4] However, the remaining 616 came from third countries (e.g., Moldova, China, Georgia, and India). Poland is a signatory of the 1951 Geneva Convention, and Polish officials are obliged to comply with the principle of *non-refoulement*. Despite that, as demonstrated by evidence from multiple sources, there were asylum seekers among persons subjected to readmission removals.[5] It fell to Ukrainian authorities to receive and detain them and, depending on details of the case, conduct their asylum procedure or deport them to their country of origin.

In February 2006 I visited Ukraine's main facility for detention of foreigners without legal status, in a village I will here call Ivanovo, near the larger town I call Vysoky Horod in the region of Transcarpathia on the external EU border (with Hungary, Slovakia, and Poland).[6] I was allowed to take part in a group visit that was part of a Polish-Ukrainian capacity-building program designed for the training of Ukrainian immigration officials and border officers. (The program is discussed in more detail below.) It is in Ivanovo that many of the readmitted from Poland and other neighboring countries are confined while their cases are pending. At the time of my visit Ukraine was preparing to reach a readmission agreement with the EU as a whole. Upon its signing, Ivanovo and other existing facilities would not be adequate for handling the larger numbers of those rejected from Europe.[7] The purpose of the visit was for the participants to appreciate on the one hand "the burden of illegal migration" already carried by the Ukrainian state, and on the other the investments that must be made to upgrade the existing system.

The day of our visit was cold. The facility, in a secluded former military garrison, held 130 men (a center for women and families is located in Vysoky Horod). Outside, the detainees as well as the guards were stomping in place and rubbing their arms to keep warm. We, the visitors, were not given permission to talk to them. One of the commanders was showing us around, accompanied by a representative of a local religious charitable organization that assisted with the day-to-day running of the center. Inside, in the dorm rooms, it was barely warmer than outside. Detainees were roughly segregated according to ethnicities. ("Those from the former Soviet republics won't stay with the Indians or the Blacks," we were told by our guide.) Some parts of the facility were being renovated, using funds provided by an Austrian religious charity. A brand-new flat-screen TV and DVD set mounted just under the ceiling in the common room bore a logo of the EU and the sponsoring charity. It was on mute, playing a film with English subtitles on the universal, worldwide problems of refugees.

This was ironic, because hardly any of the men in Ivanovo would be eventually recognized as refugees.[8] For the time being, regardless whether they were asylum seekers, "economic migrants," or persons without papers awaiting legal identification, they shared the same conditions and the same uncertainty. Most of them did not know when and where they would be released. At any point they could become subject to such ill treatment as beating and confinement to substandard conditions. Some could be refouled or denied access to an asylum procedure (HRW 2005).

On the day of my visit the grounds were covered in snow. In the courtyard of the compound a group of the detained of various ages and nationalities were building an intricate ice castle. It was probably a coincidence that their collective act of creation was as evocative of the harrowing world of Kafka as their detention itself.

Figure 5. The ice castle. Author photo.

Exclusion as Externalization

"Orderly space is a rule-governed space, whereas the rule is a rule in as far as it forbids and excludes," writes Bauman (2004: 31). For order to be achieved, and order is what the "area of freedom, security and justice" presumes, certain practices must be prohibited and certain people cannot be admitted. As this text has already shown, the area without internal borders was designed for Europeans. The people who are entitled to "freedom, security and justice" are primarily EU citizens. Some selected non-EU citizens are permitted to take advantage of some of its aspects as well—among them are visitors who have lawfully obtained Schengen visas, immigrants whose work permits have been secured by employers, and those who were able to take advantage of family reunification, repatriation, or other special programs, temporary or otherwise. A separate category, as discussed in the previous chapter, are asylum seekers. The 1951 Convention obliges EU states to accept refugees and forbids the practice of *refoulement*. But the Convention does not determine the particular mode of sifting "genuine refugees" from those who *ask to be considered refugees.* Hence, in the face of political and security pressures these criteria are becoming ever more strict, and the burden of proof—always on the petitioner herself or himself—ever more onerous. The numbers of refugees who are recognized, and thus accepted within the "area of freedom, security and justice" are dwindling EU-wide, from 49,500 in 2004 to 27,600 in 2009. On top of that, in 2004, 33,100 applicants received subsidiary protection; this number was 26,200 for 2009.[9] The Schengen ideal of order requires that everyone else be excluded from Europe's borderless area as an "undesirable migrant."

For "undesirables" who are physically present within the EU, due to a nonenforcement or partial enforcement of laws, human trafficking, unlawful entry, or some other happenstance, this means a life organized by the logic of "the new European apartheid" (Balibar 2004), in the politically and socially peripheral "spaces of non-existence" (Coutin 2003: 29) always overshadowed by uncertainty and the threat of removal.[10] There are also untold numbers of potential migrants who are repelled by the unattainable terms of entry, and who, despite the need or desire, never manage to arrive or lose their lives trying. Finally, for those who attempt to cross the EU borders but fail, the experience of exclusion in practice means removal, which can take the form of readmission, deportation, or so-called voluntary repatriation.[11] This is the fate of those I call economic migrants beyond demand, the vastly heterogeneous category which includes, as I argued in the previous chapter, those who asked for refugee status but were not deemed to be genuine refugees, along with those who perhaps would have qualified but never asked, and those who neither asked, nor would have qualified.

The fact that such categories of noncitizens dwell at the gates and on the margins of Western societies of course predates EU integration and expansion, as well as the crystallization of Schengen. The alien status of these groups is the flipside of the national citizenship model, where the relationship to the state and associated rights and responsibilities are a matter of birthright, or are conferred in the usually complex and protracted process of naturalization, which in its very name suggests that it is a mere substitute for being a natural born citizen. Citizenship is about drawing boundaries. In the course of the historical process of the routinization of the state's presence in citizens' lives, the state has assumed the right to decide which noncitizens to embrace, and which to remove or leave outside.

But the point here is that within the EU border regime, repellence, readmission, detention, and deportation, as well as "voluntary returns," are specific modes of segregation and exclusion that are increasingly accomplished beyond boundaries and within buffer zones. These are practices that demand the drawing in of those whose territories become the terrain where the repelled and the removed are most likely to end up upon failing to enter the EU. The rebordering of Europe is, among other things, about perfecting these ways of keeping certain groups on the outside. Because their fate, status, and opportunities depend on the particular conditions in these countries, this must prompt us to inquire into the arrangements between the EU and its "partners," and their consequences. This entails asking not just about the "rights of others," but also about the constitution of the murky spaces Seyla Benhabib describes as situated "at the limits of all rights regimes, [in] the blind spot in the system of rights, where the rule of law flows into its opposite: the state of the exception and the ever-present danger of violence" (2004: 163).

This cooperation and coordination that buffer zones are drawn into has two key dimensions: a political one, that is, the will of particular state authorities to engage in helping the EU keep its territory impervious to unwanted entries; and a technical one, that is, the capacity of the services of that state actually to keep up with the task. Over the course of the first decade of the twenty-first century the political will of Ukrainian authorities to cooperate with the European Union has been an exploitable resource. Kyiv might have been wrapped in political turmoil for most of the decade, with both collective emotions and political stakes at their highest during the 2004 Orange Revolution, but even though Ukrainian rhetoric concerning its relationship with the European Union hasn't been consistent, at no point has it been openly antagonistic. Even after the authority of President Viktor Yushchenko, who emerged victorious in the aftermath of the contested election in 2004, and who favored close cooperation and eventually joining the EU, began to wane, his key opponents, Yulia Tymoshenko and Viktor Yanukovych, have not decisively turned their backs on the EU. Participation in the European Neighborhood scheme carries particular rewards for Ukraine, such as recognition as a political partner, deeper economic integration, and increased mobility supported by EU funds for selected groups of citizens such as students or scientists. But the European Commission made it clear that "the pace of development of Ukraine-EU relations in facilitating people-to-people contacts and opening the common border for the free movement of people will depend on Ukraine's ability to control its borders and to address illegal migration, human trafficking, smuggling, and international organized crime" (ICPS 2006: 14). Supporting the European border regime has been essentially a transaction, albeit an uneasy and contested one. Its dynamics reflect the tension inherent in the European Neighborhood scheme, whose rhetoric of friendly cooperation cannot mask the fact that it is characterized, as James Wesley Scott observed, by competing rationales of "stability," "prosperity," "sustainability," and "security" and thus has considerable potential for exclusionary policies (Scott 2005: 429).

Fulfilling the role of a trusted border partner of Poland and the EU required of Ukrainian authorities the upgrading of their border services. In order to benefit from the technological and infrastructural capacity building that the EU was willing to sponsor, they had to meet the challenges of the new situation by abandoning their old ways, dismissed as "rigid" and "post-Soviet," in favor of flexible European ones. This meant primarily transitioning from the military-like style of patrolling the border to doing so more like policemen. It entailed entering into elaborate readmission arrangements with neighboring EU member states and, eventually, with the EU as a whole. With that came the responsibility for those refused entry into EU territory.

To provide assistance in this undertaking, a Warsaw-based think tank, which I will call the Center, in cooperation with a Kyiv counterpart, developed a project to share the lessons of adjusting Polish borders to EU standards with Ukrainian immigration and border personnel. Organized as a series of training sessions, seminars, and study visits to checkpoints and detention facilities in Poland and Ukraine, it provided me with an opportunity to observe and appreciate the politics of distributing and contesting legal and technical knowledge in the context of rebordering. It also gave me a chance to witness one real-life instance of what the European Commission and other EU bodies declare they engage in, that is, "cooperation with civil society."

By the time I was allowed to attend the Center's training in early 2006, I had already familiarized myself with a wide range of people and institutions involved in border protection, immigration, and asylum in Poland. I had also been to Ukraine several times, where one of my quests was to visit the infamous detention facility in Ivanovo near Vysoky Horod in the region Transcarpathia. But my efforts to obtain the necessary permission from the Ukrainian Ministry of Interior had failed and I was denied access.[12] I ended up spending my first visit to Vysoky Horod talking to local asylum officials and NGO activists involved, among other things, in providing legal aid to the detainees. From these previous encounters and conversations I knew that the flexible common asylum system transcends EU borders eastward, and that it is thoroughly integrated into the larger instrumentarium of the struggle against illegal migration. But it was only after I had the unique opportunity to participate in the Polish-Ukrainian training, which, among other things, finally took me inside the Vysoky Horod and Ivanovo facilities, that I could fully appreciate the intricacies and contradictions of the unfolding border and migration management arrangements.

The Nexus of Expertise

For the Europeanizing Polish society, whose support for EU membership in the years following accession only increased, to 85 percent in 2008 from the already very high 73 percent registered at the time of the 2003 referendum, (CBOS 2004, 2008) the narrative of Schengen is potent enough to offer a hegemonic framework for conceptualizing bordered space as that which is eminently governable and controllable. Naturally, like any border, it might occasionally be vulnerable to breach, but Schengen in itself provides the reason and the explanation for all exclusion carried out in its name. Therefore, no one seems to be asking what happens to the few thousand people every year who are not granted recognition as refugees. Some of them manage to find employment in the shadow economy known as the "gray zone"; others attempt crossing into Germany; many end up in deportation proceedings (Wenzel 2009). But they are invisible in the Polish public sphere, as if the very fact that they are not supposed to be there already guaranteed their absence. Likewise, no political attention is given to the half-million, if not more, "illegal migrants" who make a living in the shadows of the official economy, or are apprehended by police or border guards and enter detention and deportation limbo.

In most of Western Europe, where immigration had reached critical mass decades ago, vigorous debates on the issue engage politicians, the media, and civil society. Anti-immigrant integralists, that is, those who see themselves as defenders of the nation, tradition, and "some form of sacred patrimony" against concepts of multicultural Europe (Holmes 2000), must contend with human rights campaigners and supporters of racial and cultural pluralism. But with officially only 1.8 percent of Polish population being foreign-born, for most Poles, modern racial and cultural difference remains a rare experience and a somewhat exotic subject, associated mostly with the immigration woes of the West.[13] Thus, as I already pointed out, no significant mainstream voices within the public sphere have questioned the premises of the border regime. Similarly, few such voices have so far taken up immigrant advocacy.[14] While some semblance of a democratic "immigration debate" will probably open as the numbers and visibility of foreigners increase, in the first decade of the twenty-first century politicians and the broader public have acted as if they were convinced that the issue was already settled or didn't concern Poland. The Schengen meta-narrative and its pragmatic rationales cast a thick shadow. Obscured by this shadow, beyond public scrutiny and with only few faint objections from the civil society, a nexus of government officials, bureaucrats, and nongovernmental "independent experts" has been working to refine and sharpen the tools of the flexible asylum and immigration regime. Schengen, with its proscriptions on who is in and who is out, appears to provide all the answers; no need apparently to hash them out by democratic means.

Between Poland and Ukraine several institutional nodes uphold and advance the border regime. They are part of a network that spans the countries of united Europe and extends beyond. In previous chapters I have invited the reader into the headquarters and regional divisions of the Polish Border Guard and the offices of the Aliens Bureau. I discussed the practices of surveillance and workings of technology harnessed to the task of sorting out people. I talked of the experiences of people for whom EU's external border fractures time as much as it partitions space. The following ethnographic itinerary provides yet another perspective: an insight into the modern, EU-driven pedagogy of statecraft and its role in rebordering.

During the fifteen years between 1989 and 2004, the year of EU accession, the so-called "transition" in Poland was an arena for a vigorous transfer of Western aid and expertise. Cohorts of U.S. and West European trainers and consultants came under private or governmental aegis to spread the gospel of free markets, civil society, and good governance. As students of transition within anthropology have observed, such interventions in postsocialist countries accomplished equivocal and at times problematic results (Berdahl et al. 2000; Dunn 2004; Chivens 2006; Phillips 2005, 2008; Wedel 1998; Sampson 1996; Szmagalska-Follis 2008). But in the period leading up to Poland's entry into the EU this form of assistance was deemed as no longer needed, and the wave of "consultancy tourism" subsided (Aksartova 2006). At last, after years of being coached in the difficult arts of development and democracy, Polish officials were poised to take over the torch and carry it eastward.

It was as though through EU accession Poland "graduated" to a higher civilizational rank.[15] This fact, combined with the general Polish investment in Ukrainian affairs, constituted the context for the border services training project. This series of encounters between Polish experts and Ukrainian trainees was emblematic of the paradoxical logic of rebordering that demands the cooperation of those left behind in constructing and maintaining the conditions of their own exclusion. The official title of the project was "Enhancing the mechanisms of Ukraine's migration policy through conveying EU experience with readmission agreements."[16] In reality the training covered much more than just readmission policies. The very fact that it did so illustrated the inherent interconnectedness of all aspects of modern border regimes.

The force behind the proceedings on the Polish side was Mariusz Bożek, an affable thirty-something associate of the center who confidently called himself an "expert." At one point during the training the project staff made a name tag for me which also said "expert." I objected, preferring the more accurate label "researcher," but Mariusz admonished me saying, "there is nothing to be shy about," because the Ukrainian state needs "our" expertise. On the Ukrainian side, expert authority was vested in Mykola Danylovych Klekh, a retired senior officer of the Ukrainian border service who worked as a consultant for the Kyiv partner. The participants were an assorted, overwhelmingly male, group of about thirty Border Service personnel and officials representing central and regional divisions of the Ukrainian immigration service. Among them was an architect who would take part in designing new detention facilities in Zhuravichi near Lutsk and in Rozsudiv near Chernihiv, in use since 2008 with a capacity of 181 and 239, respectively.[17]

Also, the Ukrainian office of the International Organization for Migration (IOM) had sent a young associate to participate in the training. IOM is an intergovernmental organization whose mission statement says that it is "committed to the principle that humane and orderly migration benefits migrants and society" (IOM website). Established in 1951, it has an annual budget of over a billion dollars and operates in over 100 countries worldwide. Its central concept is that of "migration management," that is, an approach that "accepts the realities of (im)migration" and strives to regulate migration in a way characterized as "reasonable and beneficial" (Schatral forthcoming). The EU Commission relies on the IOM to implement important aspects of its external migration policies. In this capacity IOM runs a variety of programs, including policy research, migrant health assessment, "voluntary assisted returns," counter-trafficking activities, and "technical cooperation on migration management and capacity building." In Ukraine IOM is particularly active in the latter two domains. ("Capacity building" translates, among other things, into assisting with the development of detention centers.) While the IOM-affiliated participant in the training, who was Canadian but spoke fluent Ukrainian due to her family background, was eager to stress IOM's benevolence and its accomplishments in civilizing the country's immigration standards, she was also markedly unforthcoming about the details of the planned detention facilities and other forms of IOM assistance to Ukraine's border services. I did not blame her for her reticence; she did not occupy a position of power in her organization and seemed unclear on what she was authorized to talk about. However, secrecy, unaccountability, serving powerful interests, and subjecting migrants to practices that are represented as reasonable and pragmatic but in fact are coercive and erase their individual agency (for example, "voluntary assisted returns" and rehabilitation of "Victims of Trafficking"), are the key themes in critiques of IOM's work (AI 2004; HRW 2005; Schatral forthcoming).[18]

I was admitted to the training as an "independent researcher" and was allowed to observe the proceedings and participate in the study visits throughout the first and second parts of the project; the final event happened after I left Europe. The first part consisted of a three-day seminar at the think tank offices in Warsaw, supplemented with a visit to the Aliens Bureau. This spree of lectures, Power Point presentations, discussions, and meal and coffee breaks was followed by a two-day field trip to a detention center in Podleśnica, approximately eighty kilometers from Warsaw, and to a border crossing and a deportation facility in Ptaszyn nad Odrą on the Polish-German border, about 450 km west of Warsaw, on the river Odra.

The second part took place three weeks later in the city of Uzhgorod, in the southwest of Ukraine. Uzhgorod is the capital of Zakarpatska Oblast (Transcarpathia). It has a population of slightly over 100,000 and is located on the Ukrainian-Slovakian border; the borderline is three kilometers west of the city limits. The Hungarian border is 15 km to the south, and the Polish border is 45 km to the north. The organizers chose this location because "one of the main routes of illegal immigration from Asia" is said to lead through Transcarpathia. Thirty km from Uzhgorod lies the town of Vysoky Horod with the nearby village of Ivanovo, the site of a key facility for the detention of unauthorized migrants.[19] The program of the training in Uzhgorod included meetings with Slovakian and Hungarian border guards and a visit to Ivanovo. The third and final installment—the project's concluding conference—was scheduled several months later and took place in Kyiv.

The routes traversed by the Polish and Ukrainian participants in the training, penetrating deep into the territory of both countries, can only serve to augment the thesis that borders today are ubiquitous and dislocated. This itinerary in itself offered clues as to the new geography of control and security imposed on this region of Europe. Straddling the EU's external borderline along its Polish, Slovakian, and Hungarian sections, the journeys of the participants, from office buildings to checkpoints to detention facilities, at once mapped out and followed the connections between different nodes of the border regime.

Connected Vessels

Ten o'clock in the morning might not seem like a brutal hour, but on a January day in snow-covered Warsaw it turned out to be a little early to begin a day of lectures and consultations. Besides the Polish organizers, I was the first to arrive at the Center offices, located in the heart of the city, in one of the rare prewar apartment buildings where the interior had been gutted and converted into office space. Over the next three days meetings were to be held in a modern conference room on the fifth floor. Together with Mariusz, Agata, the composed and professional-looking interpreter, and a couple of other staff members we waited for the Ukrainian delegation to arrive from a nearby hotel. "It's ok," the coordinator was saying, unfazed by the delay. As she was wondering whether to adjust the morning schedule for the following days, participants started arriving. Amid greetings and apologies for the holdup, a warm atmosphere of Polish-Ukrainian amity began to emerge. "We are not in a hurry," said Mariusz. "We can do it at our pace. After all we're all Slavs here." As he later told me, he was referring to what he perceived as a cultural commonality between "our two nations." He thought that Poles and Ukrainians understood each other, and that the only difference is that Poland is "civilizationally about ten years ahead."

The chit-chat in Polish and Ukrainian, occasionally interlaced with Russian, gradually died out as the speakers took their microphones to begin the proceedings. After the requisite welcomes Mariusz gave the opening presentation entitled "Polish migration policy," which was meant to introduce the audience not just to the subject matter, but also to the further agenda of the training. He was an engaging speaker with a penchant for rhetorical questions and firm assertions. He stressed that the meeting was "not about politics" and that the issue of Ukraine's potential EU accession would not be discussed. At stake were rather Ukraine's "international commitments" to maintain control over border traffic, which must be fulfilled. To this end, he said, the organizers made an effort to provide the participants with two perspectives on the "Polish experience": a "view from the center" and "from the field." Mariusz spoke in Polish and Agata provided consecutive interpreting into Ukrainian, but the timing of the audience's nods and comments suggested that mutual understanding was independent of the translation.

Talking about the early 1990s, when after German unification Poland first came to border a Western country, Mariusz confidently crafted a narrative of symmetry and commensurability. The experience of adjusting to be a fit neighbor of Germany had to be shared with Ukraine. The "lesson" could now be transferred wholesale 700 kilometers to the east. The key element of this experience was introducing readmission. Ukraine already had a readmission agreement with Poland. It stipulated that Ukrainian authorities will accept any Ukrainian citizen or third country national apprehended after having illegally crossed the border from their territory into Poland. Ukraine was now about to negotiate a readmission agreement with the European Union as a whole.[20] Some preparation was required, and this is where the training was supposed to help.

Mariusz's narrative: Back in 1991 Poland wanted to sustain an open and friendly western border. The new democratic government lobbied also for visa-free travel. To reach an agreement with the Germans, it had to also assume the responsibility for controlling migration from and through Poland to Germany. It had to "put a dam" to border trespasses. This meant swiftly taking charge not only of its own citizens who illegally crossed the western neighbor's border, but also of citizens of third countries who did the same. Readmission agreements, Mariusz explained, are just that: "technical arrangements between competent services" that help to order flows of people and maintain control over borders. But what directly precipitated the readmission agreement? It was the ratification of the 1951 Convention Relating to the Status of Refugees during the presidency of Lech Wałęsa. This act allowed the German government to classify its postsocialist neighbor as a "safe third country" where human rights were observed. It was now possible to include it in Germany's own scheme for containing the influx of asylum seekers. With readmission arrangements in place, anyone apprehended while crossing the border could immediately be sent back. According to Mariusz, the necessary "operational cooperation" between Polish border guards and the German *Grenzschutz* "built trust" that now facilitates the ongoing integration into Schengen.

These changes went hand in hand with reforming the Border Guard and turning it from socialist army dinosaurs into a modern, European police-like force.[21] Changing the public perception of the service was critical. The officers had to acquire the trust of "regular people" so that, among other things, they could recruit informants among them. Tips from such protected sources became key to policing the smuggling of "illegals," trafficking in persons, and other cross-border crimes and misdemeanors. "I apologize for saying this," Mariusz said, "because it's obvious. Under communism we all thought that it's enough to watch the borderline. But this no longer works!" The audience responded with knowing smiles. They were on the same page.

Mariusz began listing elements of policy and practice that emerged as indispensable after the readmission agreement with Germany came into effect. Better, forgery-proof passports for improved tracking of influx and outflow; electronic databases for registering entry and departure; civilized asylum procedures and reception centers; a humane system for detention of illegal immigrants; professional management of removals. These were the things Ukraine would need to introduce and develop, following the Polish example. This was in order to be able to manage in a "proper and modern" way the stream of third-country migrants and asylum seekers traveling through Ukraine to Europe, where they will not be admitted. In return for Ukraine's commitment to do so, the EU would (maybe) lift some of the restrictions on travel of Ukrainians into the EU. It would (probably) not lift the visa requirement, but it could "simplify" the process and begin granting more visas to "certain categories of travelers."

With his metaphors of flows, streams, and dams, the image Mariusz conjured in front of his Ukrainian audience was one of complex hydraulics required for the effective regulation of human waves washing over nation-states and the EU. After his talk, I was left with the picture of connected vessels used in physics classrooms to demonstrate hydrostatic equilibrium: liquid added to one cylinder doesn't spill but flows into the next one. It was as though migration engineers imagined that such equilibrium could be accomplished also at the borders of Europe—that migrants, including asylum seekers, rather than "flooding" the EU, could be contained within the connected vessels of neighboring states. The talk also made it apparent that crafting a border regime is an elaborate game of give and take wherein the more affluent side, although it enjoys the upper hand, still has a serious stake. For admitting certain kinds of unwanted people, the less affluent governments can negotiate a slight opening of the tide-gates to their own citizens.

Democratic Pragmatism?

Throughout the training, I struggled to make sense of the affiliations and re-lationships among the people and organizations involved. Two nongovern-mental policy research institutes put the project together. State agencies were invited to participate, as were NGO representatives working on refugee assis-tance. The latter talked about their "model cooperation" with the authorities. Border guards reciprocated with similar niceties. Featured speakers included experts on government payrolls, as well as others introduced as independent. Did it make sense to consider this inclusion of civil society organizations in discussions of border security a hopeful sign of a democratic input into an area usually excluded from public debate and shrouded in secrecy, or was there something amiss? Certainly the line between "state" and "non-state" appeared thoroughly blurred.

As Pierre Bourdieu theorized about the bureaucratic field, he remarked that "one of the major powers of the state is to produce and impose categories of thought that we spontaneously apply to all things of the social world—including the state itself" (1998: 35). This power was in ample evidence at the training. All the research and expertise summoned to facilitate and justify the border regime's expansion drew on official categories and responded to state rationales, despite the purported "independence" of the setting. What Jef-frey C. Goldfarb would call "the definition of the situation" (2006) had been thoroughly accepted, and there was structurally no space for, and indeed no signs of dissenting points of view. Considering broader critiques of power and governance in the European Union, that perhaps should not have been surprising. As Cris Shore observed, EU governance relies on substitutes for representative democracy.

> Talking to nongovernmental organizations that claim to represent civil society is often a proxy for talking directly to ordinary European citizens. . . . What the Commission calls "dialogue with civil society" others would describe as an act of ventriloquism; a rigged conver-sation in which organizations financed by the EU promote political messages congenial to the EU. (Shore 2006: 716)

What is true of the way the EU is governed more generally is also a fact in rebordering. Those representatives of the civil society who, drawing on Eu-ropean Union funds, are willing to engage in promoting bureaucratic and technical solutions that are compatible with Schengen, do so. Others remain silent or on the margins.[22]

Discussing the moral and political principles behind particular modes of border management was indeed not the point of the training; the organizers cast border management as an "apolitical and technical matter." "This [the training] is not about ideology," Mariusz said to me during one of the coffee breaks. He had no qualms about this alignment of governmental and nongovernmental. He talked about how much he enjoyed working with the Border Guard and praised them for being modern, pragmatic, and "non-ideological." At one point he said: "*Capacity building* is what I really like. You get to go to the field and see *konkret*, the tangibles. You know, it's not like searching for xenophobia and discrimination of blacks, disabled, and lesbians in Rzeszowskie!"

This last comment was a quip aimed at the EU-sponsored antidiscrimination initiatives embraced by some Polish NGOs. The juxtaposition of "blacks, disabled, and lesbians" with "Rzeszowskie," a provincial and thoroughly homogeneous region in the southeast, was supposed to deliver the comic effect. Mariusz did not seem to have much patience for the idea that discrimination against minorities (sexual, racial, or otherwise) in a place like the southeast of Poland would be a problem in need of tackling. More important, he regarded it as an ideological projection, an artificial transposition of EU political correctness into a place where it was uncalled for. He was skeptical about the labor and resources that went into researching and fighting prejudice and homophobia, issues he did not perceive as particularly pressing or acute. In other words, in his view there were *real*, not made-up problems out there. He asserted his own professional investment in the technical capacity of the state to address those real problems pragmatically, for example, illegal migration. In doing so, he was responding to what he perceived as the objective (as opposed to imagined, presumably by left-wing ideologues) challenge of modernization and development.[23]

Meanwhile, over the course of the subsequent segments of the training, the Ukrainian delegation was listening to a series of lectures concerning the handling of asylum applicants and "illegal migrants." One afternoon a young NGO lawyer was giving a talk about the legal situation of migrants in Poland. He was a graduate student in his twenties.[24] He discussed the scarce forms of legalization available to non-EU citizens in Poland and began explaining the concept of subsidiary protection and "tolerated stay" as an alternative to granting refugee status, when the audience started showing signs of disorientation.

"Excuse me, *vybachte*, but I don't understand. You give status and then take it away?" a man in his forties named Vasyliy asked in a soft voice. The lawyer attempted an explanation and cited one of the EU common asylum system directives, but this only deepened the misunderstanding. "But the [1951] Convention . . . What about *non-refoulement*?" The man was pressing for clarification, as others began to whisper between themselves. This made the young lawyer visibly impatient, but Mariusz came to his aid, explaining that tolerated stay is different from refugee status and that all EU countries have instituted a similar form of protection.[25] His intervention dispersed the doubts for a little while, until, with one of the next speakers, the topic of detention came up.

The practice of detaining persons who crossed borders without authorization or were found without papers was discussed matter-of-factly as a legally grounded, necessary measure in combating illegal migration. In order to deport someone, the person must first be detained so that the authorities can confirm identity and issue the requisite documents. But immigrants often purposely get rid of their passports. If the biometric databases produce no record of the person, identification becomes a time-consuming challenge. The law generally stipulates that a person may not be detained for more than a year, but according to experts this is "usually" enough time to "execute the removal decision."[26]

The objections this information generated had to do with the expenses of maintaining appropriate facilities ("We can hardly afford prisons for *our people* in Ukraine," someone said.) The Canadian-Ukrainian IOM associate leaned over to tell me that she and her unit at the Kyiv IOM were engaged precisely in developing the infrastructure for migrant detention. But overall the audience seemed unperturbed, until later, during a visit to the Aliens Bureau, the Bureau head (still the same man I had interviewed a few months earlier; see previous chapter) mentioned that in certain cases not just illegal migrants are detained, but asylum seekers as well.

This time one of the women, an employee of the Ukrainian immigration service, raised a question, invoking the 1951 Convention again. She pointed out that detaining asylum seekers is a breach of human rights law and stated authoritatively, though incorrectly, that Ukraine does not practice it. The speaker replied that it is not a breach, because placing the person in confinement requires a court order (i.e., is not arbitrary), and because it does not impinge on his or her right to "a democratic asylum procedure." He did not mention that court orders in such cases are granted automatically, nor did he explain what precisely made the procedure "democratic." He did emphasize, however, the exceptionality of the provision: not all asylum seekers are detained, only those who are undocumented, or who illegally crossed the border into Poland. Those whose papers are in order are placed in one of the thirteen open reception centers where they await a decision. Introducing the legal possibility of detaining the undocumented was necessary "from the standpoint of state security." Finally, he rhetorically delegitimized the detainees' claim to asylum; they are, he said, "not really persecuted." In reality they apply for refugee status because "they are searching for a better life."

In their bafflement with tolerated stay and with the detention of asylum seekers, the Ukrainian delegates revealed disquiet over some of the more stark innovations in the EU asylum system. Mariusz had an answer to why it was so. "Ukrainians are recent converts to human rights," he told me. "They don't know what you can, and what you cannot do." This was why, according to him, they were questioning approaches that have been thoroughly normalized in EU law and practice. Once they were told it was OK to detain asylum seekers, and to withdraw protection after a certain time, they would adjust their practices and thinking accordingly.

While this was most likely true (it was hard to imagine that in current conditions Ukraine would tend toward a more, not less, generous asylum practice), I suggest a slightly different interpretation. What the Ukrainian participants were displaying was not a confusion about human rights, but rather an unadulterated certainty. They had entered the training with an assumption that human rights are nonnegotiable. They maintained, incorrectly, that "Ukraine does not detain asylum seekers." In doing so, they were preemptively defending the honor of their own uniformed service from an imagined or anticipated charge of human rights violations. This defense was probably an expression of loyalty as much as of discipline, only strengthened by the endurance of the Soviet habitus in the uniformed services of post-Soviet societies (Beck 2005). At the same time they were expressing the combination of civilizational aspiration and striving for democratic credentials that fifteen years earlier in Poland had prompted Lech Wałęsa's signing of the 1951 Convention. Ukrainian participants spoke on behalf of a system that was clearly marred by financial shortcomings and low awareness of refugee issues. But its agents also assumed that to make it credible, its modernization must include embracing stern human rights principles. Prior to the training, these rank-and-file border and immigration service men and women had no opportunity to learn about the flexibilization that in the 1990s and

2000s had became the defining feature of asylum practices. As the training demonstrated, Ukrainian authorities had yet to reach the point where their protection of external borders, policing of the interior, and managing all immigration would be fused into one border regime, where human rights too must be somewhat flexible.

Economic Migrants Beyond Demand

After three days of conferencing, it was time to begin a tour of detention facilities. This was the most anticipated part of the program. Ukrainian authorities already struggled with an inadequate infrastructure for detaining illegal migrants, a point that kept returning during discussions about readmission. Upon concluding the readmission agreement with the EU, the burden of handling Europe's undesirables would increase. But the EU had conditioned its promises of easing the visa requirements for Ukrainians on their willingness to, in effect, become a holder of the unwanted. The glimmering prospect of easier access to the EU was an undeniably strong incentive; while officially the Ukrainian government lamented the labor migration of its citizens, the state benefited from the remittances.[27] Moreover, Ukrainian citizens' ability to travel westward hassle-free would be a sign of modernization, and an affirmation of Ukraine's Europeanness. "Now it all comes down to money," an Interior Ministry official from Kyiv told me. "If the Evrosoyuz (EU) wants us to take these people, they have to pay for keeping them and for sending them home. We can't just do this job for them."[28] Mykola Klekh had a diplomatic term—what was needed was "financial solidarity." Visiting Polish detention centers and speaking to their managers would allow them to see how *nashy Polskiy drukhy*, "our Polish friends" handled their "illegals."

The day was freezing. A comfortable coach took us outside the city and off the main roads to get to Podleśnica, the small town not far from the capital where Poland's main Ośrodek Strzeżony, "Guarded Center," was located. The ground rules for the visit were laid on the way. We were supposed to stick together as a group. It was OK to take pictures, as long as they were not of guards or detainees. There was to be no talking to the detainees, even if they tried to talk to us. As a holdover from the past, unlike most other migrant detention facilities, this center was administered not by the Border Guard, but by the police. In the ongoing rivalry between the two services the Guard manifests an air of superiority. One of the officials had told us earlier that if our hosts would seem a little "rough," it would be because they were police-men and lacked proper training and experience in handling foreigners.

The "roughness" manifested itself immediately. The group entered the center, which was walled off behind a corrugated metal fence topped with barbed wire. Almost all the participants displayed signs of discomfort. Bod-ies stiffened, silence and solemn expressions replaced the chattiness of the bus ride. We were welcomed by a high-strung police inspector who heads the center. He ushered everyone into an austere meeting room (no more car-peted conference venues), and expressed his regrets that he could not show proper hospitality by offering alcohol. His sense of humor was acrid, and his body language and mannerisms projected a cop's mode of toughness. He an-nounced he would be explaining the day-to-day functioning of the center and started by saying that "regulations are regulations, but life is life."

The ten-year-old center, arranged in a former garrison, was comprised of two barracks. Both were two-story buildings, forming an L-shape around the snow-covered courtyard. Windows were barred, and on the bars the detainees had hung plastic bags with food to keep it cool. There were a couple of smaller buildings for storage and administration. To the side, a rusty merry-go-round stood in for a "playground." One of the buildings was for males and housed a hundred detainees. The other was for women and families with room for thirty-one. At the time of our visit the center was filled to capacity, but we were told that during summer months, when there are more illegal crossings, sometimes there is overcrowding. The inspector said that 70 percent of all "illegal immigrants" apprehended by the Border Guard end up in Podleśnica. He proudly noted that so far they've held citizens of seventy-four countries. At the time of our visit, among the detained were Indians, Pakistanis, Af-ghanis, Chinese, Vietnamese, Nigerians, Belarusians, Georgians, Ukrainians, and a large number of Russian citizens from the Caucasus.[29] Some were read-mitted from Germany. Approximately half were in different stages of asylum application procedures. Others were awaiting deportation.

"We're trying to be liberal here," the inspector said. "But not too liberal." The internal rules of the facility permit free movement inside the buildings and between rooms, but not outside. This distinguishes the center from a de-portation arrest, where those detained for short periods just prior to removal are locked up in cells. There is one hour of outdoor activity every day, when the inhabitants of the two barracks can interact. The guard to detainee ratio is one to twenty-five, and this, in his opinion, is not enough. He had advice for the Ukrainian delegation:

When you are building a center like this back home, don't skimp on security. This is a converted military facility. But these things should be built from scratch. When you design it well you can save on security manpower. Administration should be in a separate building. Only foreigners in a fenced area, so that employees don't have to enter it.

The architect and the IOM associate were taking copious notes, perhaps visualizing appropriate forms of panopticism. A few male participants were more interested in the use of weapons. The inspector limited himself to citing the laws that codify use of violence. He seemed reluctant to speak of precisely how the guards enforce order. However, in a tone that betrayed strong feelings, he described all the ways in which *cudzoziemcy*, foreigners, are a difficult and troublesome crowd. "These people are locked up," he said. "They are not happy about this. They develop a demanding attitude, they expect various things. The Chechens are the number one troublemakers."

He went on to describe the management's practice of placing the detainees in rooms together according to nationality. The guards then refer to the rooms accordingly: "Armenia," "India," "Pakistan," and "Chechnya." Cleaning duties are assigned to particular rooms, but if the people in "Armenia" or "Chechnya" have to clean, they refuse, because, according to the inspector, they expect "the Blacks" to do it. "They destroy everything," he said. "They devastate the premises and the furnishings they are given. They don't take care of anything. The Chechens took the TV into their room and don't let anyone else watch."

This rant segued into an accusation directed at NGOs that send their legal counselors into the facility. The inspector thought that these counselors' view of the situation in the center was "purely theoretical" and did not take into consideration the violent reality. "What the foreigners tell them, they believe," he said dismissively of the human rights volunteers who are allowed to visit detainees (so much for "model cooperation"). He recalled an instance when one activist in a monitoring report had gone so far as to call for his resignation. The remark was offered as a joke ridiculing the volunteers' supposed zeal. But it provoked only a few tense giggles, as there were, after all, representatives of human rights NGOs in the audience. The inspector went on, but after someone earnestly asked him about how the center makes sure detainees have access to lawyers, he appeared to restrain himself from further derogatory remarks and stiffly declared that "orderly cooperation with NGOs is very important and to some extent it even facilitates our work."

We were warned that seeing inside the barracks would not be a pleasant experience. It was going to be a mess and a picture of destruction. But this was nothing to blame the management for. The foreigners were responsible, we were told, and now they had to live amid devastation. Four guards flanked our group as we entered the male barracks. Small, diverse clusters of mostly young men, in their twenties and thirties, were peering over the banisters as we made our way through the first-floor hallway. We were shown the empty isolation cell reserved for the rowdy, and a sparse nurse's office; the doctor was not there, but apparently he held regular office hours. As we were about to walk upstairs, one of the guards shooed the men out of the way and silenced those trying to make contact. "Where are you from?" one of the detainees said in English, and again in a louder voice. "Ukraina," responded the IOM woman, to which the man replied "I'm from Pakistan," followed by a scattered chorus of other voices: "China," "Vietnam, Vietnam," "India." The guards reminded us we were not supposed to communicate across the confinement lines. But the four of them could not prevent interaction altogether. There were more than thirty of us, and many more detainees.

The members of our group peered into the disorderly rooms whose walls were decorated with chaotic drawings and posters. The prayer room had writing in Arabic. Doors had holes in them and the walls were scuffed. Mykola spoke to one of the detainees in Russian. Mariusz talked to the guards. A couple of the Ukrainian women remained downstairs. The interpreter and I talked to two young Indians, who said that they did not know how long they were going to be here and what was going to happen to them, but that eventually they were hoping to get to Germany. "If this was prison I would know for how long," one of them said. We did not get a chance to ask further questions before we were rushed out of the block.

This formal introduction followed by a visitation scenario repeated itself during the following parts of the training, in a deportation arrest on the Polish-German border, and in the facilities in Ivanovo and Vysoky Horod in Ukraine. In Ptaszyn nad Odrą, where the unit specializes in intercepting migrants on their way to Germany, we were taken on the tour by a mild-mannered Border Guard officer. The facility there was new, established in 2000, and its cleanliness and efficient design were clearly the result of adjusting to "European standards." There were four cells for women and five for men, with a total of fifty-six board beds. "We are nice to them here," the commander said with a gentle smile and a wink. Thirty-one of the spots were occupied during our visit, but we were let in only to rooms that were empty.

It was Ptaszyn, rather than the Podleśnica center, that in terms of its living conditions (very basic but new and clean), internal regulations (allowances for outdoor time, contact with the outside world, access to health care), and adherence to Schengen procedures was to constitute an example of "best practices" for the Ukrainians to emulate. The concept of "best practices," taken from the language of business, refers to a standardized way of doing things that has ostensibly proved to deliver desirable outcomes. It has been widely used in health care (e.g., benchmarking in "evidence-based medicine"), education, law enforcement, and other realms that have adopted neoliberal management practices. Best practices is also a buzzword of EU governance that comes up repeatedly in communications and regulations pertaining to immigration and borders.[30] In the official glossary of Eurojargon, the entry "best practices" somewhat tautologically explains, "one way of improving policies in the EU is for governments to look at what is going on in other EU countries and to see what works best. They can then adopt this 'best practice,' adapting it to their own national and local circumstances."[31]

As such, the notion fits in very well with the concepts of border and migration management as supposedly "apolitical and technical" realms that require pragmatic actions and practical solutions, not anything that might be construed as "ideology." But *best practices*, imposed from above and authoritatively declaring themselves superior, are nothing other than a technology of power with the capacity to impede critical thinking, evacuate the social, political, and ethical responsibility from the task at hand, and reinforce the status quo of unequal power distribution. There is also an arrogant finality in best practices; that they are "best" implies that there is no need to question, revise, or improve on them.

Later, in Ivanovo, the participants expressed a sort of relief that ultimately, though Ukrainian resources were miniscule compared to the Polish, their facility looked quite similar to the older Polish one. "Tell me honestly," Mykola asked me while we were there, "do you think Podleśnica was so much better [than Ivanovo]?" I did not think so. But then again I did not think that Ptaszyn was "better" either. It was, however, more civilized, both in the sense of being more modern, and in the Eliasian sense of being more effective at banishing violence from view. It was perhaps kinder and gentler, but still a tool for the sequestering of the unwanted, one that more closely met the European standards of Schengen, and could thus be better integrated with the flexible border regime.

In July 2007, over a year after the training and only a few months before

Ukraine's neighbors were fully admitted into the Schengen zone after the post-2004 transition period, the visa facilitation and readmission agreements between Ukraine and EU were finally signed. They contain provisions for easier access to visas to students, business travelers, and participants in cultural and scientific exchange (cf. Kirişci 2006). Moreover, visa fees for Schengen Member States were fixed at 35 euros (still a steep price, amounting to one-fifth of an average monthly salary in western Ukraine as of 2007). The agreement on readmission stipulates "the obligations and procedures for the authorities of both Ukraine and the respective EU Member State as to when and how to take back people who are illegally residing on their territories. These obligations cover nationals from Ukraine, the EU Member States and those from third countries and stateless people."[32] Franco Frattini, former vice-president of the European Commission responsible for Freedom, Security and Justice, was quoted as having said at the signing of the agreements, "these are particularly important [because] facilitating people-to-people contacts can greatly help in increasing mutual understanding and improving our relations in all fields."[33] It is a matter for future research and analysis, whether Ukraine—its border service and its authorities, as well as the people in whose name, after all, the agreement was signed—will fulfill the role of a buffer seamlessly and congenially enough for these "people-to-people contacts" and "mutual understanding" to flourish.

Externalization as a Human Rights Problem and the Problem with Human Rights

As this text has already emphasized, public sentiment toward immigrants oscillates between compassion and repression (Fassin 2005). The training of Ukrainian border services I witnessed suggests that "best practices" and other elements of neoliberal governance in managing borders and migration that come part and parcel with Schengen are an attempt, collectively hammered out by Brussels and national actors, to rein in and balance those powerful sentiments. The emphasis is on addressing the status quo—the fact that there are "undesirable migrants" out there—rather than examining the extent to which the border regime itself constructs their undesirability.

These antidemocratic features of the border regime, as well as its moral unaccountability, have been an object of sharp criticism, especially from a human rights standpoint. The key target of these critiques has been the

Common European Asylum System and its compromised capacity to ensure protection to foreigners who cannot avail themselves of the protection of their home state, as stipulated in the 1951 Convention definition of a refugee cited in the previous chapter. Today, as the UNHCR asserts, the Geneva Convention and the New York Protocol "provide the most comprehensive codification of the rights of refugees yet adopted on the international level." They are to be applied "without discrimination as to race, religion or country of origin" (UNHCR 2006: 5). But human rights lawyers and advocates worry about the fact that the EU asylum redesign might involve tinkering with precisely those provisions of the Convention that are considered most fundamental. Some of those critics adopt a law and procedure-oriented perspective. From such a standpoint, the devil is in the details. For example, one young lawyer, who introduced me to the Helsinki Foundation's program of legal assistance to foreigners, was concerned that the EU Directive on minimum standards for granting refugee status (2004/83/EC), by narrowing the formerly open definition of persecution, may modify the very definition of a refugee.[34] She was also critical of the EU-condoned practice of detaining certain categories of asylum seekers, notably the undocumented ones, as well as deporting asylum seekers who are appealing their decisions. However, she had no objections to detaining "illegal immigrants." In other words, the legal framework she was equipped with made no allowances for the ambiguity of those categories. Overall she believed that "our [Polish] regulations are pretty good," and her concerns were focused primarily on ensuring that the Geneva Convention is not undermined.

The legal scholar Sylvie Da Lomba, in her study of the right to seek asylum in the EU, offers a more comprehensive critique of the tendencies in EU legislation. She is concerned that the pragmatism which guides decision-making in the European Union may lead to systemic breaches of international refugee law. She contends that the trend to externalize asylum seekers and to detain them "casts doubts on the EU and the member states' commitment to refugee protection and human rights" (Da Lomba 2004: 16). Furthermore, she argues,

It is critical to differentiate between EU asylum and immigration policies, as their objectives vary significantly. Indeed, immigration policies put the emphasis on border control and the need to monitor migratory movements, with a view in particular to tackle irregular migration. Conversely, the provision of international protection in the absence of effective domestic protection remains at the heart of asylum. *Increasingly, however, asylum policies are shaped by immigration objectives and are absorbed by immigration policies to the detriment of their primary purpose.* The lack of provisions designed to preserve asylum seeker rights in readmission exemplify this problem. (2004: 16, emphasis added)

My own observations, as outlined above, correspond to Da Lomba's point. Immigration objectives do tend to shape asylum policy and practice, and this is a development that hurts persons in need of asylum. But it is my conviction that this criticism, like the objections of human rights lawyers whom I interviewed, remains bound by the "technocratic rationalities of law" (Riles 2006: 58) and thus can only go as far as those rationalities permit.

The 1951 Convention and the 1967 Protocol are documents that were drawn up in different times, in response to particular needs created by particular types of conflicts. Their authors did not envision a world where persons displaced by conflicts and political upheaval would be part of the same migration flows as those moving away from more generalized hardship and misery: poverty, dysfunctional socioeconomic systems, and areas devastated by natural and manmade disaster. They did not envision changing economies, terrorism-related securitization, and other factors that drive restrictive immigration policies and changing attitudes to asylum. They did not predict either the emergence of such supranational bodies as the EU with its capacity to diffuse, by the practices of externalization and buffering, rather than strengthen, the responsibility of states to protect refugees. Because of these developments, critique and advocacy focused on the preservation of the right to seek refugee status in its traditional form amounts to a very much needed, but ultimately one-sided, effort. To use Fassin's terms, it mobilizes compassion for the few, while tacitly accepting repression practiced toward the many who do not make the asylum cut. (2005) Meanwhile, the status quo at the EU borders necessitates building on the 1951 Convention and developing new ways, legal and otherwise, of thinking about the humanity, rather than ever more narrowly interpreted human rights, of all persons who are on the move, regardless of the motives that propel them.[35]

Adhering, as the EU legislation does, to mid-twentieth-century notions of refugees as individuals personally affected by persecution perpetrated by states and organizations enables excluding ever more people from the category of "bona fide asylum seekers." It relegates growing numbers to the pool of unwanted "economic migrants," that is, people whose only right is that to be treated in accordance with best practices—to be removed in an orderly and efficient manner; and even that promise falters, as Chowra Makaremi's work documents (2008). In this context the 1951 Convention, officially recognized as fundamental by the EU, is being used strategically to simulate moral legitimacy within the otherwise ethically conflicted new border regime. European Union asylum policies are both a litmus test and a fig leaf for the developing border regime. A litmus test, because their increasing rigidity reflects the overall apprehensive disposition toward non-EU foreigners. A fig leaf, because the declared upholding of the rights of the shrinking pool of recognized refugees serves to deflect attention from those in need who could not and will not be granted refugee status. Meanwhile, as the situation on the Polish-Ukrainian border demonstrates, the question of what constitutes protection and who is covered is given up to a continuous negotiation, framed by security rationales, technical specifications, and the material and mental substance of the border itself.

Chapter 7

The Border as Intertext:
Memory, Belonging, and the Search
for a New Narrative

There are not that many original ideas in the world nowadays.
Everything that can be said about Europe and its Eastern borders
has already been said, in one or another form.
I am afraid that I do not have anything specific to add.

—Yaroslav Hrytsak,
"The Borders of Europe—Seen from the Outside"

The previous chapters examined the constitutive elements of the new European border regime and the larger technocratic process of rebordering. However, there is more to rebordering, and to researching the field, than has been indicated so far. As anthropologists and other social scientists have highlighted on many occasions, field research generates both objective and subjective ways of knowing the world, where the borders of personal experience, research experience, and subjects' understandings do not separate into neat categories or conceptual limits, but instead produce and emphasize a messier, deeper, perhaps richer, set of insights (see for example Geertz 1998; Bell and Encel 1978). In this chapter I draw together a series of otherwise fragmented observations, encounters, and (mostly historical) readings that at different points in the course of my fieldwork for this project illuminated the peculiar and shifting status of the Polish-Ukrainian border. The following text thus emanates from what we might call the intertext that accumulates in the course of any ethnography. If the endeavor of "research" consists of more or less structured and recorded interviews, fieldnotes taken during and after encounters, events, and field trips, filed and annotated printed sources, and other materials that come together as "data" (and the scare quotes merely begin to hint at the arbitrariness of these concepts), what I call intertext is at once the residue and the context of those data. It includes the casual conversations with people who are not-quite-informants that touch indirectly on the subject we are studying; the assorted press clippings filed under "miscellaneous"; the unplanned and unanticipated events and encounters that unfold in the field which are not exactly "about" what one studies, but may or may not shed light on it simply because they belong to the same time and place. Ethnography necessarily produces a vast intertextual web which is all the denser if the subject matter is one that stimulates strong beliefs and emotional investments.

In what follows, I delve into this context and residue, because while Polish and EU experts, regulators, policymakers, and law enforcement agencies were engaged in constructing the border regime, the Polish and Ukrainian publics were debating other issues which had a bearing on the process of rebordering. Those issues included ways of remembering the Polish-Ukrainian conflict of the first half of the twentieth century; Ukrainian democracy, the Orange Revolution, and Ukraine's prospects for EU membership; the nature of Central European belonging and cross-border connectedness; the Europeanness of this part of Europe. While the new control apparatus (the visas, the surveillance, the entire system of border protection) was present in those debates primarily as a subplot (for example, visas as a powerful symbol of exclusion), overall they concerned the ontological status of the border. What is it? What is it *for*? What does it *mean*? What does it *do*?[1] The polyphony (or cacophony) of responses to these questions has implications for rebordering, which, let us reiterate, involves the dialectical process of defining the new boundaries of the European Union, through challenging, expanding, or otherwise altering the idea of Europe in order at once to accommodate some Eastern Europeans as new citizens of the European Union, and to account for the exclusion of others.

It has such implications, because at stake in those debates is ultimately the same issue that has been driving rebordering, that is, the question of collective and individual membership, access, and belonging to the nation-state, to the European Union, and to Europe itself. Quite independently from the Western European debates concerning security, asylum, and the desirable scope and nature of immigration to the EU, the Polish-Ukrainian frontier has been a site where the new European border was contested for its exclusionary tendencies, but sometimes also affirmed as a much-needed fence dividing Europe from the post-Soviet unknown. These sentiments have been animated by a different set of historical experiences from those informing the actions of the EU leaders, experts, and technocrats who are responsible for the regime's construction. At the heart of the construction of a united Europe is a fundamental contradiction, one that foreshadows many of the tensions discussed in previous chapters. This is the fact that from its inception the architects of the European Community have been ambivalent about its borders. Conscious of the multiple and overlapping cultural and intellectual traditions that make up "the idea of Europe" (Pagden 2002), they did not foreclose the possibility of an expansive and expanding association. However, after the iron curtain was gone, this original reluctance to set boundaries began to clash with the everyday realism and bureaucratic rationality that came to dominate the European Union as it prepared for expansion. The architects of the enlargement seemed to agree that while Europe might not have a clearly definable border, the European Union certainly does. The outer territorial borders of new member states became the boundary of the Union, and while they will continue to shift as new members are admitted (although following the 2004 and 2007 enlargements many argue that the Union is "at capacity"), the EU's external border is real and unambiguous. But it is a curious paradox that the community of states founded as a remedy to the continent's most devastating conflicts now reinforces those Central European divides where tensions produced by those very conflicts still continue to linger. The technocratic rebordering of the EU exists alongside the material and mental residues of old systems of rule and social organization, starkly visible in the discourse and practice of Polish-Ukrainian partnership. I show below that rebordering has the effect of partially depoliticizing a potentially vigorous debate between two bordering societies about the extent of their border's permeability and the nature of the movement and connections to be fostered or discouraged across it. At the same time rebordering also prompts a new set of questions and awakens a counter-hegemonic impulse in the form of a discourse of postcoloniality, here a vernacular polemic with the binarism of nationalism and reconciliation. Taking a broad interpretive angle allows one to appreciate the inherent ambiguity of the postcolonial situation—the tense histories and ethnographic encounters that this chapter draws upon show precisely this kind of ambiguity, one that technocratization is layered upon.

The Principle of National Homogeneity

To understand this paradox requires appreciation of the historical fact that the Polish-Ukrainian borderland changed hands several times over the course of the twentieth century. Chapter 1 has provided a brief outline of this history. Now I want to consider the contemporary rebordering in the context of the previous ones, which partitioned space and transferred populations. In 2004 the border itself did not shift, but the status of the bordering political entities and their citizens changed rather dramatically. This change of status (the fact that the Poles became EU citizens, while the Ukrainians didn't; the fact the Polish state ceded some of its prerogatives to a supranational body, while the Ukrainian state continued to grapple with the challenges of post-Soviet nation-building), tends to be represented as Poland's rightful "return to Europe," and as evidence of Ukraine being "not ready" to join the club. It is also sometimes narrated in terms of historical justice, where the recognition granted to Poland and other new members is a belated redress, on behalf of the Western core of the European Union, for abandoning them at the end of World War II to the mercy of Stalin. I resist these teleological interpretations and propose that, as I have argued earlier, the expansion of the European Union is only the latest reconfiguration of a social and geographic space where aftershocks of previous reborderings continue to reverberate. The projects the EU brings to the borderland, such as the modernization of infrastructure, supporting local entrepreneurship, and readjustment of border maintenance and control are the newest layers of the borderland palimpsest, consisting of contemporary modalities of social life coexisting with material and mental residues of old systems of rule and social organization. They are the newest interventions into a region haunted by the loss of its cultural and ethnic diversity, and shaped by the dialectic of grand ideologies and their disintegration.

Already in 1919 President Woodrow Wilson had hoped that a strict application of the principle of nationality (one national group within established territorial frontiers) would bring peace to the so-called "belt of mixed peoples" between Germany and Russia. However, the combination of the actual distribution of populations and the territorial ambitions of the newly sovereign states was at odds with the plan.[2] As Eric Hobsbawm observed in his reflections on nationalism after Versailles, "it simply did not work. . . . Inevitably, given the actual distribution of peoples, most of the new states built on the ruins of the old empires, were quite as multinational as the old 'prisons of nations' they replaced" (Hobsbawm 1990: 132).

In light of the problems posed by ethnic heterogeneity, the Versailles framework stipulated special Minority Treaties which constituted an integral part of the peace agreements that ended World War I.[3] Minority Treaties granted equality and limited minority rights to some (but not all) ethnically different populations living within the boundaries of Eastern European states (Poland, Czechoslovakia, Hungary, Serbia) which gained independence in the aftermath of World War I. They established a de facto division between the enfranchised "state peoples" whose belonging was ensured by virtue of their nationality, and the secondary, ethnically and linguistically different "others" to whom key rights were denied. As Hannah Arendt characterized it in *The Origins of Totalitarianism*, such an arrangement was a "disastrous experiment" whose very logic led these nationalities to be disloyal to their state governments. Government leaders, on the other hand, considered the presence of minorities a temporary situation, before they were either liquidated or assimilated (Arendt 1951: 271).

The Polish example was a case in point. In the interwar period the Ukrainian minority amounted to approximately 16 percent of the Polish population, concentrated in the Eastern districts, Jews accounted for 10 percent, and Belarussians, Germans, Russians, and Lithuanians made up the remaining 5 of the total percentage of other ethnicities (Tomaszewski 1985: 35). The state, integrating all its territories under the national banner after over a century of partitions, saw minorities as a threat to its unity.[4] Although initially they had political representation in the parliament, over the course of the 1920s their freedoms were gradually withdrawn, in keeping with the overall erosion of democracy. Finally, in 1934 Poland unilaterally withdrew from the Minority Treaty.

Political anti-Semitism rose in prominence over the course of the 1930s, and anti-Jewish agitation and policies became part of the repertoire of governance.[5] The harassment of other minorities was no less open. In Galicia and Volhynia religious and cultural freedoms of Ukrainians were curtailed, and activists of the national movement were subjected to severe persecution. Skirmishes between Polish police and fighters affiliated with Organization of Ukrainian Nationalists (OUN) continued over the course of the interwar period, most notably in Lviv. Rusini, "Ruthenians," as the Ukrainians were officially called, were not treated as a nation, but rather as an "ethnographic group," to be assimilated with time into the Polish nation (Hrytsak 2000: 191). In these conditions, Ukrainian activists and fighters periodically organized demonstrations and attacks on local Polish institutions and assassinated local officials. OUN was deemed a terrorist organization; in response, in 1930, the authorities carried out a violent campaign targeting Ukrainians in Galicia. The army and the police "pacified" Ukrainian villages in the entire region. "The principle of collective responsibility was applied to the entire Ukrainian community. . . . Following this logic, being Ukrainian meant being a politically uncertain element" (Hrytsak 2000: 191). The account of this universal victimization of the Ukrainians by the Polish state in the 1920 and 30s is one of the shared acts of suffering that in post-1991 Ukraine became "raw material for nation-building" (Etkind 2010), especially in the west of the country. It is one of the foundational traumas whose memory lies at the heart of contemporary Ukrainianness, right next to memories of violence inflicted by the Soviets, notably the famine of the 1930s.[6]

Arendt wrote that the "nationally frustrated peoples" believed that true freedom, sovereignty, and guarantee of their human rights would come only with national emancipation. Further, she observed, "in this conviction, which could base itself on the fact that the French Revolution had combined the declaration of the Rights of Man with national sovereignty, they were supported by the Minority Treaties themselves, which did not entrust the governments with the protection of different nationalities but charged the League of Nations with the safeguarding of the rights of those who, for reasons of territorial settlement, had been left without national states of their own" (Arendt 1951: 272). The League of Nations in turn provided meager protection, considering that it was composed of "national statesmen whose sympathies could not but be with the unhappy new governments which were hampered and opposed on principle by between 25 and 50 percent of their inhabitants" (272). However, it is precisely in the fact that an international body guaranteed minority rights that Arendt sees the significance of the Treaties. "The recognition that millions of people lived outside normal legal protection and needed an additional guarantee of their elementary rights from an outside body"—this was something new in European history. We may observe that this awareness informed also the postwar history of human rights. For example, even though the 1951 Convention is almost universally ratified, the UNHCR is still given the mandate to oversee and intervene in the protection of the displaced.

"The Minority Treaties said in plain language what until then had only been implied in the working system of nation states, namely, that only nationals could be citizens . . . that persons of a different nationality needed some law of exception until or unless they were completely assimilated or divorced from their origin" (Arendt 1951: 275). This is what Lydia Morris termed "Arendt's paradox" (2010). The state, from being an instrument of the law became an instrument of the nation. This in turn was a harbinger of events to come in the 1930s (Benhabib 2004: 54). But, rather than acknowledging this elevation of particular national interests over the universal rule of law, the exception established by the Minority Treaties was defended on the grounds that it was temporarily needed in countries where constitutional governments were in early stages of development. This illusion was shattered as statelessness became a widespread phenomenon:

> The framers of the Minority Treaties did not foresee the possibility of wholesale population transfers or the problem of people who had become "undeportable" because there was no country on earth in which they enjoyed the right to residence. The minorities could still be regarded as an exceptional phenomenon, peculiar to certain territories that deviated from the norm. This argument was always tempting because it left the system itself untouched; it has in a way survived the second World War whose peacemakers, convinced of the impracticability of Minority Treaties, began to "repatriate" nationalities as much as possible in an effort to unscramble the "belt of mixed populations."
> (Arendt 1951: 277)

Indeed, in order not to repeat the mistakes of the Versailles Treaty, some 27 years and one world war later, Churchill and other heads of victorious states argued that the cycles of violence of 1920s and 1930s would not repeat themselves if nation-states were nationally uniform. The architects of the post-World War II order decided to pursue the alignment of ethnolinguistic borders with political ones in the name of future peace.

But before they had the chance to do that, the latter years of World War II saw a disastrous coda to the interwar friction between the Polish state and the Ukrainian minority. As Wilson documents, the Organization of Ukrainian Nationalists had had contacts with the Nazis since the 1920s (Wilson 2000: 132). But it wasn't until "the Soviet occupation of eastern Poland/Western Ukraine (1939–1941) brought a definitive end to constitutional politics, and the German invasion of the USSR a real possibility of displacing Soviet power" that new opportunities for the OUN begun to open up (132). They symbolically declared national independence in 1941 in Lviv, and announced cooperation with National-Socialist Germany, under whose auspices they envisioned the establishment of Ukrainian statehood. That expectation was soon thwarted, and OUN leaders were arrested. Despite earlier hints that Germany would support Ukraine as a "buffer state" between itself and the Soviet Union, racial theories won out with geopolitics. During the war the Nazis saw Ukrainians, like other Slavic peoples, as *Untermenschen*, and their lands as nothing more than *Lebensraum* for the Germans.[7]

Once the lack of German support became clear, OUN and its military arm, the Ukrainian Insurgent Army, UPA, changed tactics and disowned its fascist roots, but the Polish underground Home Army never ceased to view them as enemies and Nazi collaborators. Mutual attacks started in 1942, but in 1943 UPA began the action of eliminating the minority Polish population from Volhynia and Galicia that would become part of the envisioned Ukrainian state. Mass killings, which, as Snyder argues, are best thought of as ethnic cleansing, took place in Volhynia (Snyder 2003), while in Galicia Polish inhabitants were initially expelled under the threat of death, but later (in 1944) also exterminated. According to Grzegorz Motyka, a Polish historian and an advocate of a "balanced" approach to this history (as opposed to supporters of unapologetically nationalist interpretations), "UPA mobilized local peasants, who participated in the attacks frequently armed only with axes and pitchforks. Acts of inhuman cruelty often ensued" (Motyka 2008: 1).[8] As I indicated in Chapter 2, the numbers of victims are contested, but the most likely figures appear to be fifty to sixty thousand victims among the Polish and two to three thousand among the Ukrainians (although higher for both populations if the entire period of the Polish-Ukrainian conflict, from 1943 to 1948, is considered).

Confusion and anxiety mark the present borderland with its embedded conflicting memories. Everything in this story is the subject of dispute, starting with historical factuality, matters of culpability and justification, the final assessment of the events, and ending with the need for potential apologies and the most desirable form of remembrance. Yaroslav Hrytsak, the most prominent Ukrainian partner for Polish historians who, like Motyka, seek reconciliation, emphasizes above all the Soviet-induced amnesia that prevents an open discussion of these events in Ukraine, but admits that "according to the national framework of Ukrainian history, the anti-Polish action of UPA in 1943 in Volhynia was an act of forced self-defense, a response to the anti-Ukrainian terror of the Polish underground, which had begun earlier" (Hrytsak 2009: 121). In Poland in turn, "the issue of the Polish retaliation is the most divisive one for historians. Some researchers who are vigorously supported by the national-Kresy circles disregard the problem of Polish actions against Ukrainians, and they attempt to represent their scale as mini-mal" (Motyka 2008: 6).[9]

Regardless of the controversies concerning its contemporary interpre-tation, the tragic futility of the whole conflict is indisputable. No indepen-dent Ukrainian state was constituted after World War II, and the ethnically cleansed territories became neither Polish nor Ukrainian, but part of the So-viet Union. The postwar establishment of new boundaries propelled massive displacements and resettlements of the remaining inhabitants. Such late nine-teenth and early twentieth-century forms of social organization as the small landholding, the Jewish *shtetl*, the *petit-bourgeois* town had already been de-stroyed over the course of the war, and the region was divided and actively remade to fit the ideology of the new political entities—the Soviet Union and the nominally independent but de facto Soviet-controlled People's Republic of Poland—that emerged in place of the old. Just in the areas directly adjacent to today's borderline, that is, in Eastern Galicia and Volhynia, and in West-ern Galicia and the Western Carpathians in Poland, over 1.5 million people were either forcibly removed from their homes, or resettled on a supposedly "voluntary" basis. The overall numbers for Poland and Western Ukraine were much higher (Magocsi 2002: 189–91; see also Snyder 2010: 327–28). These shaken and uprooted populations soon filled the blockhouse neighborhoods of newly industrialized towns and cities on both sides of the border, collec-tive farms (primarily in Ukraine), and thoroughly reorganized urban centers, with state-controlled commerce, public schooling, and health care, and an repressive socialist administration.

Many ethnic Poles expelled from Ukraine by the new Soviet administra-tion were resettled to formerly German territories that had become the west-ern part of the Polish People's Republic. This area was officially called the "Recovered Lands" (Ziemie Odzyskane), on the grounds that they had been part of Poland in the Middle Ages and were only now "recovered" from the Germans. This area in 1945–47 was purged of its German inhabitants.[10] Their forced departure was represented as a rightful retribution for German atroci-ties during the war.[11]

Since Polish-Ukrainian tension on the borderland continued to brew well after the final demarcation of the border, and violent incidents con-tinued into the late 1940s, the new Polish authorities in 1947 conducted an additional wave of resettlements: the so-called Akcja Wisła (Operation Vis-tula). It was then that they forcibly relocated over 140,000 Ukrainians and Lemkos (Carpathian highlanders of the Orthodox faith) to the Recovered

Lands and other places, where, unsupported by their traditional communities and churches, it was believed that they would quickly assimilate. Akcja Wisła was justified by the need to liquidate the still active divisions of UPA, but for the thousands of civilians who had no connections to the national movement it was a sheer act of ethnic-based persecution. As in the case of the earlier Polish-Ukrainian struggles, the precise course of events and number of victims of Operation Vistula remain contested to this day.[12] It left the Ukrainian community shattered and decimated. Many of its members, in order to escape harassment, adopted Polish as their language and abandoned the Greek Catholic rite in favor of Roman Catholicism. With their national origins concealed from the outside world, many of the originally resettled, as well as their children, to this day recall living in terror of being exposed as Ukrainians.

Thanks to socialist nationality policies and enforced isolation, the aftermath of this succession of violence and displacement settled into a lasting status quo. That it was lasting is not to say it was static—as Hann (1998) has shown, the process of assimilation and the evolution of nationalism continued to unfold both despite and because of the constraints of socialism. By 1948 Poland was a Communist-ruled state whose population was almost exclusively composed of persons claiming Polish nationality and speaking the Polish language. Between the last prewar census in 1931 and the first one after the collapse of Communism in 1991, the proportion of Poles within Poland increased from 69 to 97 percent, and that of national and ethnic minorities dropped from 31 to a mere 3 percent. The new Ukrainian Socialist Soviet Republic, on the other hand, became an area where Russian settlement was encouraged and the proportion of ethnic Russians reached nearly 20 percent, concentrated, however, primarily in the east and Crimea (Hrytsak 2000).[13] However, in the USSR ethnicity was supposed to dissolve, or be transcended by the larger Soviet community of nations.[14]

In other words, the post–World War II international order in Europe was built upon the outcomes of policies of mass killing, military campaigns, and complex negotiations between the victorious powers, not any kind of justice for the nationally disenfranchised. And it was the Versailles Treaty with its minority clauses that charted the path for the rigid way in which the principle of nationality was applied in Eastern Europe after 1945.[15] Resettlements and reborderings in the region were part of the Versailles legacy. By sorting out populations into nationally enfranchised citizens and separate groups of minorities, the rebordering of Europe between 1918 and 1921 had also laid the groundwork, to Hannah Arendt's deep concern, for the proliferation of special categories of persons: besides the minorities themselves, also refugees, stateless and displaced persons, and migrants who due to their own actions or circumstances beyond their control find themselves deprived of protection and vulnerable to violence and exploitation.[16]

This is not to say that since the end of World War II there are no vulnerable spots in East and Central Europe, where the presence of ethnic minorities would be a source of tension. The borderland between Slovakia and Ukraine, as well as Transylvania, are notable examples of such areas, although as Brubaker and his research team have shown, intense elite-level nationalist conflict need not go hand in hand with popular ethnic mobilization (Brubaker et al. 2006, see also Kűrti 2001). The former Yugoslavia, the most horrifying case of ethnic violence in late twentieth-century (Eastern) Europe, may be the one case that shares the most features with the ethnic cleansing in Volhynia in 1943 (Snyder 2003: 233).

In fact, it has been noted that the states in the region that were the most ethnically mixed were most likely, after 1989, to take the path of authoritarian nationalism rather than liberal democracy. Hence, the ethnically homogeneous Poland, Czech Republic, and Hungary experienced the least internal turmoil in the course of the transition (Ash 1999). They were also the first in line to join the European Union. Consequently, in the Polish-Ukrainian borderland the EU inherited the status quo of "dismembered multiethnicity" (Redlich 2002: x). National minorities are sparse; apart from the Ukrainians, there are Belarusians and tiny Jewish communities. Their legal status is largely settled. But, contrary to the efforts of Soviet propaganda, nationalism itself and its frustrations survived under socialism on both sides of the border. Postsocialist democracy opened new avenues for its expression, but with the opening of the public sphere it also provided new imperatives to challenge it. Present-day consternations of memory, which I discuss below, are a belated reckoning with the implications of dying and killing in the name of ethnic purity and territorial sovereignty; the concurrent anxieties of European belonging yield an idealization of a multiethnic Europe that once ostensibly thrived on diversity.

While these tensions linger, after the EU enlargement, the issue of other special categories of persons and their need for recognition has come to the surface. Nonnationals who are "unable or unwilling," as the 1951 Convention puts it, to enjoy the protection and guarantees of citizenship of their own state today are protected by International Human Rights, but, as I have shown earlier in this text, that protection is often incomplete. As Liisa Mal-kki has so persuasively shown in her account of the condition of exile, the principle of nationality, or what she calls the "national order of things," cre-ated a logic which continues to abhor ambiguous categories (1995: 6). The European Union, as a novel type of political body, attempts to modify the national order of things by creating a new layer of inclusion in the form of EU citizenship. But ambiguity of membership remains no less troubling. At the Polish-Ukrainian frontier today there are EU citizens and non-EU citizens, but the latter category includes the confounding cases of citizens of nowhere who may even be in possession of valid passports, but not of anything that would qualify as a viable home. This is another way in which the legacy of Versailles haunts today's rebordering of Europe, and reminds us that the flaws in the international system of rights are far from resolved.

Consternation and Anxiety

Since the end of the Soviet Union and Ukrainian independence in 1991, neighbors on both sides of the Polish-Ukrainian border have been getting to know each other anew. From the perspective of these cross-border en-gagements, the Polish-Ukrainian frontier looks quite different from the way it does when seen, say, from Brussels. Its role as a barrier protecting the Eu-ropean Union from unwanted migratory flows recedes into the background, and it emerges as an interface of more localized twofold tensions. The first one is the consternation over some of the more divisive memories that haunt the borderland and the ongoing clashing efforts to overcome them on the one hand, and to keep them politically potent on the other. The second manifest tension is grounded in an alternative interpretation of the past and orients itself toward the future. It can be classified under the rubric of the anxiety of European belonging.

The object of the first tension is the memory of the Polish-Ukrainian struggle of the first half of the twentieth century, which encompasses such events as the 1943 killings of Polish civilians in Volhynia and Galicia perpe-trated by the Ukrainian Insurgent Army (UPA) and the subsequent Polish retaliation, but also the earlier record of persecution of the Ukrainian minor-ity in the interwar Polish Republic and the Ukrainian response to it. In the context of this memory of conflict, calls for reconciliation come up against competing claims of victimhood and charges of barbarity. Dead bodies take on new political lives amid disputes over cemeteries, exhumations, and memorials (cf. Verdery 1999).

"Europe benefits profoundly from an understanding of the often *subterranean cultural trafficking* of traumatic memories along the eastern border of the EU," wrote the Russian literary scholar Alexander Etkind. "These memories, if left to fester, threaten to destabilize Eastern Europe; they transform workaday political disputes into pitched battles for 'national souls'" (Etkind 2010). Etkind's metaphor of trafficking suggests that the flow of historical trauma across the border is toxic. Douglas Holmes has called this form of discourse "illicit" (Holmes 1993). "Battles for 'national souls,'" full of historical recriminations and often fought by proxies of unsavory political lineage, are unwelcome in the European Union that ostensibly has disowned combative nationalisms. Etkind implies that such conflicts can be dangerous at the community's edges, causing them to fray and possibly disintegrate.

Indeed, even though since 1989 Eastern Europe has been experiencing a hyper-awakening of its historical consciousness, not all identities forged through the experience, memory, and postmemory (Hirsch 2008) of violence have been equally accommodated in the region's emerging public spheres. While Polish-Ukrainian animosities were being tamed through the project of mutual reconciliation carried out at the level of highest state authorities, local resentments were muted, and latent hostility on both sides remained unacknowledged. Despite having been officially commemorated, once the collapse of the Soviet Union made it possible, the three decades of the at times latent and at times violent conflict, roughly from 1918 to 1948, have so far defied closure.

The handshakes of Polish and Ukrainian presidents, the "dialogue of intellectuals," (Hrytsak 2009: 126) and the declarations of good will at sites of mass graves failed to appeal to (and appease) everyone.[17] Many of those, in both Poland and Ukraine, who construct their identities based on unrectified historical wrongs, notably members of organizations of the resettled inhabitants of Kresy in Poland, and veterans and sympathizers of UPA in Ukraine, refuse to accept the conciliatory agenda adopted in neighborly politics in the early 1990s. They invoke displaced histories to reveal what they consider the deficits of the official reconciliation approach. They reject the proposition that the new neighborly relations be based on forgiveness and acknowledgment of mutual wrongs. Instead, they seek "truth" and commemoration free from the mendacities of "moral relativism" that purportedly sacrifices accounting for atrocity on the altar of contemporary politics.[18] In response to the supposed silencing of their narratives of suffering, some of them engage in what I call the politics of horror and abomination. This is a politics that dehumanizes the opponent, relies on an emotive discourse of grisly and corporeal aspects of violence, and delegitimizes efforts at a democratic dialogue. It strives "to introduce the unvoiced and unspeakable into political discourse. Established political forces resist these 'illicitudes', defining those who articulate them as racists, terrorists, bigots, or as some other form of essentialized pariah" (Holmes 1993: 258). The Polish agents of this discourse depict Ukrainians as coldblooded killers, and Poles as a benign civilizing force in the erstwhile Polish Kresy. The Ukrainian "traffickers in trauma" frame Poles as ruthless exploiters and occupiers, and the Ukrainian side of the conflict as righteous freedom fighters. Ultimately, these participants in the struggle over memory are the heirs of the region's nationalisms of the first half of the twentieth century. Their fight is ultimately one of the strands of a larger cultural front aiming to reassert national sovereignty and membership in ethnonational terms.

The second tension, the anxiety of European belonging, is rooted in a different imaginary. It stems from the larger narrative of Central Europe as the area where Western Christianity meets the Byzantine tradition and Islam, and where "there is neither a maritime nor a terrestrial frontier permitting us to say where Europe leaves off and Asia begins" (Pocock 2002: 61). It is about once having been a multiethnic and multilingual borderland that has now been ruined and dismembered, and about longing for the (now romanticized) cultural riches of this vanished past. It is finally about occupying the precarious space "between East and West" (as the cliché goes), civilization and barbarity (Wolff 1994), and feeling at the mercy of larger historical forces that decide how the boundary is drawn, and who find themselves on which side.[19]

"It is like this with the border: when I'm being told that I cannot just go whenever I want to Vienna, Warsaw, or Berlin, it feels the same way as if someone locked me out of the rooms in my own house." This frustration was expressed to me by Yuri Andrukhovych, a Ukrainian writer and intellectual from the western Ukrainian town of Ivano-Frankivsk. I met Andrukhovych at a book fair in Warsaw in 2005, where I came to browse the plentiful supply of Ukrainian fiction, poetry, and history books. His magical-realist novels and essays about Central Europe earned him in Poland the status of a literary celebrity equal to that which he enjoys in Ukraine. He claims a rightful belonging to Europe as a geographic entity and a cultural whole. The most upsetting aspect of current EU border policies for him is being subject to regulations that effectively cut him off from membership and participation in a universe he considers his own. Andrukhovych's irritation with the present border regime goes beyond impatience with endless visa application processes, rude border guards, and intrusive customs officers. When I talked to him at a promotional event for a new anthology of Ukrainian poetry, he told me that he was mostly concerned with what he referred to as "mental borders":

> We are talking about the border in the sense of mentality, right? Such border exists for Western Europeans, and not only for them. Many Poles, Czechs, and Hungarians think so too. . . . That Asia begins in our country, the Wild East. So, this real border, the political border, represents the frontier of consciousness (*granica świadomości*). People continue to perceive Ukraine as a part of the Russian world, part of the Soviet Empire. They cannot open up to larger Europe, the true perspective of Europe.

In his use of the metaphor of a house where access to certain rooms is restricted, as well as in his aggravation with the practical inconveniences presented by the border regime, Andrukhovych expressed his worry that, not unlike the Iron Curtain that divided the continent sixty years earlier, the new border seals, legitimates, and solidifies the vague and shifting frontier between Europe's West and East. Like many other Eastern Europeans who after the expansion of the European Union found themselves on the "wrong" side of Schengen, he not only resents the exclusionary force of the new geopolitical arrangement, but also strongly opposes equating "Europe" with the European Union.

Andrukhovych's objection to what he considers a narrow, or closed concept of Europe has been a continuous trope in his work. It is emblematic of the Central Europeanist consciousness that I shall discuss further in this chapter. It is a dread of being not only walled off from the Western world, but also somehow unwanted, or in Milan Kundera's words "hidden, even further, by the curtain of strange and scarcely accessible languages" (1984:5). *Latynka* (The Roman Alphabet), a poem by Andriy Bondar, who moves in the same literary circles as Andrukhovych, poignantly plays on this theme, with the second stanza as follows:

odyn mij znajomyj vvazhaje
scho z perekhodom na latynku
nash narod stane menshe krasty
tobto kudys odrazu raptom
podinetsia tsia rozkhrystana vizantijschyna
tsia khamska sovietchyna tsia bezbereha fino-uhorschyna
(sorry, uhorci, sorry, finy)
i v holovi schos tilky "klac"—i my evropa

one of my friends thinks
that if we switch to the roman alphabet
our people will steal less
and immediately
our messy byzantinisms
our obnoxious sovietisms our endless ugro-finnisms
(sorry ugrics, sorry finns)
will disappear and something will snap in our heads
—and "voila!" we are part of europe[20]

The reinforcement of the EU border accentuates and amplifies the relevance of this trope of vacillation between asserting Europeanness and acknowledging its tenuousness at the undefined edges of the continent. The anxiety of European belonging is experienced daily on the borderland, and not only by the elite of savvy intellectuals. (Andrukhovych, like other privileged cosmopolitans who happen to carry non-EU passports, sometimes does encounter exasperating difficulties, but after all usually manages to obtain the required documents and travel where he chooses.[21]) A sense of unease and an acute awareness of being shut out underpin the quotidian lives of people who lack the cultural capital and monetary resources to navigate efficiently the complex regulations of entry and access, but to whom work west of the border appears as the sole opportunity of earning a living. The question of their own identity, European or otherwise, may not be foremost on their minds, but they resignedly bemoan their "second class" status, underscored by the heavy presence of the border, inscribed in the passports they carry, the language they speak and write, and the work clothes they carry in their luggage.

Surviving Atlantis

In *The Native Realm* Czesław Miłosz portrays the powerful tension between the nationalist Polish right wing and the Jewish, Lithuanian, Ukrainian, and Belarusian minorities in the 1920s and 1930s. In the postscript to a chapter on nationalities in his native Vilnius he writes,

> A country or a state should endure longer than an individual. At least this seems to be in keeping with the order of things. Today, however, one is constantly running into survivors of various Atlantises. Their lands in the course of time are transformed in memory and take on outlines that are no longer verifiable. Similarly, between-the-wars Poland has sunk beneath the surface. In her place a new organism has appeared on the map, with the same name but within different borders, an ironic fulfillment of the nationalist dream, now clear of its minorities or at least with a very negligible number. (Miłosz 1968: 106)

It is not nostalgia for the Atlantis of prewar Poland that informs Miłosz's perspective; he was, to the dismay of his inexorable detractors, an unrelenting critic of the virulently nationalist politics that—following the overall political atmosphere in Europe—gradually dominated Polish scene between the wars (see also Miłosz 1999).[22] Irony is the key trope in his thinking about Poland's borders, for the nationalists who dreamed of ethnic purity *and* demanded that their claims to Kresy be honored were forced to absorb the brutal historical lesson that they could not have both. At the same time, over the course of the twentieth century in this part of Europe individuals did endure longer than states. After the war, even the trace presence of Ukrainians, Jews, and other Atlantis survivors in Poland posed an inherent challenge to the socialist order, which strived to obliterate the record of their particular suffering and, more generally, of their respective collective memories.

As I followed the rebordering of Europe, I have, like Miłosz, repeatedly run into such "survivors of Atlantis." For example, in Lublin and Warsaw—two cities with particularly active Ukrainian minority communities—I was welcomed to the local Greek Catholic churches, which have enjoyed a revival in recent years. These inconspicuous parishes for years were sustained by small groups of descendants of Ukrainians who remained in Poland after the war. Today they provide an oasis of familiarity, spiritual guidance, and networking opportunities also to recent Ukrainian immigrants and temporary workers.[23] At a Sunday mass in Warsaw I observed a mixed crowd of old community members and newcomers. Grandmotherly women whose unaccented Polish signaled that they had spent their whole lives in Poland stayed close to one another. Ukrainian-speaking men and women of all ages came as much to pray as to peruse the job announcements tacked to the bulletin board in the church's foyer. Ukrainian students who had come to Warsaw to get their degrees at the university mingled after the service with Polish-Ukrainian intellectuals, whose faces I recognized from their media appearances. Week-old newspapers from Ukraine were for sale at the entrance, along with Svitoch chocolates and other Ukrainian sweets, vastly superior to Polish ones, according to the vendors.

Through the Greek Catholic parish in Lublin, I met Mirosław, a man in his sixties who was a natural scientist by training, but whose personal passion was regional history. His family survived Akcja Wisła by preempting the resettlement and moving to Lublin from their village on the border before it was liquidated. He hosted me in his cozy apartment in one of Lublin's blockhouse neighborhoods and, while his wife served tea and homemade cake, he told me about the stigma of being Ukrainian under socialism.

> We were scared. Not of violence. But we were scared, in the fifties and sixties, of people pointing fingers, of ostracism. There was no honest discussion then, you could not stand up and openly speak about who you were. Not like now. . . . Nowadays it is fashionable to be different, to have an *identity*. But that is a privilege of your generation. We are still like we were before.

Claiming an "identity" was not an innocent personal choice for Mirosław, as he imagined it to be for younger people today. Although he no longer feared ostracism, he was reluctant to manifest his Ukrainianness openly and accept the label of a member of a national minority. He opted for caution, suggesting that tolerance and acceptance of difference cannot be taken for granted, regardless of Poland's (after all quite recent) embrace of democratic principles.

Mirosław suspected that I was Ukrainian too. This would have seemed to him the only logical explanation of my interest in, as he referred to it, "our affairs" (*nashy spravy*). I explained that I was not, and tried to convey that in my view, my nationality did not make a difference to my research. But I was wrong, for to him it did. I did not want my research to be seen as privileging any particular national agenda, but had initially failed to grasp that my naïve cosmopolitanism was out of place. There was no escaping my nationality, necessarily representing one of the sides of the perhaps dormant, but not quite dead, conflict. Mirosław wondered why, as a Pole, I would want to talk to a representative of a "national minority." This only underscored the durability of the alienation he felt as member of the latter. I tried to convey that what was at stake in my research was an understanding of the future of the European Union as a political entity, as opposed to the future of the Polish, or the Ukrainian, nation-state only, and that how Ukrainians moved, voluntarily and forcibly, across borders in the past and present was supremely relevant to my interests.

A couple of days later I was getting ready to leave Lublin. I went to the local Greek Catholic church to say goodbye, after mass, to the members of the local Ukrainian community whom I had met over the course of my visit. Mirosław came up to me, grasped the drawstring at the collar of my jacket, tugged at it gently, and warmly looking me in the eyes asked, "Are you absolutely sure that you're not Ukrainian?" When I said that I was as sure as anyone in Central Europe can be sure of their ancestry, he let the string go and responded after a pause, "That's good. That's very good. Perhaps people over there [in the U.S., where I was based at the time] will finally understand something about us [Ukrainians] from your research. It will be different from when we speak for ourselves." I could not shake off the feeling that I would probably disappoint Mirosław. But he struck me as an Atlantis survivor who thought that he and his fellow survivors must be spoken for, or else "people over there" would think that Atlantis was just a figment of their imagination.

Father Michał was a Greek Catholic priest of Ukrainian background, who grew up in the Mazury region in the northern part of Poland, where his family was resettled during Akcja Wisła. They never renounced their religious rite, and sending one son into priesthood was a family tradition. I spoke with him at the Warsaw church in spring 2005. He bemoaned the fact that the two groups of parishioners—the "minority" and the "immigrants"—seem to have little in common. He expressed his belief that "Polish Ukrainians" should help "Ukrainian Ukrainians" integrate and feel at home. "But maybe they don't want the association. Maybe they feel that they are better than someone who comes here to clean and cook," he wondered aloud, seemingly puzzled by this idea. With time I noticed that Father Michał's observation was correct. The succession of reborderings had created such divergent historical experiences that for those two groups it left ethnicity eviscerated of its potential to be a source of solidarity. In the first decade of the twenty-first century, the

"Polish Ukrainians" and the "Ukrainian Ukrainians" inhabit different historical continuums; they are different categories of persons. Legally, the former
are a "minority"—a recognized "culturally different" community of Polish,
and thus EU, citizens with a set of special cultural rights and protections. The
latter are constructed as "aliens." What they can and cannot do or expect from
the host state and its citizens depends on further variables of their status. The
"minority" is constructed as carrying a particular baggage of memories and
having a vested interest in the protracted historical debates. Through their
status they are, so to speak, permanently implicated in the binary nationalist
logic, while at the same time paradoxically transcending it, owing to the fact
that they are now EU citizens. The "aliens" have a more distant relationship to
the conflict, but the divide between them and their Polish hosts is more immediate, experienced as economic and political, not historical and cultural.
They have a much stronger investment in discussions about their belonging,
or otherwise, in Europe, and the exact terms of their access to the European
Union.

Dressed in Orange, Drenched in Blood

Despite the baggage of nearly a century of post-Versailles history, over the
course of the past decade or so, Ukraine has come to be represented in the
Polish public sphere as a culturally close neighbor who, mostly due to the
misfortune of having been a part of the Soviet Union, ended up impover-
ished and civilizationally backward. The cultural proximity to Poland has
been also emphasized in Ukraine, particularly in the west. As mentioned in
Chapter 1, these representations have been largely driven by the elite project of Polish-Ukrainian reconciliation and the influential ideas of thinkers
and essayists associated with the émigré journal *Kultura*.[24] The imperative
to promote close ties gave rise to a narrative whereby Ukraine, regardless of
the hardships suffered by vast sectors of the Ukrainian society and in spite
of the oft-mentioned specter of Russian domination, is developing along the
same trajectory of democratization and free market economy as Poland has
since 1989. Therefore, as liberal politicians, NGOs, and development experts
argue, Ukraine needs and deserves the same kind of support from Poland as
Poland had received, between 1989 and its EU accession, from its western
neighbors and allies. This stance was bolstered by the protests against the rig-
ging of presidential elections that swept across Ukraine in 2004, known as the

Orange Revolution. A media blitz in Poland elevated the Ukrainian upheaval to the status of a popular democratic cause. In the fall of 2004 and winter of 2005, the numbers of people wearing orange and supporting the presidential candidate Viktor Yushchenko in Warsaw all but equaled those in Kyiv.[25]

The Polish backing of the Ukrainian struggle was intense and emotional, thoroughly marginalizing the few voices that questioned whether such strong involvement on the side of one politician was desirable. And this politician, Viktor Yushchenko, a few muted voices from the political right suggested, could after all be plausibly described as a Ukrainian nationalist, and as such deserved no trust. In the streets, volunteers handed out orange ribbons symbolizing support for the protests in Kyiv. In most large cities university students organized rallies. In Warsaw, Polish and Ukrainian students set up a tent colony in front of the Ukrainian Embassy, a miniature of the one established by protesters in Kyiv. On television Polish politicians of all stripes delivered speeches in praise of Ukraine's "democratic awakening." They emphasized the democratic credentials of Viktor Yushchenko, his embrace of a pro-European and pro-NATO agenda, and his commitment to the Polish-Ukrainian alliance. Indeed, in Poland there seemed to be far less ambiguity as to what was good for Ukraine than there was in Ukraine itself.[26]

It was in early 2005, at the height of this media-fuelled excitement over all things Ukrainian, that I launched the main, year-long stint of my fieldwork. When I arrived in Warsaw in January, only weeks after Yushchenko finally won the presidency, I could still spot orange ribbons on people's winter attire. Graffiti and banners with signs (in Polish) "Free Ukraine" (Wolna Ukraina) were still up on fences and walls in the vicinity of the Ukrainian Embassy. The cultural scene featured a flurry of Ukraine-related events, such as talks, poetry readings, book signings, art openings, and rock shows, all featuring artists from the other side of the border.

But this collective pro-Ukrainian enthusiasm did not reach into every corner of Polish society. In early 2005, a traveling exhibition entitled Eastern Borderland Drenched in Polish Blood (Kresy Wschodnie we krwi polskiej tonące) attracted favorable publicity from right-wing media and prompted the liberal daily Gazeta Wyborcza to issue a protest.[27] The exhibition was organized by a group of Kresowiacy, that is, persons claiming Kresy origins. The group was called the Society for Volhynia and Polissia (Towarzystwo Miłośników Wołynia i Polesia). Their exhibition was shown in Kraków, Warsaw, and Lublin between January and April and consisted of two parts. The first was documentary, including photographs, papers, and handwritten notes of Polish victims of Ukrainian independence fighters in Volhynia in 1943. Yellowed pictures of the "before" showed whole Kresy families, their houses, and other property, as well as many Catholic churches. They were juxtaposed with photos of the "after"—ruined buildings, rummaged property, exhumations, and human skulls with triangular holes from blows delivered with a special tool for killing cattle.

The second part was a collection of anonymous painted illustrations; their author, according to the catalogue, was an unprofessional artist who depicted the 1943 events in Volhynia based on eyewitness accounts. The series title was Tortures exercised on the Polish by the Organization of Ukrainian Nationalists (OUN)—Ukrainian Insurgent Army (UPA) (dutifully translated into English). Each numbered image contained a graphic illustration of a particular form of torture rendered in bright colors and expressionist strokes. Captions were simple matter-of-fact descriptions, such as "Poking out eyeballs and cutting the tongue in half," "Hammering a big and thick nail into the head," "Cutting a child with a knife into pieces and throwing them around," "Cutting open pregnant women's abdomens and throwing broken glass inside."

To be sure, the composition of the photographic part of the exhibition, which portrayed Polish families together with their entire material world as victims of illegitimate invaders, deserved criticism for being one-sided and for failing to contextualize the Kresy martyrology. But the painted illustrations, clearly intended as "evidence" of unquestionable Ukrainian barbarity, hit a new extreme. The blatant inflammatory intent was all the more striking because of the timing. The exhibition could not but be read as an attempt to spark a backlash against the swelling excitement in neighborly politics.

The exhibition was on display at the otherwise respectable Society for Fine Arts in Kraków. On the day I visited the atmosphere inside was tense. As I talked to an elderly woman in front of the photographs, who was lamenting what she described as the destruction of "all traces of Polishness" in Kresy, a man in his thirties exclaimed to everyone in the room: "The worst thing is that the *skurwysyn* (son-of-a-bitch) [President] Kwaśniewski is with them [the Ukrainians]!" In front of the gory illustrations he delivered a tirade against the Polish president's pro-Ukrainian politics in general, and the recognition that he had extended to the Ukrainian victims of Akcja Wisła in particular. The woman I had just spoken to nodded approvingly. The man's angry outburst fell on fertile ground as another male visitor cried out: "And those Jews from *Gazeta Wyborcza* are with them [Ukrainians] too. That's strange, isn't it, after all Ukrainian nationalists snuffed out the Jews as well!"

At the same time as he was denouncing the Ukrainian Insurgent Army for its collusion with the Nazi extermination policies, he was also expressing the belief, popular on the nationalist right, that Poland's main liberal newspaper *Gazeta Wyborcza*, supportive of Polish-Ukrainian reconciliation, was "in Jewish hands" and therefore not "truly" Polish or loyal to "Polish interests."

With its incendiary content, and its capacity to provoke hateful comments and to attract excitable viewers, the exhibition constituted a prime instance of politics of horror and abomination. In their reactions, these viewers drew on an entrenched nationalist framework where Ukrainians, Poles, and Jews constitute bounded, mutually exclusive, and irreconcilable groups, almost distinct species. They were projecting these categories onto current affairs, filtering the complex politics of memory and neighborhood through the timeless prism of inherent antagonism. The idea that either the Poles or the supposed Jews (who, when invoked in such rants, are nothing but a figment of the anti-Semitic imagination) could conduct dialogue with Ukrainians burst the frames of reference available to these visitors of the Kresy exhibition.[28]

The nationally reported controversy surrounding the exhibition was only beginning to unfold, but it was stopped in its tracks by the death, on April 2, 2005, of Pope John Paul II. For two weeks national mourning replaced political life. By mid-April the controversial show was dismantled and everyone seemed to forget about it. But the exhibition was not a momentary lapse into extremism. It combined deliberately shocking charges of barbarity with a strong pretense to objectivity (the respectable exhibition halls that admitted the production, the inclusion of an ostensibly documentary part consisting of papers and photographs). It might have been inconsistent with the mainstream theme of reconciliation and alliance that in the years 2003–2006 dominated the discourse, but not accidentally so.[29] Rather, it reflected a steady nationalist current combined with the unresolved claims to the recognition of victims that continue to undercut overcoming the legacy of conflict. These sentiments, while seemingly distanced from debates on the European Union, its role, and its boundaries, in fact speak directly to them, in the sense that they are part of a larger cultural front that privileges national allegiance over any other forms of belonging, and asserts the nationalist interpretation of the borderland's history. In some way, the Kresowiacy who put up the exhibition, as well as their sympathizers who were moved by it, are still struggling with the consequences of the previous rebordering. They hardly seem to notice that the current one has rendered their discourse illicit, and thus strangely potent and subversive.

Expectations of Central Europeanism

And so the different and conflicting stories about the history of the rifts and connections across the Polish-Ukrainian frontier animate antagonistic politics and competing imaginaries of the future. Nationalist ideologues, disinclined to abandon old hostilities and anxious about the prospects for national sovereignty, may feel embattled by Europeanizing forces and discourses, but they have no shortage of sympathizers in either country. However, there are other accounts at work. After 1991, many (especially western) Ukrainian intellectuals, writers, and their students and readers set about reaffirming the theme of Ukraine's belonging to Europe, and its ties to neighboring nations. Their project bore family resemblance to the Central Europeanist interpretation of Polish identity which had its heyday in the 1980s, but which remained relevant in the context of EU accession as well (Fiut 1999; Toruńczyk 1987). Ukrainian Central Europeanists however emphasized also new tropes, such as the postmodern appreciation of hybridity and peripheries. As they eschewed markers of Soviet identity and bid their farewell to empire, many became invested in the Central European ideal of cultural diversity and self-consciously provincial cosmopolitanism rooted particularly in the "retrospective utopia" (Hnatiuk 2003: 191) of Habsburg Galicia.[30]

As Czesław Miłosz as well as my informants Mirosław and Father Michał remind us, the effects of changing border regimes are not just temporal, spatial, political, and bureaucratic, but also live in cultural and individual consciousness. Amid the twentieth-century experiences of fascism, socialism, two wars, and their aftermaths, Eastern Europe produced a venerable body of literature that emphasizes its cultural commonalities and shared belonging despite the uncertainty of its boundaries (see for example Drakulić 1997; Kundera 1984; Miłosz 1968; Stasiuk and Andrukhovych 2000; Riabchuk 2004). This tradition probes the ambiguous senses in which this region belongs to "Europe" (or the West), understood as a putative cultural whole. Miłosz, Kundera, Havel, Brodsky and others make claims on behalf of a *Central* Europe, conceived of as an antidote to a rigid East-West duality. In their optic the identity of the region is not determined through imposed demarcations, bureaucratic procedures, or market indexes. Central Europeanness is metaphysical, established through the region's imperial histories and the cycles of ruination and reconstruction that they engendered. It is an essence that accounts for the region's cultural vibrancy despite repeated destruction (Andrukhovych 2000). It is within such Central Europeanism that the project

of Polish-Ukrainian reconciliation is nestled, and its benign discourse sup-
plies the vocabulary of "brotherhood," "neighborhood," and "shared fate."

Svetlana Boym writes that "[Central Europe's] ironic prophets dreamed of
marginalizing the border and questioning the heavy inevitability of the Iron
Curtain" (2001: 228). That quest was avowedly political, and as such it had
tangible political effects—for example, it brought together dissidents from
neighboring countries and spread awareness of their resistance beyond the
Soviet bloc. But with the ascent of Europeanization (in Borneman and Fowler's 1997 sense of a "strategy of self-representation and a device of power"
wielded on behalf of the European Union), Central Europeanism seems to
be losing relevance. It has attracted criticism for being "lifeless" (Huelle in
Hnatiuk 2003: 173) and overly romanticized. The sense of common fate and
solidarity that used to buoy Eastern European intellectuals has waned. (Maziarski 2001) "Economists and cheerful technocrats" (Boym 2001: 224) displaced writers and artists as the representatives of national will. The legal,
bureaucratic, institutional reality of the EU superseded the chimera of the
"heart of Europe," leaving parts of it behind a high-tech border fence.

A new, technologically sophisticated, and institutionally complex border
divides the region which corresponds to the geopoetic space of the Central
European ideal. Do the ideal itself, and its adherents, have any power left to
"question the heavy inevitability" of the new external EU border? And what
would that questioning entail?[31] Or has Central Europeanism lost, or is it
bound to lose, whatever political edge it might have had? After all, the rebordering of Europe, replete as it is with developmentalist, technocratic, and
instrumental elements, works somewhat like James Ferguson's "anti-politics
machine" (1990). In the following sentence we could replace the word "development" with the word "rebordering": "By making the intentional blueprints
for 'development' so highly visible, a 'development' project can end up performing extremely sensitive political operations involving the entrenchment
and expansion of institutional state power almost invisibly under the cover
of a neutral, technical mission to which no one can object" (Ferguson 1990:
256). It ought to be sufficient to recall the discourse and practice of Polish-
Ukrainian partnership as actualized in the service of rebordering, along with
its constructs of "capacity building," "best practices," and "technical arrangements" such as detention and readmission policies (all discussed in the previous chapter), to appreciate how it achieves what Ferguson would call "the
suspension of politics" (256).

A Border of *Posts*

And so rebordering does, at least to some degree, depoliticize what ought to be—especially in light of the vexing history—a vigorous debate between two bordering societies about the extent of their border's permeability and the nature of the movement and connections to be fostered or discouraged across it. However, by altering the status of those neighboring states, rebordering prompts also a new set of questions and awakens a counter-hegemonic impulse in the form of a rather new—in this place and time—discourse of postcoloniality. This discourse is a homegrown polemic with the binarism of nationalism and reconciliation, a response to EU expansion, and it also implies a critique of the overly romantic Central Europeanism. It converges with a broader scholarly project to study contemporary Eastern Europe and the former Soviet Union from a postcolonial perspective (Buchowski 2006; Cavanagh 2004; Carey and Raciborski 2004; Moore 2001; Verdery 2002b).

The consequences of wars and breakdowns in the borderland have outlived the states and empires that caused them. This condition of protracted living in the shadows of massive historical shifts is indeed reflected by the use of various "posts" to describe the region: it has been alternately conceptualized as postpartition, postwar, and postsocialist or post-Soviet. And indeed the area can accurately be conceived of as postcolonial, due to the historical ebb and flow of political, economic, and cultural domination of Poles over Ukrainians as well as of Russia, Nazi Germany, and Austria over both groups and other minorities (Janion 2006; Riabchuk 2004).

Literary scholar Maria Janion and historian Daniel Beauvois argue that Poland, with its history of several occupations and an unresolved complex of a formerly multinational state, is a peculiar instance of a postcolonial country. In different times in its history it acted as a colonizer toward the peoples of today's Ukraine, Belarus, and Lithuania, while the Polish population itself experienced colonial-like domination and occupation at the hands of the neighboring Prussia, Austria, Russia and later Germany and the Soviet Union (Janion 2006; Beauvois 2005; cf. Cavanagh 2004).

The current rebordering of Europe, animated by a new set of imperatives to reorganize territory and populations, revalorizes space. In so doing it introduces new possibilities, while foreclosing others, in this postcolonial borderland. It frames the historically embattled societies as participating in and benefiting from the civilizing process of the EU-animated spread of democracy, peace, and prosperity, and accords to the Polish society and institutions the role of a dispatcher of these values. As one expert has written in the context of a call for better access to visas, "personal experiences of traveling in Poland and other EU countries are most effective in teaching the rules of democracy, and help create a pro-European attitude among our eastern neighbors" (Wasilewska 2008: 19). At the same time, the ambiguous and fraught process of reinforcing the boundary between a European inside and outside produces exclusions that show telling continuities with otherwise seemingly vanquished forms of power inequalities.

But the extension of notions of empire and the postcolonial to Eastern Europe and the former Soviet states must not imply a mechanical transfer of categories from different imperial contexts. Rather than constituting a definitive framework, it ought to provide a broad interpretive angle that allows one to appreciate the inherent ambiguity of the postcolonial situation. It should draw attention to the tensions between repudiating and celebrating the past, expressions of inferiority and superiority, expectations of a better future and a sense of abandonment and powerlessness, "the desire for autochthony and the fact of a hybrid, part-colonial origin," and "between resistance and complicity" toward larger political forces (Moore 2001: 112).

The tense histories and ethnographic encounters that this chapter draws upon show precisely this kind of ambiguity. For example, was the Polish rush to support the Orange Revolution a sheer emanation of democratic consciousness, or did other nostalgias lurk within it? What genealogy can be traced in the developmental discourse eagerly adopted today by NGOs, entrepreneurs, experts, and officials who travel east to promote current modernization schemes?

Maria Janion's concern in recent years has been the reframing of narratives that Poles tell themselves about their history and its various Others (Jews, women, and now Ukrainians). Her point of departure is the observation that, although Polish territory was partitioned and colonized in the nineteenth and twentieth centuries by the more powerful regional empires, local literary tradition and elite discourse tended to praise and glorify Polish colonization of others. Not only that—Polish claims to belonging in Europe were grounded precisely in these acts of domination.

> Looking from this perspective at our contemporary cultural consciousness allows us to decipher a certain convoluted pattern that is present within it. We are a postcolonial country which at the same time—what frequently happens – experiences a sense of superiority

toward its colonizer—Russia. It is here that we felt and continue to feel European, involved in a struggle against Asian barbarity. (Janion 2006: 328; translation mine)

Janion goes on to emphasize that Roman Catholicism prevents the Polish from identifying "too much" with the Slavs, and sustains a distance from what is perceived as their "inferiority,"

> however, being a postcolonial country, we are not after all genuine Europeans, for—as Slavs—we are secondary to them, the Russian-Slavic adulteration having taken its toll on us. *We were simultaneously a colony, and a colonizer of our brotherly Slavs. Till this day we feel superior to them, while at the same time sensing kinship with their "inferiority."* (Janion 2006: 328; translation and emphasis mine)

Janion argues for a reassessment of the theme of Kresy as a "mythic-symbolic complex," reflecting the colonial position of Polish nobility in the Ukrainian borderland.[32] She asserts that there is a need to reevaluate the notions of "civilizational mission" in the East. This is an especially urgent task, considering that the postulate of Polish superiority and essential Europeanness toward Ukrainians and other neighbors is widely accepted without much reflection or criticism. This she ascribes to the enduring "Kresy mentality."[33] The memory of these advances became a key ingredient in national pride, which in turn helped build resistance to Poland's Russian, Prussian, and Austrian overlords during the eighteenth and nineteenth- century partitions. It also bolstered the self-righteousness that used to justify the persecution of the Ukrainian national movement between the wars.

Not unlike colonial apologists in other contexts (e.g., Ferguson 2003; D'Souza 2002), many defend the centuries-long Polish domination on the borderland on the grounds of its overall beneficence. Theirs is a narrative where Polonization was positive, for it equaled Europeanization. Assertions that Polish rule in the East provided the conduit for European ideas and values are not limited to the political right. They are often brought up by professional historians and political analysts in debates on European boundaries (Kieniewicz 1990, Najder 2003). But, as Janion retorts to such assertions, "the beauty of the affluent landholders' estates, the culture of noble mansions, advances in modernizing agriculture, as well as industrialization in the second half of the nineteenth century and beginning of the twentieth, cannot balance out the ruthless exploitation and oppression of Ukrainian peasantry and the betrayed and expropriated landless nobility" (Janion 2006: 173). Yet what she calls "the most basic element" of the Kresy myth, the sense of superiority and civilizational and religious mission (172), appears also to be its most enduring one.

The Kresy myth was at work at the Kraków exhibition that I described above, animating a malignant politics of memory. But the notions of a civilizing mission morphed also into a curious drive once again to posses Ukraine, though this time by different means and on different terms. The seemingly benign and dry language of eastern "strategy" or "policy," with its claims of "expertise" in "eastern matters" and calls for "friendly monitoring," is, to be sure, quite different from the nineteenth-century insistence that Polish nobility in Ukraine was the bastion of civilization and Christianity.[34] Assertions of superiority and overt condescension are no longer part of acceptable public speech.[35] But while the idiom and the practices have changed, the underpinning sentiment shows some continuities with the Kresy complex.

"Partnership" was a keyword in the vocabulary of the Western agents of aid and development supplied to Eastern Europe after 1989.[36] Here it emerges once again as the politically correct way of referring to the fundamentally unequal relationships forged between persons, organizations, enterprises and institutions as part of the "strategic alliance." "The Ukrainian side is the weaker side, what can I tell you," I was told by a program officer at a Warsaw-based grant giving agency which administers funds for Polish-Ukrainian cooperation projects. This, of course is not per se an incorrect assertion. The point is that it is taken up, maintained, and reinforced through what Thomas Chivens described in the context of American aid to Poland as the "pedagogical framework of transition," that is, the "mundane conference-style 'exchanges,' presentations, loan negotiations, advice, grants, question and answer periods, training programs, and the distribution of forms, pamphlets, instructional materials and overhead slides" (Chivens 2006). Thus the Polish "experts" mimic and reproduce the didactic mode to which they themselves have been subject, once again transferring "European" or "Western standards" eastward. But even in this highly scripted practice, the frontier mentality and adventurous streak of the Kresy nobleman are not altogether lost. Another program officer in the same grant-giving agency shared the following perception:

It's just that my impression is that our people who enter Ukraine today are enthusiasts, adventure seekers, in business and otherwise. You can't deny it, it's not a fully stable market. In order to be successful there, that calls for a particular type of an entrepreneur. A foolhardy nature (*zawadiaka*), with a penchant for risk, someone who would take it as an adventure.

The predilection for risk-taking is of course a prerequisite for any daring capitalist in the twenty-first century who is interested in venturing to the various "developing" or "emerging" markets of this world. It has also been part of older frontier narratives such as that of the American West, whose similarity to the Kresy myth Maria Janion also picks up (2006: 169). But in this context the masculine foolhardiness (*zawadiackość*) one supposedly needs to thrive on the frontier is consistent, down to the choice of noun, with the traditional portrait of the Polish Kresy nobleman.[37]

For a Counter-Hegemonic Narrative

"Much as the Treaty of Versailles impelled an era of experimentation, the European Treaties are framing 'new' identity projects—projects that infuse Europe with diverse and at times contradictory political significance," writes Douglas Holmes (2009: 55). What is the potential of such postcolonial critique to contribute new local interpretations of the contemporary reborder-ing of Europe, and, in doing so, to inject new politics into the discussion; to repoliticize it beyond national preoccupations and the zero-sum game of European inclusion and exclusion? Is the European Union itself an impe-rial formation whose effects at its new frontier resemble colonial ones? How does its expansion complicate the already convoluted pattern of inferiority and superiority, power and powerlessness, and layers of different aftermaths? Is it possible to discern "the colonizer" and "the colonized" in this newest configuration?

    The largest of these questions, that is, whether or not the expansion of the European Union is an instance of imperial politics, is part of a separate dis-cussion that is largely the reflection of competing normative beliefs regard-ing where the European Union comes from, where it should be headed, and what ought to be the status of the new (and, more broadly, all) member states within it. Engaging this question would require addressing such matters as the history and nature of EU governance, national sovereignty of members versus central EU authority, the concept of federal Europe, competition between different political centers as well as peripheries, internal heterogeneity and relationships between constituent regions, and standing vis-à-vis other world powers (from the perspective of Eastern Europe, Russia being the critical one). These issues must remain bracketed, although it wouldn't be rash to say that the answers are multitiered and equivocal (see, for example, Anderson 2007; Zielonka 2006).

However, on the micro level that my ethnography can speak to, this perspective of qualified postcoloniality, or rather, what I prefer to think of as the layering of different *posts*, helps us appreciate that the easternmost frontier of the EU's 2004 expansion historically has been a terrain of incomplete, contradictory, and paradoxical engagements with a series of projects of European modernity. Internal colonization, multinational empires, the nation-state, expansion and occupation, mass killings, and Soviet socialism were all actualizations of more or less coherent, and more or less perilous, ideas about how to divide and govern people and territory in the face of changing conditions in Europe and the world between the eighteenth and the twentieth centuries. One inherent element in this series of shifts were the arbitrary and desperate reborderings that rendered space and time fragmented and discontinuous. The repeated redrawing of territorial boundaries imbued people's lives with fear and uncertainty derived from the experience or intersubjective memory of killings, resettlements, and struggles over land. It also produced a particular sense of space, marked by the internalized and naturalized knowledge that territory on different sides of the border is far from being the same. Historically, no matter where exactly they happened to be located, frontiers dividing the borderland, like those splitting Eastern Europe in general, always cut somewhere across binary axes. They would leave the West, Europe, civilization, development, wealth, and power on one side, and the East, Asia, barbarity, underdevelopment, poverty, and powerlessness on the other.

The enlargement of the European Union and the rebordering that it brings about, irrespective of its relative faults or merits, may be viewed as the latest instance of a hegemonic intervention into this fragmented social terrain. To describe it thus is in no way to deny the fact that Poland's joining the European Union was the result of democratic politics. I shall insist that it was, from the victories of the democratic anti-Communist opposition in 1989 that first advocated it, to the accession referendum in 2003. But the day-to-day dynamics of EU governance—especially with regard to borders—are notoriously lacking in democratic accountability. The Europeanizing narrative that accompanies these changes overwhelms and blots out other stories.

EU institutions, through their Polish "partners," who more accurately ought to be called proxies, foster a latter-day "civilizing mission" in the East, among whose vital objectives is rendering the "East" congenial to and co-operative with the vision of internal security embraced by the EU. Rebordering appropriates "Europe" for the European Union. It sorts people who dwell in the borderland into categories with variable rights and opportunities. Ukrainian itinerants in Poland, as well as other migrants, experience time and space as regimented and discontinuous, even though this time the borders didn't shift, and their journeys are for the most part not forced. But the relative stability and coherence of life-worlds remains a privilege that is unequally distributed on the two sides of the border. Its distribution is affected not just by citizenship or immigration status, but also by the combined play of class or economic status, gender, and nationality. Nothing can compare to the intense cruelty exercised in this region by Hitler and Stalin, but violence has not been completely eradicated from the borderland, although its actors, victims, causes, and motives have changed. For example, persons who have been trafficked or smuggled suffer at the hands of the traffickers, but sometimes also at the hands of law enforcement; detainees in centers for illegal migrants experience the brutality of guards and the arbitrary force of the system itself. Economic migrants, both the desirable and the ones beyond demand, suffer exploitation, racism, and various humiliations of low status, from dependence on charity to homelessness and dispossession. Politicizing and contesting these effects of rebordering requires a counter-hegemonic narrative (or narratives) that will highlight them. Such a narrative would have to subvert the dominant stories of rebordering, without reverting to the binds of the ethnonational definition of membership, and without essentializing Europeanness. It will not get anywhere looking for a "colonizer" and a "colonized" on the EU frontier, for such categories are far too static to correspond to the realities created by a European governance which locates power, not in singular sovereignties, but in the web of rules, expertise, funding channels and bodies, practices of monitoring and evaluation and other Foucauldian "political technologies." However, this repoliticizing narrative would have to recognize and bear witness to the gradations and variability of subalternity, understood here in its key sense as that against which the hegemonic discourse defines itself (cf. Bhaba 1996; Spivak 1988).

As for the consternations of memory and the anxieties of European belonging, the antiteleological reading of the borderland's history leads to the conclusion that neither can be resolved. The former have flared up, and in the foreseeable future will periodically do so again, as a reminder of the potential of historical trauma to upset established politics. The latter is also here to stay. The EU is and always will remain in tension with its immediate neighborhood, because, regardless of whether it expands again, there will always be those left at its doorstep claiming a stake in the European idea, be it on the basis of their Christianity, or geography, or history, or because of a commitment to a particular concept of modernity, and thus challenging their exclusion from the European Union. The harder the access and flow between Europe's centers and its outskirts, the stronger the resentment and loathing it will produce. But while the border may create the illusion of a decisive division between an outside and an inside, that is a mystification, for in reality it already penetrates outward, delivering European tools, rules, and technologies right into the heart of its buffer zones.

Chapter 8

Conclusion

The suffering of men must never be a silent residue of policy.
—Michel Foucault

I opened this text with the juxtaposition of the unstable situation of one circle of mostly female Ukrainian migrant workers in Warsaw, and one expert account of the efficacies of border policing on the Polish-Ukrainian border achieved in the context of EU expansion in 2004. I argued that in Poland, the new European border regime substitutes expansive and technically advanced forms of border control for explicit policies regulating immigration and other forms of movement across its frontiers. In doing so, it merges and conflates vital matters of human mobility, legality, and territoriality. Throughout the preceding chapters, I have highlighted some specific practices and discourses that are symptomatic of this elision. I found them to be the effects of a dialectic of bordering and rebordering, in a region long exposed to frontier changes and shifting territorial ideologies. Some of the practices that I write about, such as the externalization of migrants and asylum seekers, the restricting of the definition of a legitimate refugee in the European Union, and the buffering of the border regime, constitute more universal intrinsic features of bordering in the Western world today, but this ethnography illuminates their locally and historically specific manifestations.

In the remaining few pages, I shall briefly revisit the key findings of this research and suggest what they might imply for a broader understanding of the role borders and mobility play in the making of the "actually existing European Union." That these issues are at the heart of Europeanization, and that they are a source of much unease, is underscored by an anecdote recalled in passing by Cris Shore in an interview occasioned by the EU enlargement on May 1, 2004:

> In a recent speech to the European Parliament, [UN Secretary General] Kofi Annan delivered a scathing attack on "fortress Europe" and its "dehumanizing" policies towards immigrants that are leading many to their deaths. Paradoxically, MEPs gave him a standing ovation. (Shore and Abélès 2004: 13)

The picture of MEPs fervently agreeing with a condemnation of practices that they themselves are implicated in through the EU legislative process is quite telling.[1] It captures the ambivalence of European parliamentarians toward Europe's borders, and hints perhaps at their readiness to delegate these matters to the Eliasian "specialist groups" who would take care of them quietly and out of sight (Elias 1994: 372). By and large attached to their self-image as enlightened politicians, committed to human rights principles at least in the realm of declarations, and more often than not receptive to some qualified form of multiculturalism in the EU, few in this political elite want anything to do with the image of EU borders as deadly insurmountable walls. They would happily disown representations of EU policies as heartless and repressive. And yet, across the continent, particularly in countries with large nonwhite immigrant populations, political capital is increasingly accumulated by the rhetoric of immigration control as well as calls for tight limits on the dependency of aliens on the state.

This brings us back to the tension between universalism and exclusionary tendencies at the heart of European unification, and between segregation and freedom of movement at the heart of Schengen. To suggest that these tensions could ever be resolved would be fundamentally to misunderstand the agonistic nature of the politics of European integration, and perhaps of politics more generally. However, conceding that the conflicting imperatives will never go away is not the same as a fatalistic resignation to the damaging effects of the frictions between them. It behooves us to trace, name, and document such effects in particular human lives and experience, as well as at the specific institutional nexuses where they are produced. Ethnography is particularly well suited to both of these tasks. By delivering fine-grained details of the border regime's operation in specific lives and locales, it can contribute to informed advocacy on behalf of a rethinking of the philosophical and legal foundations underpinning the "area of freedom, security and justice."

Producing the Inside and the Outside

The borderland between Poland and Ukraine has been exposed to a succession of territorial ideologies. I have argued that the new configuration entailed by the Schengen territory without internal borders ought to be interpreted as the latest among them. It arrives, however, in an area where the aftermaths of previous borderings continue to be felt. These left durable imprints on the landscape, the infrastructure, and the consciousness and memory of people on both sides of the current borderline. As such traces were being reworked and reinterpreted by the second post-World War II generation, rapid changes associated with the disintegration of the socialist economy and post-1989 economic reforms initiated dense and frequent cross-border movements, which I have referred to as postsocialist mobility. This mobility has succeeded in repairing some of the ruptured connections between communities on the two sides of the border, and in establishing new ones. But, as I have shown, it has also introduced new fractures and discontinuities, particularly into the lives of the relatively more economically disadvantaged Ukrainian participants in this traffic. Those fractures and discontinuities were subsequently exacerbated by the current rebordering of Europe.

As my work among itinerant Ukrainian women working in Poland documents, rebordering creates a particular time-space in which migrant lives unfold. Time becomes subject to the regimentation imposed by such devices of the border regime as visas and work permits. Space becomes discontinuous, with home and work divided not just by a border but also by a temporal *korydor* that doesn't lend itself to an easy passage. These obstacles can be circumvented, but at the cost of sinking into a legal nonexistence whose corollaries are a heightened vulnerability and penumbral practices of migrant survival. And yet this price appears to be worth paying, for it opens up access to employment that is largely beyond the reach of failed asylum seekers and other irregular migrants who are deemed to be "economic migrants," but for whom the new European border regime has no place and no demand.

But before those economic migrants beyond demand can be "processed" outside the European Union territory, they have to be spotted, apprehended, and detained. To accomplish those goals, rebordering reorients the way the state sees. It supplants the border guards' imperative of protecting the *national* territory with that of protecting the territory *of the European Union*, continuous and devoid of internal borderlines all the way from the river Bug to the coast of Portugal. It equips them with new technologies that extend their capacity to see beyond the physical limits of the frontier, thus facilitating the externalization of undesirable migrants. But for all the Euro-talk of cohesion and integration, this fusing of the national and the supranational does not happen seamlessly. Rather, it produces puzzling contradictions and dilemmas for those in charge of protecting and enforcing borders. Polish practitioners of rebordering address those dilemmas by circumventing the EU goal of an external border that would repel non-EU economic migration. They exercise their own situated judgment over who gets in and who doesn't. In this way they respond to the political and economic impracticality of the rigid boundary but remain both indifferent to and, at the level of the border guards patrolling the border, also powerless toward the structural inequalities and individual hardships it perpetuates.

Naturally, the designers of Schengen have been under no illusion that the external borders of the EU could ever be sealed tight. Hence the deterritorialization of borders, that is, the proliferation of new sites, situations, and events for the control of aliens and their movements, and the creation of exceptional spaces for the enclosure and holding of those who are found to belong elsewhere. Such spaces—detention facilities for various categories of unwanted migrants of varying degrees of securitization—are constructed both within and outside the EU territory. I have discussed examples of the congenial cross-border cooperation of Polish and Ukrainian experts, bureaucrats, and border services, which facilitates the establishment of externalizing arrangements. This discussion has highlighted the paradoxical situation that the authorities of a non-EU state contribute to the maintenance of a border regime that leaves their own citizens on the outside. It has also shown that by politically and financially encouraging the increased involvement of Ukrainian authorities in policing EU-bound migration, the EU provides incentives for a punitive approach to irregular migrants while abdicating its responsibility for the actual fate of the detained and the deported.

The Banality of Exclusion

This question of moral and political responsibility amid the conflicting imperatives that drive rebordering is ultimately the critical one. Within the EU's new border regime, legality and protection become scarce resources beyond the access of most migrants traversing the margins of Europe. At the same time, my research shows that in Poland, the safe and internally open European space within secure boundaries is promoted as such an unquestioned social good that hardly anyone asks what price is paid for it and by whom. What emerges is a banality of exclusion, by which I mean officials, border guards, experts, and regular citizens expressing an uncritical acceptance of the premises of the border regime. I do not intend to imply a direct parallel between Hannah Arendt's notion of *banality of evil* (Arendt 1963) and the *banality of exclusion*; instead, I want to suggest a conceptual kinship. It is the ground-level mechanism of these phenomena that is similar—persons responsible for the day-to-day operation of the border regime, like most perpetrators of more extreme forms of state violence, are complicit with conditions that discourage, if not directly preclude, critical thought. I emphasize mechanisms such as the distancing of the rejected migrants and asylum seekers, or the sanitization of language pertaining to repressive practices (for example, "capacity building," "migration management," "return policy," "best practices"). These are the patterns of discourse and practice wherein official, as well as popular, thinking about "aliens" is largely confined, and whereby the hardship and suffering of migrants is framed as inevitable.

Thus exclusion becomes banal, its causes and consequences unremarkable and necessary, overshadowed by the splendor of new freedoms associated with European Union and Schengen membership. And this exclusion has multiple dimensions. There is the exclusion from access to EU territory, the a priori closing off of the continent to those deemed not to belong. There is the social and economic exclusion of migrants who do find themselves without papers in the Polish/EU territory; their inability to access state services and health care, scarce opportunities to integrate with the communities they inhabit, and other foreclosed routes that are the function of their "contingent mobility" (Blank 2004). In this way the vast majority of them are quite effectively trapped where they already are, that is, in low-status, exploitable positions.

I speak also of legal exclusion, that is, the unavailability, or scarce availability, of legalization of work and residence that would partially open up avenues leading out of social exclusion.[2] Various aspects and degrees of socioeconomic and legal exclusion are experienced by both the largely desirable Ukrainian itinerants and the unwanted failed asylum seekers and other "illegals." But there is another dimension of exclusion, from the broad category of the "European" that has been appropriated by the hegemonic discourse of the European Union. This phenomenon, the shutting of doors in Andrukhovych's metaphorical house that I described in Chapter 7, is a hegemonic imposition that can engender subjective perceptions of inferiority, unwantedness, insult, and outrage. Such exclusion could be framed as "merely" symbolic. But in fact the sentiments it provokes could potentially disrupt banality and repoliticize the discussion of rebordering, were they to be mobilized on behalf of a counter-hegemonic border narrative.

Governance by Exclusion

It is in the making and perpetuation of all these exclusions, however, through the process of charting a path between national and supranational imperatives, that European integration takes place. Jacques Delors, the French politician and two-term president of the European Commission (1985–1994), has famously called the European Union *un objet politique non identifié*, an unidentified political object (Zielonka 2006; Shore and Abélès 2004). Indeed, the community's apparent indeterminacy has become a cliché of Europeanist literature. But attention to the EU's borders, particularly the multiple dimensions of rebordering, can help demystify this political UFO. It can bring into focus the quotidian effects of both the Brussels-originating supranationality and the decentered transnationality practiced by various categories of border-crossers. Away from grand rhetoric of European identity, national versus community interests, and putatively compromised sovereignties, an ethnography of rebordering reveals how at its borders European content is produced alongside discontent, and how modest and tenuous is the transnationalism that breaches the boundary.

But while nation-states are being integrated though this governance by exclusion, there is and will be resistance toward the European Commission's encroachment on the traditional domains of national authorities. Such resistance is usually couched in the discourse of sovereignty. But what matters more from the perspective of the "actually existing EU" is how the daily embedded practices of border-making and maintaining are changing in the face of Schengen, and with them the realities they confront and reproduce, as discussed throughout this text. The tacit acceptance of postsocialist mobility by Polish authorities described in Chapter 4 might be deeply objectionable for its makeshiftness and failure to address matters of migrant rights and welfare, but one must recognize that it does address vital human needs in a flawed yet workable way. There is no one reason that prevents the Polish state from openly addressing the issues of migrants by an explicit policy of inclusion instead of through the exclusions of the border regime. It is a combination of factors that involve geopolitical rationales, neoliberal economics, fear of immigrant dependence and associated costs, internal populisms, and the logic of Schengen whereby the Polish state cannot guarantee that those coming *to* Poland will necessarily stay *in* Poland. But the border regime provides a handy excuse to disengage from these problems.

Special Area of Human Hope?

Rebordering is morally and intellectually unsettling, not only because of the harm, hardship, and uncertainty it inflicts on so many, but also because it is a sign and a symptom of the fact that International Human Rights, specifically their provisions concerning asylum and refugees, as documented in this text, can hardly make up for the limits and deficiencies of the national and EU model of citizenship. Questions concerning asylum, the role of migrant workers in the integrating economy, and their rights outside their countries of citizenship are made all the more urgent by the fact that the EU, as represented by its governing elites, seeks to transcend its reputation as a politically vacuous, excessively techno- and bureaucratic body. However, internal tensions—not least those related to borders and human mobility—have forced this elite to abort the effort to craft and ratify a constitution, and replace it with a less symbolically significant and a more technical treaty. Hence, for the time being, the EU dodged the call to legitimate its own existence by invoking some set of values as a basis for a shared political identity. But the defunct draft Treaty Establishing a Constitution for Europe, the product of a Constitutional Convention headed by former president of France Valèry Giscard d'Estaing and struck down in the French and Dutch referenda of 2005, stands as an awkward reminder of such aspirations. As Alessandro Ferrara observed about the draft Treaty, it was very parsimonious with phrases capable of impressing the collective imaginary, phrases such as "life, liberty, and the pursuit of happiness,'" or *"liberté, égalité, fraternité."* The only exception to this expressive restraint is the sentence that concludes the "Preamble," where Europe is identified as a "special area of human hope." (Ferrara 2007: 316)

What is, Ferrara asks farther, the exact nature of the hope for whose realization Europe supposedly constitutes a special area? And why is this political space "so exceptionally conducive" to its fulfillment?

Ferrara addresses these questions by pointing out that the Treaty, in its outward prohibition of including the death penalty into law as well as the prohibition to deport, expel, or extradite anyone "to a state where there is serious risk that he or she would be subjected to the death penalty, torture or other inhuman and degrading punishment" (part II, art. 79) forcefully expresses "an ethical intuition which unites the whole European continent" (2007: 318).[3] Based on this commitment, combined with other constitutional promises such as bioethical protection, respect for privacy, gender equality, consumer protection, and social welfare, Ferrara concludes that "the European Union . . . proposes itself to its own citizens and to the rest of the world as the political space in which the dignity of the human being, *not just of the citizen*, is protected in the most complete way available on the planet" (Ferrara 2007: 320, emphasis mine).

This commitment is no longer officially framed in terms of a "special area of human hope." One way to interpret the silencing of this vision, and of the constitutional push more generally, could be to observe that rebordering reveals the impossibility of reconciling the promise of universal protection of human dignity with the myriad conditions, qualifications, and restrictions which permeate the EU's daily practices and documents regulating human mobility.

Exceptionality, detention facilities for the undesirable, and other exterritorial *korydors* hardly fit with the "special area of human hope." European Union citizenship might be a privilege, albeit one that is rarely valued for signifying the ethos of a political membership. Instead it has practical applications for its holders. Among them the key one might be the freedom from arbitrary discontinuities of space, and from the regimentations of time, such as those experienced by Ukrainian itinerants in Poland.[4] As for the other non-EU citizens who make their way into the European Union across the Polish-Ukrainian and other borders, their hope is even more scaled down.

The moral and political responsibility for their lives is written into the EU's regulations and, in token forms, actualized in various nodes of the border regime. However, it is trapped on the one hand in the limited twentieth-century notions of refugeeness, and on the other in the concept of "economic migration" that assumes economic rationality and free will. As long as that is the case, their rights will devolve into "best practices" whose "bestness" has yet to receive proper scrutiny.

In the introductory chapter I declared that to write the border is to attend to the specific places, agents, and practices whereby the sorting of different categories of migrants entering the territory of the European Union is performed on a day-to-day basis. I stated that it entails the interrogation of the material and symbolic force of the emerging categories and practices of citizenship, entry rights, residence, and other forms of (non)*being* relative to boundaries. Given that the border between Poland and Ukraine has now become part of the external boundary of the European Union, and that this entails a new relationship between centers of power and borderland locations, I chose a hybrid methodology of field research in multiple sites combined with a study of printed and online-based source materials, such as EU- and Schengen-related documents, governmental and nongovernmental publications, newspapers, and magazines. This was an experimental approach that had its limitations but also has yielded a payoff. (And may the reader be the judge of its extent.) Explaining the methodological approach for his ethnography of European integralism, where he engaged with informants across a range of institutional and other sites vital to his topic, Douglas Holmes wrote, "I have avoided making broad methodological claims for this . . . multisited maneuver, because I think the reader will see why these moves were necessary given the specific issues I was pursuing and the circumstances that presented themselves during the research" (Holmes 2000: 4). I echo Holmes, and hope that in the preceding chapters, the reader has seen how my moves across places on and away from the Polish-Ukrainian frontier were prompted by the specific questions I wanted to answer.

When this study began, with preliminary fieldwork in the summer of 2003, the initial idea, to investigate what the European Union means for Poland's eastern border, prompted me to visit the border itself. At the time, I imagined a circumscribed kind of fieldwork that would focus on the changing "boundaries and connections" (Barth 2000) in selected localities in Poland and Ukraine. However, my inclination toward such research soon dissipated. As I have stated in the introductory chapter, the decisive shifts reconfiguring life on the borderland had less to do with the inherent dynamics of the local relations between Poles and Ukrainians, and more with the larger transformations that have swept across Europe in the last few decades. From the collapse of Communism to EU expansion, such shifts have originated in centers far removed from the peripheral frontier locality. Contemporary modes of governing the border, for example, are being developed in Brussels and adapted in Warsaw to the specificities of the Polish situation. Migration policy experts, lawyers, technocrats, and politicians debate these issues in sterile conference rooms. They do so without ever setting their feet on the muddy banks of the river Bug, which since May 2004 delimits a section of the EU's eastern border.

With these factors in mind, I had to conceptualize the border so as to probe the multiple new ways of regulating movement, migration, and citizenship status. The EU law aims to integrate the management of external borders with other forms of policing. Thus, the frame of this study had to be wide enough to include the multiple sites and levels of significant adjustments in Europe's security scheme. With this in mind, I extended my interests to local and central border management institutions, the Aliens Bureau in Warsaw, and NGOs involved with rebordering. All the same, embracing the concept of "ethnography on an awkward scale," understood as an effort to account for phenomena that are "*both* global in [their] reach and localized in [their] protean manifestations" (Comaroff and Comaroff 2003: 158), I attended to the micro-effects of these regulations, so that their localized human consequences could be identified and named. As the Comaroffs remind us, built into such venture is "an effort to engage at once with the general and the particular, with variance and simility, with continuity and rupture." (158) Hence my focus on the routes of itinerants, from their homes in Ukraine through border checkpoints to bazaars and workplaces in Polish towns and cities.

Building on my preliminary observations, in 2005–2006 I conducted twelve months of field research in Poland and Ukraine, supplemented with a follow-up in summer 2008, among border guards and immigration officials as well as in migrant communities and civil society organizations. Following legal anthropologist Carol Greenhouse, I understood ethnographic fieldwork as "a relational practice linking knowledge production to the historical and local specificity of experience" (2006: 187). Questions animating my research were informed by contemporary theories of governmentality, borders, and legal subjectivity (as discussed in Chapter 1), but I embraced the ethnographic emphasis on close encounter and a search for situated points of view. Thus, as a participant-observer of cross-border human traffic, I collected a range of diverse vernacular accounts of crossing, policing, and subverting the border. As an anthropologist educated and living in the U.S., and a Polish citizen and native speaker, I was confronted with frequent misapprehensions of my status and of my project, mostly by officials and border guards, who repeatedly inquired who exactly commissioned my research. Accustomed to utilitarian studies of institutional efficiency, and to their work being monitored for compliance with EU and Schengen standards, they found quite unconvincing my awkward explanations that changing border practices are worth studying for their own sake, because they are a reflection of broader societal and political change.

Nevertheless, I obtained official clearance to conduct fieldwork in border locations and in the headquarters of the Border Guard, as well as in other institutions governing the receiving of migrants. Ukrainian itinerant workers, Polish and Ukrainian petty traders, border guards, ministerial and local officials, and NGO activists and personnel on both sides gave me access to their subjective and experiential knowledge of various aspects of negotiating the border. For example, Ukrainians illegally working in Poland explained effective methods of smuggling tobacco and circumventing border requirements. Some of them shared intimate details of their lives lived in multiple locales and variously marked by the condition of illegality. Polish border guards at various levels of institutional hierarchy introduced me to protocols for returning, deporting, and detaining illegal migrants and to the specific settings where these protocols operate. Also, more or less reluctantly, they allowed me to familiarize myself with selected aspects of their daily work of patrolling the border, in this way revealing their own perspectives on what it means to manage and enforce a supranational boundary. I drew on historical sources, legal texts, policy papers, official statements, and independent reports, as listed in the Bibliography, to situate the accounts I have gathered within the larger context of the ongoing debate on what is "Europe," who belongs in it, and how to define its limits. In the process, I came to think of my research as the ethnographic zooming in and out—from close focus on particular lives affected by rebordering to a panoramic picture of national strategies of Europeanization.

Notes

Chapter 1. Introduction: Rebordering Europe

Epigraph: Seyla Benhabib (2004: 6).

1. Poland, Hungary, the Czech Republic, Slovakia, Slovenia, Lithuania, Latvia, and Estonia were the first eight postsocialist countries included in the European Union. Malta and Cyprus joined the same day. Romania and Bulgaria became EU member states on January 1, 2007. As of 2010, Turkey, Iceland, The Former Yugoslav Republic of Macedonia, and Croatia have the status of Candidate Countries. The official list of Potential Candidate Countries includes Albania, Serbia, Montenegro, Bosnia and Herzegovina, and Kosovo under Security Council Resolution 1244. Ukraine is not currently considered for EU candidacy.

2. Anna's name, as well as names of most informants who appear in this book, most institutions (save for singular ones, like the Polish Border Guard) and some locations, have been changed to protect the privacy of everyone who provided information and shared not always officially authorized opinions. Changes of place names are indicated in the text; where no such indication appears, the reader should assume the authentic name has been preserved.

3. This was assuming she worked without interruption 6 days a week and made approximately 1,900 Polish *złoty in* the course of a month. At the time the average salary in Warsaw was approximately 3,000 *złoty*. Anna shared a 600-*złoty* room with two other people. One U.S. dollar was worth 3.2 Polish *złoty*, and most cleaning jobs in Warsaw paid 8 to 10 *złoty* per hour.

4. The higher estimates of unemployment—10, 13, even 20 percent—were mentioned in interviews and casual conversations with journalists and researchers in Lviv. See also Szerepka and Jaroszewicz 2007 and the Economic Statistics Archive of the Centre for Policy Studies in Kyiv, http://www.icps.com.ua/eng/arh/admin/es.html.

5. These numbers are imprecise and estimated on the basis of the numbers of border crossings, visas issued, and other data (IOM 2004; Herm 2008). The higher number circulates in Ukrainian media (see, e.g., Shokalo 2005) and was often mentioned by my Ukrainian informants; the lower one by the Polish officials. Officially only 1.8 percent

of the population of Poland is foreign-born (Główny Urząd Statystyczny 2009; Herm 2008).

6. Overall economic growth spurred by EU accession and the exodus, between 2004 and 2007, of approximately two million Polish workers to Western Europe, after EU borders and some labor markets were opened, exacerbated labor shortages in these sectors. As of data collected in 2009, 340,000 have since returned to Poland (see Frelak and Roguska 2008; GUS 2009).

7. Significant numbers of Ukrainians do it, however, the most popular destinations being Italy (500,000), Greece (200,000), and Portugal (200,000), due to a system of temporary work permits (Shokalo 2005).

8. Many observations in this book also apply to Belarusians and the Polish-Belarusian border. Estimates of the numbers of Belarusians in Poland are even harder to come by than for Ukrainians. Due to the tense political situation between Poland and Belarus, and an anti-Western dictatorial regime in the latter, there are also far fewer bilateral cooperative initiatives along the Polish-Belarusian border.

9. Among the documented cases of migrants bound for Europe dying at sea was that of a boat of North African refugees fleeing in the aftermath of political unrest in March 2011. According to the *Guardian*, 61 of the 72 people on board died after the boat ran out of fuel and was adrift for days. Several military units, including a NATO ship, ignored calls for help. The turmoil in the region in early 2011 fueled a sharp rise in attempts to reach Europe by sea, with up to 30,000 migrants believed to have made the journey across the Mediterranean between January and April 2011. The main destination has been the Italian island Lampedusa, off the coast of Sicily (Shenker 2011).

10. A more immediate predecessor of contemporary European integration was the Pan-European movement of the 1920s, inspired by the devastation of the Great War and by the growing strength of the United States and the budding Soviet Union. While the movement had important backers among the political elites of interwar Europe, the rising influence of fascism swept it to the margins in the 1930s (Dinan 2005: 14).

11. There are, of course, other interpretations of EU enlargement, such as the historical-materialist argument that its purpose was to secure externally the neoliberal restructuring in East and Central Europe (Bieler 2002). While there is no doubt that representatives of transnational capital had an influence over the direction of economic transformations in the region, this interpretation neglects the broader political and symbolic context wherein such influences could be realized.

12. The challenge goes both ways, as Willem Maas convincingly shows, pointing out that EU citizenship, based on ethical and moral conceptions that are not necessarily universally shared, could and may be repealed (Maas 2007: 95).

13. Some features of this East-West intra-EU flow are discussed in Favell 2008b; Garapich 2008.

14. The discontents of postsocialist transformations have been captured by an array of ethnographies written from standpoints critical of triumphalist interpretations of the year 1989. From early assessments of the social consequences of socialism's collapse

(Berdahl et al. 2000; Bridger and Pine 1998; Hann and Dunn 1996; Petryna 2002; Ries 1997; Sampson 1996; Verdery 1996; Wedel 1998; West 2001) to more recent, fine-grained accounts of everyday life under rapidly advancing capitalism (Dunn 2004; Hann 2002, 2006; Ost 2005; Ries 2002; Verdery 2002b), the general tendency in this literature has been to transcend traditional area studies and understand postsocialist transformations comparatively, as manifestations of global social, economic, and political phenomena (Buyandelgeriyn 2008).

15. The Common Market was functional by 1992. By then the customs union was in effect, and technical and physical barriers to trade had been abolished. The European Monetary System, launched in 1979, preceded the gradual introduction of the Euro— the common European currency—in 2002.

16. Under the Treaty of Amsterdam (1997) the Schengen legislation was incorporated into the European *acquis communautaire.*

17. Poland formally joined Schengen in December 2007, but internal border controls were removed only in March the following year. The same schedule applied to eight other countries that joined the EU in 2004 (seven postsocialist states and Malta, but not Cyprus). Bulgaria and Romania, both admitted in 2007, remain, as of 2011, outside Schengen. Various technical and legal challenges have prevented the roll-out of SIS II, projected to come online in 2013. In its stead Schengen states are using an enhanced version of the previous database, SISone4all.

18. The draft Treaty Establishing a Constitution for Europe was adopted by the European Convention in June 2003. Subsequently it was subject to ratification by the member states, in referenda or by parliamentary approval. The French and Dutch referenda on May 29 and June 1, 2005, brought negative results (55 percent rejection in France and 62 percent in the Netherlands). In 2007 renewed constitutional efforts were taken up by Angela Merkel, head of the German EU Presidency. At the EU Summit in June that year it was announced that the Treaty would be scaled down, revised, and called not a Constitution but a Reform Treaty. These efforts eventually led to the Treaty of Lisbon.

19. On the expiration of the Hague Programme, it is being replaced with the 2009 Stockholm Programme, which carries the original agenda farther.

20. For an overview of "transit migration," including main routes into Europe, see Düvell 2006. Due to heavy policing, Poland's eastern borders are secondary entry points, compared to the Southern Carpathian route, the Aegean Sea, and the waters between Libya and Italy.

21. Tentativeness as a feature of the present is remarked upon by many students of what Paul Rabinow has usefully called the "near future/recent past" (2003: 56). See, e.g., Steve Collier and Andrew Lakoff on the "regimes of living" (Ong and Collier 2005: 23); see also Bowker and Star 1999; Ong 1999; Petryna 2005.

22. In *The Socialist System: The Political Economy of Communism*, János Kornai argued for studying "actually existing socialism" as it historically emerged as opposed to "the fancied socialist system that operates efficiently and fairly" (1992: 12). Similarly, while the cohesive, fair, and human rights-respecting European Union remains

a contested object of desire, the emergent everyday forms of integration demand study and analysis.

23. As Rabinow writes, "The anthropologist of the actual seeks to identify emergent assemblages and to set them in an environment that is partially composed of apparatuses and partially of a variety of other elements, such as institutions, symbols and the like. A central task . . . is to identify conjunctures between and among these diverse objects and between and among their temporalities and their functionalities" (2003: 56).

24. See Case 2009 for a particularly interesting discussion of the strategic uses of claims of European belonging.

Chapter 2. Civilizing the Postsocialist Frontier?

Epigraph: Pamela Ballinger (2003: 11).

1. The referendum capped the period of Poland's EU candidacy and negotiations which began in 1994 with the formal application for membership. It took place over two days (June 7 and 8) rather than just one, because the authorities feared the embarrassment of a low turnout. In the end 58.85% of the voters cast ballots, 77.45% voting "yes" and 22.55% voting "no" in response to the question "Do you give your consent to the accession of the Polish Republic to the European Union?" (National Elections Commission, http://referendum.pkw.gov.pl/sww/kraj/indexA.html8, accessed September 30, 2009; see also Clem and Chodakiewicz 2004).

2. TIR (Transports Internationaux Routiers; International Road Transport) refers to all cargo transport that conforms to standards established by the 1975 UN/ECE Convention on the International Transport of Goods. In Polish *tir* is a generic term for any large truck. Derived from it is the word *tirówka*, a roadside prostitute.

3. Diana R. Blank (2004) describes them in the context of the southern border of Ukraine and Moldova. Onions, I was told by a farmer in western Ukraine, are expensive to grow, so the low domestic supply accounts for the relatively high prices in Ukraine.

4. In 2003 the Finance Ministry launched a campaign to curtail corruption in the Customs Service. Before then, according to Zbigniew Bujak (personal communication, June 29, 2004), a former dissident and one of the first reformers of customs after 1989, the problem of corruption and lax enforcement of the eastern border was an intractable problem. Colluding with the smugglers' networks provided incomparably better income than being an employee of the state.

5. The Polish-Belarusian and Polish-Lithuanian borderlands had similar demographic characteristics, with Lithuanian and Belarusian populations striving for self-determination in the interwar period.

6. The demarcation line between Soviet Union and Poland approximating the shape of today's border was originally proposed in 1919 by British foreign minister George Curzon, hence referred to as the "Curzon line." However, the Riga Treaty of 1921 established a boundary line that left Galicia and Volhynia on the Polish side. The Curzon line

was eventually accepted, with few alterations, in Yalta as the eastern border of the new Polish People's Republic.

7. As part of its regional policies, the EU encourages establishment of "Euroregions"—transborder cooperation structures linking two or more territories in adjacent countries. They have no political or legislative power, only administrative arrangements facilitating joint projects of local administrative structures. They are also a conduit for EU funding. Poland and Ukraine have two Euroregions, Bug, established in 1993, and Karpaty, established in 1995, encompassing the northern and southern sections of the Polish-Ukrainian borderland.

8. Huyssen emphasizes that reading palimpsests "is not some imperialism of *écriture*. . . . It is rather the conviction that literary techniques of reading historically, intertextually, constructively, and deconstructively at the same time can be woven into our understanding of urban spaces as lived spaces that shape collective imaginaries" (2003: 7). While the density of art and architecture attracts Huyssen to cities (Berlin, New York), there is no reason not to extend his notion of palimpsest to nonurban spaces, especially when their landscapes—like that of the borderland—feature prominently in national mythologies and nationalist narratives.

9. Germany attacked Poland from the west on September 1, 1939. Based on the Ribbentrop-Molotov Pact, the Soviets entered from the east on September 17. Disregarding the Pact, in summer 1941 Hitler launched Operation Barbarossa—an attack on the Soviet Union whose ultimate goal was the overthrow of the Soviet government and inclusion of the European part of the Soviet Union into the Nazi German sphere of influence.

10. These numbers pertain only to Volhynia. Overall, the Polish-Ukrainian conflict lasted from 1943, the year of the killings in Volhynia, to 1947, when the leadership of the Ukrainian underground was destroyed in Communist Poland. Motyka estimates the total number of deaths throughout this period at 100,000 among Poles, and 10,000 to 15,000 among Ukrainians (2011: 446–47).

11. For an English-language account, Timothy Snyder (2003) offers a comprehensive, yet succinct, discussion of this "obscure but important" episode of ethnic cleansing, which he characterizes as "a story of multiple occupations and of cleansing within cleansings" (2003: 198). Snyder stresses the immediate and particular local causes, showing how the specific political and ideological context of the triple occupation (Soviet, German, and again Soviet) enabled the mobilization of nationalist Ukrainian partisans against Polish civilians. He also notes that before the outbreak of the war Volhynia was actually a site of relative cultural and religious autonomy for Ukrainians designed to limit the popularity of communism, and hence a place where the Polish minority and Ukrainian majority coexisted in a state of relative accord (202).

12. No attempt "to trim the frontiers to the wishes of the population ever succeeded, until, at Soviet instigation, it was decided in 1944–45 to trim the population to the requirements of arbitrary frontiers" (Davies 1982: 543). Approximately 1.25 million Poles were resettled from the now Soviet Volhynia and Eastern Galicia to the newly acquired western territories of the Polish People's Republic, from which their German inhabitants

were expelled. A little under half a million Ukrainians were transferred east of the new Polish border and a further 150,000 resettled in former German territories (Magocsi 2002: 190).

13. At the war's end there were still about 225,000 Jews living in Polish territory, but between 1945 and 1948, in hope of escaping endemic persecution and horrific memories, the majority (150,000) left for Palestine or Western Europe. Of the remaining 75,000 some left on their own in the 1950s and 1960s, and the majority were expelled during the 1968 anti-Semitic campaign spearheaded by Władysław Gomułka, nationalist leader of the Communist party. The largest other minorities were the 2 percent of Ukrainians and under 1 percent of ethnic Germans, concentrated primarily in the region of Silesia.

14. This was true about other people's democracies as well. Leszek Jesień notes, "In fact, travel from some countries of the former Soviet bloc (like Poland, Hungary, and Yugoslavia) to the West was at times easier than between them" (2000: 190).

15. As Brown writes, "The Pole in the Russian empire loomed large as the chief enemy. Poles were depicted as a threat to the Ukrainian and Belarusian peasantry (both of which were seen by tsarist-era intellectuals as Russian) and to the existence of the Russian state itself. . . . Poles were also depicted as the ultimate subversives of the monarchy . . . [they] were especially dangerous because they had links with the Roman Catholic Church and with fellow Poles in the German and Austro-Hungarian empires" (2004: 5). For the image of the Bolshevik in interwar Poland see Miłosz 1999; for the more contemporary relationship between stereotypes and national identity see Zarycki 2004.

16. The Greek Catholic Church, also known as Uniate Church, was established in 1596 based on an agreement between a splinter group of Orthodox bishops and the Roman Catholics. The Greek Catholics recognize the authority of the Pope and are bound by Catholic dogma, but they retain autonomy in matters of rite and tradition. This means they follow the Byzantine rather than the Latin rite. Today Greek Catholicism remains strong mainly in the Ukrainian part of Galicia, where it reestablished itself in the late twentieth century after the so called catacomb period of over forty years of underground existence in the Soviet Union. The dominant religion in the rest of Ukraine is Orthodox Christianity. Evangelical movements have grown significantly in recent years as well (Wanner 2003).

17. See Allina-Pisano and Simonyi 2011.

18. I use the term geopoetics to denote a critique of geopolitics that is based on an embrace of alternative notions of a particular space. In her work on United States-Mexico borderland narratives, Rosemary A. King (2000) defined geopoetics as the artistic expression of place and space. I take geopoetics to encompass discourses and practices that articulate political (in the broadest sense), cultural, and moral agendas in tension with those that stem from the hegemony of the allegedly objective geopolitical facts.

19. The vouchers, supposedly documenting that the person had booked a holiday in Poland, could be bought cheaply in every kiosk on the border. In the early 1990s failure

to present a voucher or an invitation was not necessarily a cause for being turned away from a border crossing. Rather, it was an opportunity for the guards to extract a small bribe. This changed in the late 1990s, when as part of pre-EU reforms Polish authorities introduced stricter controls, including checking for false documents, and began to require possession of a certain sum of money to enter the country. This caused a fall in traffic around 1998, which quickly rebounded.

20. Statistics made available by the Border Guard, on file with author.

21. In his account of the post-Soviet reopening of the Georgian-Turkish border Pelkmans offers a vivid description of a similar dynamic there (Pelkmans 2006: 176).

22. This study does not discuss the profits from the sale of tobacco and alcohol.

23. As of 2007, there were 76,000 foreigners legally resident in Poland. Ukrainians were the largest group, at 21,500. Data made available by Urząd do Spraw Repatriacji i Cudzoziemców (Office for Repatriation and Foreigners), on file with author.

24. Both quotations drawn from http://europa.eu/pol/socio/index_en.htm.

25. Recent examples here include the Employer Sanctions Directive 2009/52/EC, and the Schengen Borders Code Regulation (EC) No 562/2006. EU regulations have binding power. Directives are also binding as to the effect that must be achieved, but the choice of methods is left up to the member states. They are incorporated into national legislation through a process known as transposition (Treaty on the Functioning of the European Union, art. 288).

26. Przemyśl has a population of 70,000. In the 1990s approximately 2,000 of its inhabitants declared themselves Ukrainian (Hann 1998: 846).

27. The 2005 turn to the right in Poland precipitated many examples of this resistance through the discourse of "Polish exceptionality," emphasizing the role of "tradition" and Catholicism in social life. Among other issues, this discourse supports the Polish opt-out protocol from the Charter of Fundamental Rights that allows it to withdraw unilaterally from provisions concerning "morality and the family" (issues such as gay marriage, abortion, in vitro fertilization).

28. This frequency and price of rides remained unchanged as of 2010.

Chapter 3. I'm Not Really Here: The Time-Space of Itinerant Lives

Epigraph: Piotr Lachmann, author of "The Boundaries of the Borderland" (1998) from which this excerpt is taken (17), is a Polish-German poet, translator, and essayist. The theme of Central European borderlands has been one of his key concerns in the 1990s.

1. For the economic and cultural aspects of markets and petty trade in postsocialism see Humphrey 2002; Mandel and Humphrey 2002, especially the contribution by Kaneff (2002).

2. Such studies, for example by Düvell (2007); Bieniecki et al. (2005); Korczyńska (2005); and, offering a comparative perspective, Szczepanikova et al. (2006) are key for understanding the "push" and "pull" factors animating the movement of people across

borders, and the mechanisms of oppression and exploitation almost universally suffered by migrants in low-wage jobs. Scholarship on the gendered dimension of migration and on the political economy for migrant domestic work has also informed my work in this chapter. I have learned a great deal particularly from the work of Leyla Keough (2006); Bridget Anderson (2000); Annie Phizacklea (1986); and Mirjana Morokvasic (1991, 2004).

3. Anderson cites a German NGO report that somewhat one-sidedly calls these mutual dependencies arising in the context of the new border regime a "continuum of exploitation" (Forschunggesselschaft Flucht and Migration, "Germany, Poland and Ukraine: Asylum-Seekers and the 'Domino Effect,'" cited in Anderson 2000: 182).

4. Despite EU-mandated changes to labor law, intended to facilitate women's return to work after maternity, public supports for working mothers and persons with other care responsibilities are sparse. Toward the end of the century's first decade, the government considered commercialization of care services a panacea for the problems of working mothers. For example, the solution to the shortage of nurseries was loosening state oversight over creation of new facilities.

5. Contemporary Polish feminist scholars tend to be restrained in their praise of this equality, critiquing its top-down nature or calling it a myth altogether (Fuszara 2002; Titkow 2001, 2003). Most students of women's issues in Poland would admit, however, that the benefits of the socialist equal rights policy lie in the fact that at the very least the "socialist version of equality politics created a legal and structural basis . . . facilitating further actions for an authentic parity of the rights and opportunities for women and men" (Titkow 2001: 55).

6. For comparison, according to figures assembled by Einhorn, the corresponding figures were 55 for West Germany (1987), 57 for France (1989), and 68 for the UK (1990) (1993: 266). The overall participation of women in the workforce in Poland grew from 30 percent of all employed in 1950 to nearly 46 percent in 1988 (Budrowska 2003: 36). The figures in West Germany were 38 percent (1988), France 43 percent (1989), and UK 43 percent (1990) (Einhorn 1993: 266). I have rounded the figures to the nearest whole number.

7. As Małgorzata Tarasiewicz wrote in 1991, "the motivation for most [working women] was not the hope of fulfilling career ambitions or the intention of being financially independent but a much more mundane need to make ends meet" (1991: 182). For other discussions of women's work under socialism and after see Matynia 2003; Einhorn 1993; Gal and Kligman 2000.

8. Some anthropological critiques of neoliberal reforms in Poland and East and Central Europe are found in Berdahl 2000; Bridger and Pine 1998; Dunn 2004. A contemporary wellspring of academic-cum-political vernacular critique of post-1989 economic reforms is the journal *Krytyka Polityczna*, published in Warsaw since 2002, and the associated network of cultural centers fostering leftist intellectual debate (http://www.krytykapolityczna.pl/).

9. Things are not quite the same with Ukrainian men: they are often stereotyped

as shady, criminal types and tossed in one bag with the disliked Ruskie, technically a disparaging term for Russians, but commonly applied to all citizens of the former Soviet Union, or people speaking *ruski*, the Russian language. On the perceptions of Ukrainians in Poland see, e.g., Konieczna 2003. This account, however, also bypasses issues of gender.

10. Adrian Favell attributes the fact that migrants from countries such as Ukraine, Turkey, and Morocco will continue arriving within EU boundaries to the broader "concentric logic of an externalizing, 'neighborhood'-building EU" (2009: 171).

11. On this point Greta Uehling incisively noted that "If we examine migrants' descriptions of their experiences alongside discussions of irregular migration in policy and position papers, there are interesting slippages. For example, whereas migrants lament the necessity to leave their homes and search for sources of livelihood in unfamiliar and sometimes hostile cities in Europe, officials and workers in nongovernmental organizations (NGOs) often picture irregular migration in terms of an inexorable striving to live lives more like theirs, in Europe. It is certainly possible to both lament the need to leave *and* experience a justifiable desire to meet needs elsewhere. The point, however, is that it is dangerous and misleading to overly inflate the desirability of European lives" (2004: 78).

12. In the village Lena was from, Pentecostalism has almost fully displaced the traditional Orthodox rite. As opposed to mostly Greek Catholic Galicia, Volhynia and Polissia were traditionally Orthodox. However, since the early 1990s evangelical missions have started coming to promote conversion; Pentecostal and Baptist are the most popular denominations (Wanner 2003).

13. Lena's base salary was paid in U.S. dollars. As Alaina Lemon documents, reliance on "hard currency" in shadow market transactions was a widespread practice in the former Soviet Union in the 1990s. She argues that U.S. currency was valued not simply for its buying power and relative stability, but that the patterns of handling and exchanging dollars were about communication, self-understanding and aesthetic pleasure (1998). To a lesser extent this was the case also in Poland (Pine 2002b). In the 2000s this practice was on the wane, for a host of economic and cultural reasons, such as the weakening of the dollar in relation to local currencies, emergence of the euro, and the fading allure of all things American. Nevertheless nearly all of the Ukrainian itinerants I encountered discussed their earnings in dollar amounts, regardless of the actual currency they were paid in. As a rule, savings would be kept in U.S. dollars. When queried, they described this practice as a "habit," explained that dollars were "safe," but, a couple of the older informants (in their 40s or 50s), acknowledged that the dollar is "not what it used to be."

14. Needless to say, "Bulba" Borovets, like other UPA commanders, would be regarded as a villain on the other side of the border. The post-1991 glorification of UPA in Ukraine (and its vilification in Poland) is among the thorniest issues in contemporary Polish-Ukrainian relations; see Chapter 7.

15. In keeping with the general logic of Ukrainian mobility patterns reprising those of Polish mobility from the early 1990s, similar arrangements were common also among Polish women working in Germany (Morokvasic 1991).

16. Ukrainian teachers of English have actually left western Ukraine in significant numbers to teach in Polish public schools, primarily but not exclusively in rural areas. The Polish education system for years has suffered a shortage of English teachers. (The Peace Corps ceased its operations in Poland in the early 1990s; meanwhile English became compulsory.) Polish English teachers chose employment in private language schools and in nonteaching occupations in Poland and elsewhere in the EU over the poorly paid public school jobs. The vacancies became attractive to Ukrainian educators, and this narrow but important segment of the labor market is one where the legalization process is smooth and facilitated by the authorities. There are no country-wide statistics on this phenomenon, but in Lubelskie, one of the districts adjacent to the border, there were more than 100 Ukrainian English teachers in 2004, many of them actively recruited in Ukraine by the Polish school principals (Reszka 2004).

17. Despite recent gentrification of some parts of the right bank (Praga), its northern part still sharply contrasts with the rapidly developing left bank. Rentals are significantly cheaper than elsewhere in Warsaw, and until its final closure the market at the stadium contributed to the area's (not always justified) shady reputation.

18. In 1991, the year of the Soviet Union collapse, the most alarmist predictions estimated that nine million citizens of the former USSR would head west seeking opportunities to settle and find work (Iglicka and Sword 1999: 2). But the anticipated "wave" did not materialize, save for the challenge of the estimated 600,000–800,000 refugees who fled former Yugoslavia in 1991 and after.

19. The Hague Programme states that the "European Council underlines the need for further development of the common visa policy as part of multi-layered system aimed at facilitating legitimate travel and tackling illegal immigration through further harmonization of national legislation and handling practices at local consular missions" (26). In the long run, the Council envisions an establishment of common visa offices.

20. EU states that are part of the Schengen group (old members minus the UK and Ireland, who opted out, and including Norway and Iceland who joined, despite not being EU members) issue so-called Schengen visas, which allow travel within the entire Schengen territory. These visas are required of citizens of 101 countries. Some of the countries whose citizens are exempt include Croatia, which is a candidate for EU membership (but not Turkey), as well as Australia, Canada, Japan, New Zealand, and the United States (Council Regulation No. 539/2001). Procedures for issuing visas are regulated by Common Consular Instructions (2002/C 313/01). EU member states have autonomy with respect to regulating labor migrations. They can establish quotas and select sending countries from which they receive migrant workers. However, after EU expansion, the governments of most Western European countries concluded that there was now an ample supply of labor within the Union's own boundaries. In fact, the fear of an oversupply prompted the majority of member states to maintain restrictions on hiring "new" Europeans for transitional periods of up to seven years.

21. A selection of press commentary on this issue is available at http://www.isp.org .pl/?v=page&id=152&ln=pl; see also http://www.wprost.pl/ar/?O=50239. Zarycki cites

opinion poll figures that show that while overall 45 percent of the population considered visas beneficial for Poland, and 30 percent thought they would be harmful, in border regions the proportions were reversed and the majority considered them harmful (2004: 596).

22. Between late 2003 and late 2007 Polish consulates in Ukraine issued free visas valid only for Poland. In 2006 in Lviv, I talked to a consular official who compared the process of granting them to labeling bottles on a conveyor belt. He said that the process was strictly mechanical, that it would be "simply impossible" to vet every applicant. Since Poland's accession into Schengen, Ukrainian citizens are eligible for short-term Schengen visas, which replaced the 90-day national ones. I discuss the ramifications of this change in the Epilogue to this chapter.

23. In 2004 and 2005 both consular facilities in western Ukraine (in Lviv and Lutsk) were marred by shortages of space and allegations of corrupt practices (Kowalski and Forostyna 2005; Kowalski 2005). High demand created delays and added tension to the already burdensome experience of waiting for permission to enter Poland. In the following years the Polish press repeatedly reported on piecemeal "improvements" (*usprawnienia*) at the consulates, but the underlying shortage of space remained an issue.

24. Around the same time the Lviv facility introduced online registration for visa appointments (ostensibly to curtail the chaos of the lines). The queue entrepreneurship instantly branched into computer services. The majority of rural applicants had no access to the Internet and no computer skills, presenting another niche to be exploited.

25. Ministry of Labor and Social Policy, http://www.mps.gov.pl/index.php?gid=1047, according to data accessed January 10, 2006. It had fallen to 15 percent in 2007 and 9 percent in 2009, due to an improved economy and large numbers of the young unemployed falling off the register due to emigration.

26. Gradual changes began in 2007, with the introduction of legal measures facilitating seasonal employment of foreigners (see note 37 below). That year saw also the introduction of an abolition act attempting to regularize foreign citizens who had been living illegally in Poland for an uninterrupted period of ten years or more (Dąbrowski 2007). But this program changed nothing in the lives of itinerant workers, because it required, among other steep criteria, that the applicant present a documented promise of legal employment. This would have been very difficult to obtain for an immigrant without legal status. Only 1,800 people acquired legal residency owing to this law. As of the summer of 2011, a new abolition bill for illegal migrants has been passed by parliament, partially as a result of the lobbying of the Ukrainian Association in Poland. It will come into force on January 1, 2012 and it aims to regularize the legal status of people who have resided illegally in Poland since accession to Schengen (2007). The application window will be open for six months. The drafters of the bill aimed for a more effective program than the one in 2007 and did not make legal employment a condition. Persons whose status will become legal under the bill will have the right to legal residency for two years, during which time they will not need additional work permits. To extend legal residency beyond the initial two years they will need a long-term or permanent

employment contract. The key requirement is an uninterrupted stay of minimum three years, which excludes seasonal workers and those who practiced the *korydor*. NGO analysts have pointed out that irregular migrants detained by the Border Guard and persons without identity documents are not eligible either; however, some categories of failed asylum seekers do qualify (Słubik 2011: 8). The Ministry of Interior expects that "ten-odd thousand" of migrants illegally resident in Poland will acquire legal status through the program, http://www.mswia.gov.pl/portal/pl/2/9316/Abolicja_dla_cudzoziemcow, accessed October 25, 2011.

27. See the discussion of the "deficit of care" in Ehrenreich and Hochschild 2004.

28. For example, the coveted visas to Western European countries were costly and, the rejected applicants reported, very difficult to obtain. Ukrainian women between ages eighteen and forty were particularly unlikely to be granted visas to travel to Germany or France, perhaps because of the perception that they would engage in sex work, or seek to settle abroad via marriage (sham or otherwise). This informal policy, not confirmed by the consulates but consistently reported by visa applicants, prompted potential migrants to search for alternative ways to enter the EU. During the same period Ukrainian observers of migration started noting an increase in numbers of Ukrainians traveling for work to Russia. Russia maintains a practically open border between its territory and the former republics and imposes no visa requirement. This fact has reportedly been juxtaposed in Russian propaganda with the rigid EU border policy to make a point that Russia, not the West, is a true friend to Ukraine (Ihor Markov, Yuri Andrukhovych, personal communication).

29. The 2000 UN Protocol to Prevent, Suppress and Punish Trafficking in Persons, Especially Women and Children, Supplementing the UN Convention Against Transnational Organized Crime, Article 3a, gives the following definition of trafficking: "Trafficking in persons shall mean the recruitment, transportation, harboring or receipt of persons, by means of the threat or use of force, . . . of the abuse of power or of a position of vulnerability, or of the giving or receiving of payments or benefits, to achieve the consent of a person having control over other person, for the purpose of exploitation. Exploitation shall include, at a minimum, the exploitation of the prostitution of others or other forms of sexual exploitation, forced labor or services, slavery or practices similar to slavery, servitude or the removal of organs)." On the politics of anti-trafficking discourse see Day 2010.

30. The vast majority of Ukrainians in Poland come from western Ukraine, from the *oblasti* of Lviv, Ivano-Frankivsk, Ternopil, Rivne, and Volhynska. Thus their homes are generally located within 500 kilometers of the Polish border (see Frelak 2005).

31. Claudia, October 2005, http://www.kobieta.claudia.pl. The quoted article is unfortunately no longer accessible.

32. The link between "kindness" and power in the experience of domestic workers in the colonial context is analyzed seminally by Ann L. Stoler (2002) as part of the broader genealogy of the intimate in colonial rule. Bridget Anderson connects the patronizing expressions of kindness to the legacy of slavery (2000: 144–46).

33. Such comments overlook the fact that it is not the high buying power of the money earned in Poland that will make it possible to "feed the family," but rather the highly developed skill of stretching all income as far as it can go. This notwithstanding, it is worth noting that the justifications of low pay for the work of Ukrainians are not just a sign of social acceptance of pay inequality and discrimination, but also a reproduction of the very same form of marginalization that Polish workers abroad were, and continue to experience.

34. Radio TOK FM, Popołudnie Radia Tok FM (Afternoon show), December 12, 2005.

35. An earlier trigger for similar questions was the controversy over an EU directive that eased restrictions in the service market. The directive would have made it possible to sell services throughout the EU while having a business registered only in the country of origin. The fear that this would undercut local job markets gave rise to the famous figure of the "Polish plumber," which became a symbol of "old" Europe's objections to open circulation of labor. "Polish plumber" loomed large over the debate before the French referendum in May 2005, underscoring the ambivalence in the old member states over the post-2004 wave of migrants from the East. As Favell puts it, these migrants "are making a new European space of movement and fulfilling a new idea of European citizenship; but they are also being shuffled into economic roles in the West European economies assigned in the postwar to traditional non-European immigrants" (2009: 172).

36. She got married as planned and had a daughter in 2011. She was working in Poland until nearly the end of her pregnancy but returned to give birth in Ukraine. The birth was complicated, and Lena was hospitalized for several weeks with an infection. As this manuscript is being finalized, she and her daughter are living in her small apartment, while the husband is working in Poland.

37. The new policy requires a prospective employer to register laborers in a regional Labor Office. This regularizes their status in Poland for three months. Old rules of issuing visas applied until the 2007 accession to the Schengen zone. Afterward, visas ceased to be free, and each applicant must be interviewed in person by the consul.

Chapter 4. Seeing like a Border Guard: Strategies of Surveillance

1. For an empirical study of European free movement see Favell 2008a. Elsewhere, this author argues that "In theory European free movement could be an avenue for building a very different [overcoming the nationalizing logic of nation-states] Europe. Yet, numbers of such migrants have historically been small. Still, today, less than one in fifty Europeans lives outside their country of origin, and numbers have not grown appreciably with any of the major steps toward European integration" (2009: 178). Furthermore, he asserts, based on his findings, that this kind of mobility "will remain an exclusive property of elites . . . and European spatial mobility opportunities will not lead to dramatic new social mobility or the emergence of a more widespread cosmopolitan sensibility (as the theorists dream)" (181).

2. January 1990 was the original target date when the Schengen Convention

abolishing checks on internal borders was to enter into force. However, the system collapse in Eastern Europe and governments' fear of inundation with illegal migrants from the region "prompted second thoughts about the abolition of member state controls" (Dinan 2005: 565). The anticipated "wave" did not materialize, save for the challenge presented by the estimated 600,000–800,000 refugees who fled former Yugoslavia in 1991 and after; see UNEP map, http://maps.grida.no/go/graphic/refugees-and-displaced-people-from-the-former-yugoslavia-since-1991. It took several more years until the political and technical obstacles to full implementation of the agreement were settled and the internal-border-free Schengen zone became a fact.

3. Before 1989, crossing the Poland-USSR border required an invitation. After the dissolution of the Soviet Union the old system remained in place, though mostly not enforced. The transit rules with Ukraine were even more liberal; the only requirement was showing a certain small amount of money (Iglicka 2001).

4. Before 1980 travel to the GDR was strictly controlled but possible. In 1980, in fear of Solidarity influence, Erich Honecker sealed off the GDR-Poland border, making entry the privilege of carefully screened official visitors. The visa requirement for Poles traveling to Germany was abolished in 1991 (Chessa 2004). Residents of border towns were allowed to use pedestrian crossings with minimal controls, but vehicle crossings remained burdensome. The common practice of smuggling tobacco and alcohol contributed to increased policing. The highest priority for Polish and German border guards, however, was preventing entry into Germany of migrants from the former Soviet Union and Asia, for whom Poland was a transit country (see the 2003 film *Lichter* by Hans-Christian Schmidt for a fictionalized, yet realistic depiction of the social dynamics on the Polish-German border).

5. The names of all Border Guard and other state officials who appear in this and the following two chapters have been changed.

6. William Walters noted that Schengen is among place names like Westphalia, Vienna, Versailles, Potsdam, and Maastricht that correspond to a particular historical moment in the formation of Europe as a space of territories, sovereignties, economies, and cultures. Thus, in this chapter and elsewhere in this text I use "Schengen" to refer to the practices and concepts that emerged and were developed in the original Schengen system (Walters 2002: 561).

7. In 2008 the numbers of Poles working abroad started to shrink, but there were only temporary fluctuations in the number of Ukrainians coming to Poland (Frelak and Roguska 2008; Herm 2008).

8. Similar shows air in the UK (*UK Border Patrol*) and in Australia.

9. Fassin makes a similar, if more nuanced, argument about the parallel between contemporary European refugee camps and Auschwitz and Guantanamo. Such parallels might be implied in Agamben's proposition that the model of social organization embodied by the camp is the "biopolitical paradigm of the West" (1998). However, to Fassin "mere analogy" is not historically justified. What does give ground for pursuing the comparison is the fact that camps in general "correspond to a specific response to

problems of public order by instituting small territories of exception" (2005: 379). We may add a further caveat, that it remains vital to pay attention also to the ways in which "problems of public order" get defined as "problems" in the first place.

10. Eurodac, to which Poland has been connected since 2003, gathers data on asylum seekers entering EU territory. Its purpose is to help authorities determine the country of first asylum for persons applying for refugee status. Based on the Dublin Regulation, every EU state is responsible for processing the applications lodged by those who first entered its territory. Schengen Information System (SIS) is a database of undesirable persons and objects. All third country nationals entering the EU at its external borders are checked against SIS. Additionally, a VIS database stores information on all visas issued by Schengen countries. As of this writing, the EU is developing the second generation SIS. It will be based in Strasbourg, and will facilitate integrating future new EU members into the Schengen zone.

11. Any such dating must be slightly arbitrary. I take the beginnings of modern migration regulations to be the key point (Torpey 2000). But the beginnings of the biopolitical border can be dated to much earlier times, even as far as the Byzantine Empire (Walters 2002: 571).

12. It is worth pointing out that what is new here is not the technology itself, after all "no more sophisticated than the technology of automatic banking machines" (Walters 2002). What is new is the mode of its application and the tethering of databases to such instruments as the Dublin Regulation. Above all, however, it is the fact that "the EU for the first time has undertaken to collect and coordinate personal information on a massive scale" (Snyder 2000: 222).

13. The Museum of the Berlin Wall, known as Haus am Checkpoint Charlie, in Berlin exhibits the documentation concerning some of the more spectacular escapes and commemorates the persons who were shot in attempting to make a crossing. (As of 2006, the German institution Center for Contemporary Historical Research was able to confirm 125 such deaths; see http://www.chronik-der-mauer.de/, accessed June 16, 2007.)

14. The Warsaw Pact, whose full title reads Treaty of Friendship, Cooperation and Mutual Assistance, was the Soviet response to NATO. It was signed May 1, 1955, by the governments of the People's Republic of Albania, People's Republic of Bulgaria, Hungarian People's Republic, Democratic Republic of Germany, Polish People's Republic, Romanian People's Republic, Union of Soviet Socialist Republics, and Czechoslovak Republic. It was orchestrated in response to what was described as the "remilitarization of Germany" and "integration of Western Germany in the North Atlantic bloc, which increases the threat of another war and creates a menace to the national security of the peaceloving states."

15. A person's plea to leave the country for professional reasons was in most cases an opportunity for the secret police to attempt recruiting an informer. I have discussed this in more depth elsewhere (Szmagalska-Follis 2009).

16. Apart from "official" visits, I conducted participant observation of the traffic

by repeatedly crossing the border in both directions, alone and in the company of itinerant workers and tobacco runners.

17. The tasks of the Border Guard are regulated by the Border Guard Act of October 12, 1990. Since its initial passing it has been amended several times to adjust to the demands of EU integration. The current version of the act was published in the *Official Journal of Laws* on May 11, 2007.

18. 52 million euro was the estimated cost of setting up the virtual fence along the eastern border (*Rzeczpospolita*, May 20, 2005).

19. While formally Frontex is not an EU border service, it does coordinate joint operations, and since 2007 it deploys Rapid Border Intervention Teams (RABITs), particularly in the Mediterranean and Aegean Areas. Frontex actions have been subject to criticism on the grounds that the agency's mandate is unclear and its human rights responsibilities are not clearly set out (ECRE 2007). My own experience with Frontex is one of a secretive and uncommunicative institution, offering (unsurprisingly) only the most platitudinous responses to any inquiries about its actions and plans.

20. In 2005, of the 30 million registered crossings on the external EU land border, 18 million took place on the Polish-Ukrainian stretch (Border Guard 2005). This number is so high because it includes crossings by petty traders who, as I described in Chapter 1, sometimes cross the border several times a day.

21. Enforcing customs regulations is the responsibility of the Customs Service, who search vehicles for contraband after the border guard has finished passport control. But these authorities cooperate, and when border guards determine that a car is suspicious they may also conduct a search.

22. This is not to say that docility is the only effect of this disciplinary technique; it is, however, the implicit objective of arbitrary refusals. I stay mindful of Foucault's qualification that "there are no relations of power without resistances; the latter are all the more real and effective because they are formed right at the point where relations of power are exercised" (1980: 142).

23. As I learned later, another similar device under consideration was the CO_2 detector—a machine with a sensor that measures the CO_2 level in the air inside the container to determine the presence of a living, breathing body (cf. Fassin 2005). Walters also offers an account of the operation of such detectors in the Belgian port of Zeebrugge (2006: 192).

24. I followed up a couple of months later, but the delivery was postponed. Formalities related to the schedule of spending EU money also delayed some of the other elements of the modernization. Nevertheless, the guards at local units were eager to embrace new technology. Meanwhile, in mid-2006 the European Commission announced there were obstacles to the quick implementation of the Schengen Accords on the EU eastern border. This further extended the time by which the Polish border must become fully equipped and ultimately ready for its role of the eastern flank. Finally the heartbeat detectors were purchased in 2007.

25. Cited from the section on Eurodac contained in the summary of legislation

pertaining to immigration and asylum, http://europa.eu/scadplus/leg/en/lvb/l33081.htm.

26. Dublin Regulation is shorthand for Council Regulation (EC) No. 343/2003 of February 18, 2003, establishing the criteria and mechanisms for determining the Member State responsible for examining an asylum application lodged in one of the Member States by a third country national.

27. The press releases are available through the RAPID section of the EU portal, at http://europa.eu/rapid/

Chapter 5. Economic Migrants Beyond Demand: Asylum and the Politics of Classification

1. This chapter has been adapted from an earlier essay in *Citizenship, Borders, and Human Rights*, ed. Rogers M. Smith (Philadelphia: University of Pennsylvania Press, 2011).

2. The Aliens Bureau decision can be appealed to the Council for Refugees. The Council decision is final and can be appealed only on formal grounds to the Administrative Court of the appropriate voivodship.

3. Among the legal instruments that restrict and impede access to international protection are Council Regulation (EC) No. 343/2003 of February 18, 2003, establishing criteria and mechanisms for determining the Member State responsible for examining an application lodged in a Member State by a third country national (commonly known as the Dublin Regulation); Council Directive 2004/83/EC of April 29, 2004, on minimum standards for qualification and status of third country nationals or stateless persons as refugees or persons who otherwise need international protection and the content of the protection granted; Council Directive 2005/85/EC of December 1, 2005, on minimum standards on procedures in Member States for granting and withdrawing refugee status.

4. For a general overview of the right to seek asylum in the EU, see Da Lomba 2004. For a detailed discussion of the new politics of compassion toward refugees in France see Fassin 2005 and Ticktin 2006.

5. Approximately 600 Bosnians applied for refugee status in 1992; it was granted in 75 cases (interview at UNHCR Warsaw, April 2005). Incidentally, just as Poland and other Eastern European countries for the first time in their post-1989 history experienced playing host to the displaced, in Western Europe the influx of the victims of the Yugoslav conflict was the trigger of the strong anti-refugee sentiment that since then has only intensified.

6. *Goniec Lubelski*, August 2, 2006.

7. As this manuscript is being finalized, a new parliamentary campaign is getting underway, ahead of the October 2011 election. The Polish political scene experienced a massive shock as a result of the crash of the presidential plane near Smolensk, Russia, in April 2010, which killed president Lech Kaczyński and 95 other people, many of them politicians. In the aftermath, politics became more polarized than ever before, with the crash itself the key divisive issue. The right-wing opposition party Law and Justice draws

voters who believe the crash was the effect of a conspiracy against the staunchly patri-
otic president; the center-right governing Civic Platform and the shrinking left have
documented that it was a tragic accident. This conflict between two right-wing parties
is intensely personal, a fierce animosity between the opposition leader, twin brother of
the deceased president, Jarosław Kaczyński, and prime minister Donald Tusk, and has
largely displaced ideological disputes between electoral rivals. Immigration again does
not seem to come up in the campaign. However, a pragmatic abolition bill, offering legalization to some, but not all, migrants illegally resident in Poland, is due to come into
force in 2012 (Chap. 3 n 26).

8. This thought was expressed by Janusz Grzyb: "We don't want to repeat the mistakes that the French committed with the Arabs and the Germans committed with the
Turks. These immigrants do not adapt well to life in their new countries," *Dziennik*, July
25, 2007. I encountered similar sentiments expressed by high-ranking officials at the
Border Guard and Aliens Bureau.

9. This leaves no room for the kind of ambiguity that usually characterizes migrations precipitated by war or political instability. Indeed, it may be the case that not all
persons fleeing Chechnya and other post-Soviet republics are victims of *direct, individual* persecution. Many are seeking to escape generalized hardship, destruction, and
insecurity created by the two Chechen wars. Some, especially those who take advantage
of legal aid provided by human rights organizations, based on that fact are able to obtain
"tolerated status" and thus avoid deportation.

10. An innovation stipulated in Council Directive 2005/85/EC of December 1, 2005,
on minimum standards and procedures in Member States for granting and withdrawing
refugee status.

11. Especially in the years preceding accession, the eastern border issue was receiving a lot of attention, notably in Germany. On March 1, 2000, the *Deutsche Presse Agen-
tur* ran a headline, "Hundreds of thousands of foreigners are poised outside Poland's
eastern border waiting to enter illegally on their way to the western Europe." These fears
resurfaced in 2007, as the final checks on the new members' western borders were being
abolished.

12. In practice this approach creates a situation in which often neither the genuinely
persecuted nor the economically desperate succeed in entering Europe. This becomes
apparent particularly when analyzing the Mediterranean transit route, where thousands
of migrants and refugees travel by sea from the Middle East to Italy. Based on the agreements between Silvio Berlusconi, the Italian prime minister, and Muammar Gaddafi,
the Libyan leader, in 2008, joint Libyan and Italian patrols began patrolling Libyan territorial waters and summarily returning boat migrants to Libya. Human Rights Watch
published a report on the Libyan-Italian mistreatment of migrants (2009). According
to the report, irregular boat migrants to Sicily including Lampedusa and Sardinia fell
by 55 percent in the first six months of 2009 compared to the same period the previous
year (24), giving Berlusconi the opportunity to brag that the arrangement is "working."

13. Bunyan points out also that the summit was an instance of highly undemocratic

decision making, where the manner of debate excluded civil society and national parliaments from the opaque process of vetting security priorities. He quotes a remark by British Interior Minister Jack Straw that "whenever two or three Interior Ministers are gathered together, they tend to talk about nothing else than asylum and migration" (1999: 3).

14. Based on the Dublin Regulation, there are several criteria for determining responsibility: where the first application was lodged, where the applicant first entered the EU, which country gave him or her a visa, and/or where he or she has legally residing relatives.

15. To this end, the EU Council adopted two key directives for harmonization of national laws. (1) Council Directive 2004/83/EC of April 29, 2004, on minimum standards for the qualification and status of third country nationals or stateless persons as refugees or as persons who otherwise need international protection and the content of the protection granted; (2) Council Directive 2005/85/EC of December 1, 2005, on minimum standards on procedures in Member States for granting and withdrawing refugee status.

16. Dublin has been the subject of sustained criticism by immigrant rights activists, who emphasize that when the opportunity to apply for protection is limited to the country of first arrival, asylum seekers who happen to arrive first in countries with underresourced and poorly functioning systems are at a disadvantage and will likely sink into the limbo of unregulated status. Critical discussions of Dublin can be found, for example, in the archives of Statewatch (http://www.statewatch.org) and in Migreurop 2009, a report focusing on southern European borders, containing particularly alarming findings about Greece. A theoretically oriented critique is offered by Walters (2010), who places Dublin in his genealogy of deportation as a political and historical practice, a disciplinary tactic and an instrument of population control.

17. A summary of the relevant acts which exemplify this trend is available at http://www.europa.eu/scadplus/leg/en/s17000.htm#ASILE, accessed July 3, 2007.

18. I am not disputing that there are clearly instances where refugees want to and can return to their homeland. But in many situations the period of displacement is very long and withdrawal of protection amounts to a personal crisis for the refugee, a fact ignored by policy and allocation of resources geared toward eventual return. Cf. The Green Paper on a Community Return Policy, Hague Programme.

19. One notable step in promoting returns is the Voluntary Assisted Returns program operated by European governments in close collaboration with the International Organization for Migration (IOM). The program allows persons no longer eligible for temporary protection to return "voluntarily" to their home countries, avoiding forcible repatriation. In return for choosing voluntary return they are granted small stipends for relocation and reintegration.

20. 1951 Convention Relating to the Status of Refugees (Art. 1, par. 2).

21. Data provided by the Aliens Bureau, on file with author. In 2009, however, the Bureau received 8,138 applications in January 1–October 1, in comparison to 8,517 over all 2008.

22. Legal assistance is available to asylum claimants through pro bono organizations, for example Caritas, the Helsinki Foundation for Human Rights, or the Halina Nieć Human Rights Association (these organizations have the status of UNHCR implementing partners). According to the UNHCR representative I spoke to, developing a system of legal aid for refugees ought to be a key task for Polish authorities.

23. Safe country of origin is the alien's country of origin where, due to the legal system and its application as well as due to political relations, there is no persecution due to race, religion, nationality, belonging to a particular social group, or political beliefs, and where nongovernmental and international organizations are able to conduct activities for observance of human rights. Safe third country is a country not the alien's country of origin which ratified and applies the Geneva Convention and New York Protocol; points (a)–(f) list additional stipulations such as availability of asylum procedures, availability of human rights NGOs, *non-refoulement*, and ban on torture and inhuman or degrading treatment, Art. 2, para. 2 & 3, Act on Granting Protection to Aliens, Official Journal of Laws 128, position 1176.

24. See note 4. On the specific case of Chechens, the humanitarian organization Refugees International did report in early 2005 that there are "some cases" when asylum seekers fleeing the Chechen conflict were returned from the border, http://www.refugees international.org/content/article/detail/7442/, accessed 7/18/2007.

25. This changed markedly in 2009, when in the first ten months nearly 45 percent of the applicants were Georgian citizens (in comparison to 8 percent in 2008).

26. The sources of the highly specific data on which the office relies to perform its tasks include information sent by embassies, databases with access restricted to state personnel, publications of the governmental Center for Eastern Studies, news from press agencies, local libraries, and EU-sponsored conferences and trainings on situation in countries of origin.

27. Anthropologists, trauma scholars, and other social scientists who have studied asylum systems empirically would dispute this claim. For example, in *Rejecting Refugees* Carol Bohmer and Amy Shuman offer several examples drawn from legal practice of applicants having tremendous trouble conveying their experiences to asylum officials in a manner that conforms to their expectations. They argue that establishing the credibility of asylum applicants is rife with cultural, linguistic, and psychological problems which are exacerbated by the strictures of bureaucracy, case overload, and pressures on case workers to recognize ever fewer people as refugees (2008; see also Malkki 2007; Fassin and d'Halluin 2007).

28. I am grateful to Professor Michael Katz, who commented on an earlier version of this chapter, for his observation that drawing distinctions between those entitled and not entitled to a benefit is a fundamental act of public policy that has a long history of relying on "scientific" methods only ultimately to produce discriminatory results. See Katz 1996 [1986]: 60–88.

29. As Fassin observed in his analysis of the values and norms by which immigration and asylum are thought of and acted on in France, the political treatment of aliens

"oscillates between sentiments of sympathy on the one hand and concern for order on the other hand, between a politics of pity and policies of control" (2005: 366).

30. Inaction about immigration persisted through the period of the nominally left-wing but actually neoliberal government that ushered Poland into the EU and the subsequent conservative rule of the Kaczyński twins. Immigration was not a polarizing factor between them. Both governments worried that an open welcoming of immigrants would have been unpopular, due to the fact that Poland's economic growth did not translate into improved economic conditions for vast sectors of the population. The perception of Polish society as generally impoverished and in need of protectionist policies made inaction the safe way to go throughout the first decade of the twenty-first century.

31. Until 2007 legalizing an employee for low-skilled work was obstructed by bureaucratic constraints and prohibitive cost. Since mid-2008, Ukrainians can be legally hired in Poland for vacancies that fail to attract Polish employees. The period of employment cannot exceed 6 months in any calendar year, in two nonconsecutive intervals (three months at work, three at home, three months at work, three at home). Given these restrictions, few employees and migrants go through the effort of obtaining a permit.

32. The development to watch in this regard is the new immigrant abolition in Poland due to enter into force in 2012. It extends the opportunity to acquire legal status to some failed asylum seekers, notably those who do not pose a threat to public order and security, and who fulfill a continuous residency requirement since 2007, although certain specific procedural conditions must be met. See also note 7 and Chap. 3 n 26.

33. Even though the Border Guard boasts—in the words of one unit commander—"nearly 100 percent efficiency in catching illegals," there are of course ways to sneak in successfully. Smuggling immigrants is a developing business, and every now and again the press reveals cases of collusion of corrupt guards with the smugglers. A report focusing on the Vietnamese in Poland prepared at the Warsaw University (Międzykulturowe Centrum Adaptacji Zawodowej 2008) estimates that 15,000–25,000 illegal immigrants from Vietnam live in the country. The majority are thought to have entered with the help of smugglers.

34. Similar arguments for compassion for immigrants based on the national experience of emigration are often deployed in Ireland. However, in the first decade of the twenty-first century immigration-weary populists there registered an important victory in the form of the notorious Irish referendum of 2004 which removed jus soli constitutional rights to citizenship from Irish-born children of immigrants. Ultimately, Irish political parties share institutional inability to engage with immigrant constituencies (Fanning and Mutwarasibo 2007), a situation comparable to that in Poland.

35. Cited in *Dziennik*, July 25, 2007.

36. Tolerated status is subject to annual review and can be withdrawn if the reason for granting it has ceased; the alien voluntarily requested protection from authorities of the country of origin; the alien has permanently left the territory of the Polish Republic; the continuation of tolerated status could cause a serious threat to the security of state or

public safety and order (Act on Granting Protection to Aliens, Art. 102, Official Journal of Laws no. 128, position 1176).

37. Others like him deploy different tactics to dodge deportation and remain beyond the gaze of the state, within EU boundaries yet hidden from view. *Harragas*, the Arabic name for North African migrants who attempt to immigrate into Europe in makeshift boats, comes from the verb *haraqa*, "to burn," and refers to burning documents to preempt identification and forestall deportation (Kapllani 2010: 39).

38. For comparison see Castañeda 2010 on the institution of the *Duldung* in Germany.

Chapter 6. Capacity Building and Other Technicalities: Ukraine as a Border Zone

1. See also http://www.statewatch.org/news/2003/jun/07eubuffer.htm.

2. A significant new development in this field took place in 2008, when Italy signed a friendship treaty with Libya. Based on the treaty, persons intercepted when attempting to enter Italy by sea are now handed over without screening to Libyan authorities. The Eurodac database has shown that the number of those caught trying to enter Italy illegally fell from 32,052 in 2008 to 7,300 in 2009. The practice of turning immigrants and asylum seekers back without screening has drawn severe criticism from Human Rights Watch, Amnesty International, and other organizations. See http://www.hrw .org/en/news/2009/09/17/italylibya-migrants-describe-forced-returns-abuse, accessed June 8, 2010.

3. The concept is formalized in a Council Directive on minimum standards on procedures in member states for granting and withdrawing refugee status, Council of the European Union, Brussels, November 17, 2005, arts. 27, 30.

4. This number was 3,278 in 2005, 2,751 in 2006, 1,914 in 2007, and 3,448 in 2008, according to statistics made available by the Polish Border Guard. The tables made available, however, do not break down the numbers by citizenship. The proportion of Ukrainian citizens in the total number of the readmitted is cited from HRW 2005: 15. It is important to note that initially, in the 1980s and early 1990s, readmission agreements covered only reciprocal return of citizens of contracting states. The Polish-Ukrainian readmission agreement is "second generation," in that it covers also third-country nationals.

5. In principle asylum seekers should only be returned to the next "safe country" if they have been determined to have a legal right to be there (a visa or passport stamp showing they were admitted). In practice these guarantees are not always observed. Svetlana Marintseva and Natalya Dulnyeva of the organization Human Rights Have No Borders, based in Lviv, told me about persons who have been sent back to Ukraine with no consideration for their asylum request in Poland. The lawyer I spoke to at the Warsaw-based Helsinki Foundation for Human Rights attributed such cases to Border Guard reluctance to accept asylum claims in the first place. However, at the time of our conversation in summer 2005, she described the situation as "much improved." Human Rights Watch also cites such cases (2005: 15), as does Uehling (2004).

6. Out of respect for the anonymity arrangements made with those granting me access to these research sites, I have changed most of the identifying names in this chapter. Regardless of the names they go by, however, these places exist and are important primarily as sites of the very real experiences of those who dwell in them.

7. The Agreement was signed in October 2006 at the EU-Ukraine summit in Helsinki.

8. During our visit we were told that about 30 percent of the 130 detainees were seeking asylum (had an active claim being processed by Ukrainian authorities). An average of 1,000–1,400 people apply for asylum in Ukraine each year. The recognition rate is 4 percent (HRW 2005: 31).

9. EU-wide statistics are available starting in 2009 (Eurostat 2009). For 2004, see Chalmers 2006: 648.

10. "The spaces of non-existence occupied by the undocumented derive from the conflation of and disjuncture between physical and legal presence. Physical and legal presence are conflated in that citizens are presumed to be located within particular national territories, physical presence confers certain legal rights, and periods of continuous residence are often perquisites for legalization and naturalization. A disjuncture between physical and legal presence arises when individuals cross or remain within borders without legal authorization" (Coutin 2003: 29).

11. Voluntary repatriation is a form of repatriation that is increasingly adopted by EU governments. The undesirable immigrants are offered incentives and assistance (free ticket, a small amount of money) to return home, ostensibly of their own volition. In Poland, as in many other European countries, the Border Guard has an agreement with the International Organization for Migration to execute Assisted Voluntary Returns. For more information see http://www.iom.int/jahia/Jahia/activities/by-theme/regulating-migration

12. Later, the retired Ukrainian Border Service officer who now consults for the Kyiv think tank and who eventually authorized my visit to Vysoky Horod told me informally that the Ministry officials were puzzled by my request, saw no reason why a Pole from a U.S. university should be interested in Ukraine's internal security affairs, and rejected me, as he said, "just in case."

13. This is not to disregard the fact that Poland has a history of cohabitation of ethnic, religious, and linguistic minorities, as well as a record of persecution of those minorities, especially in the 1930s, as the next chapter discusses. This is why my comment pertains specifically to "modern racial and cultural difference," that is, the result of contemporary migrations, as opposed to cultural diversity as a general phenomenon. The often problematic memory and the curious afterlives of Polish interwar diversity, especially with regard to Polish Jewish and Polish Ukrainian relations, are mostly outside the scope of this study (for discussion of some aspects of these memories see Chapters 1 and 7). Therefore, although the genealogy of contemporary Polish integralism undoubtedly can be traced to the interwar anti-Semitic national-Catholic right, I shall not speculate if and to what extent today's low awareness of immigrant issues as

well as the racism and discrimination that immigrants experience is sui generis or a product of that history. For a related discussion of cultural differences in postsocialist Latvia see Dzenovska 2010.

14. There are a number of NGOs that provide much-needed assistance to immigrants, mostly free legal counseling, interpretation services and language courses, limited material assistance (distribution of donated goods), as well as play and study groups for refugee and asylum-seeker children. There have also been a number of ad hoc initiatives that emerged in response to cases that gained media exposure. For example, in 2008 Polish media reported extensively on Svetlana Jakovleva, a single mother, cancer patient, and Ukrainian immigrant who has lived illegally in Poland for fourteen years, ineligible for treatment under the Polish public health care system and with poor chances of survival. Jakovleva's four children, born and raised in Poland, would be deported to Ukraine and placed in institutional care on her passing. Reports on her situation elicited a massive outpouring of compassion. Proksenos, the foundation established with the purpose of helping Svetlana, collected 350,000 PLN (nearly U.S.$120,000) in donations; President Kaczyński granted the children Polish citizenship; an adoptive family was found (Frontczak 2009). Proksenos subsequently defined its mission as assistance to foreigners in Poland who find themselves in similarly desperate situations. This form of help aimed at identifiable individuals, while very much needed, is also a symptomatically apolitical way of responding to the problems of (particular) immigrants. It does not address the collective plight of immigrants, does not respond to systemic issues, or criticize the Polish/EU border regime.

15. I did not invent this metaphor. I've heard it used by employees of American aid agencies in Ukraine. When a particular developmental assistance program ends and a final report is submitted, the country, region, or industry in question is said to have "graduated."

16. Unless otherwise noted, citations in this section are from unpublished materials circulated among training participants (on file with the author).

17. The global expansion of detention infrastructure is monitored by the Global Detention Project at the Graduate Institute in Geneva, http://www.globaldetentionproject .org/.

18. See also the grassroots anti-IOM action of No Border, http://www.noborder.org/ iom/index.php, accessed July 17, 2007.

19. Smaller detention facilities are located in Mostyska near the Polish border and in the vicinity of Kyiv. Two other centers were in the planning stages at the time of my research; the IOM was the government's partner in their construction. According to Svetlana Marintseva, an Amnesty International human rights advocate in Lviv, in many places in Ukraine asylum seekers and persons deemed to be "illegal immigrants" are held in regular jails.

20. This is a curious example of the underdefined nature of EU sovereignty. In terms of striking readmission agreements, the EU acts like a state, arranging to remove people from the territory of the whole Union. This capability has been in force since the Treaty

of Amsterdam. As previously discussed, this not the case with other aspects of regulating migration, notably policies toward economic migrants.

21. The military genealogy of the Border Guard remains a source of pride for many functionaries I spoke to, who liked to emphasize the army-like discipline that positively distinguishes their ranks from other uniformed services.

22. Once, during a visit to the headquarters of the Border Guard, I overheard a phone conversation in which a German NGO was refused access to a deportation arrest. When I inquired about the reasons for the refusal, my informant declined to discuss them. Some time afterward, I mentioned the incident to a Polish associate of the UNHCR. He explained, insisting he was speaking off-record, that such refusals are issued because in the past "some organizations" published false reports accusing Polish border services of *refoulement* and other illegal practices. Therefore, "after such experiences it isn't surprising that the Border Guard refuses access to organizations whose only purpose is to criticize." My UNHCR informant offered this interpretation: "German organizations suffer, from this, let's call it, identity crisis. We are talking here about extreme left groups, whose purpose is to undermine the entire system of protection from illegal immigration developed by the EU. They are not interested in constructive criticism, but in spreading disorder (*sianie zamętu*) and accusations, and delegitimizing solutions worked out by the international community. These actions belong to the sphere of politics, and not assistance to the needy."

23. Of course, it is precisely in all the "Rzeszowskies" of Poland that historically sedimented forms of prejudice are most entrenched. But this is not a problem that can be solved through "capacity building."

24. Providing legal assistance to refugees and immigrants is not a professionalized domain. Most NGO legal counselors whom I met in Poland and Ukraine were law students. Some of them felt passionate about refugee issues; others considered this work to be an opportunity to build a résumé and acquire experience. Either way, there appeared to be little continuity in the staffing of such organizations and too few volunteers to reach out to all asylum seekers in need.

25. In fact Ukrainian law also has a provision for temporary protection (political asylum, *politychny prytulok*, as opposed to refugee status, *status bizhentsa*).

26. A UNHCR report of 2004 NGO monitoring of detention facilities pointed out that there are instances when administrators obtain court orders to extend detention that lack an adequate justification, http://www.unhcr.pl/publikacje/zobcejziemi/nr21/raport.php, accessed February 23, 2006.

27. According to the IOM, the gross figure of remittances for 2008 was U.S.$5,769,000, http://www.iom.int/jahia/Jahia/activities/europe/eastern-europe/ukraine/cache/offonce/, accessed March 7, 2010.

28. Eurosoyuz, the Ukrainian word, echoes Radiansky Soyuz, the term for Soviet Union. This occasionally leads to slips of tongue and provokes jokes that play on the notion that the EU, like the USSR, is a hegemonic power.

29. The inspector did not reveal exact numbers, but a 2004 Helsinki Foundation

report states that of the 279 detainees held in the center between September 2003 and January 2004 there were 50 Russian citizens. The practice of listing them this way makes it impossible to say how many were Chechen. It is likely that most were, but some could be Ingush or Dagestani.

30. For example, the Green Paper on the Future of Common European Asylum System (COM (207) 301) calls for developing systems for the dissemination of best practices in handling asylum cases; the Council and Commission Action Plan implementing the Hague Programme on Strengthening Freedom, Security and Justice in the European Union (Council ref. 9778/2/05) calls for professional workshops with a view toward establishing best practices in realms such as the legal professions, customs administration, and law enforcement cooperation; the Proposal for a Regulation of the European Parliament and of the Council establishing a European Asylum Support Office (COM/2009/0066) calls for establishment of a central body that would serve as a best practices hub in the realm of asylum.

31. http://europa.eu/abc/eurojargon/index_en.htm, accessed August 30, 2010.

32. More details of the agreements are available at http://europa.eu/rapid/press ReleasesAction.do?reference=IP/07/849&format=HTML&ag, accessed September 30, 2008.

33. See http://ec.europa.eu/commission_barroso/frattini/media/default_en.htm, accessed September 30, 2008.

34. In Chapter III, Qualification for Being a Refugee, persecution is qualified as (a) sufficiently serious by nature or repetition as to constitute a severe violation of basic human rights, in particular the rights from which derogation cannot be made under Art.15(2) of the European Convention for the Protection of Human Rights and Fundamental Freedoms; or (b) an accumulation of various measures, including violations of human rights, which is sufficiently severe as to affect an individual in a similar manner as mentioned in (a). 2004/83/EC, http://eur-lex.europa.eu/LexUriServ/LexUriServ .do?uri=CELEX: 32004L0083: EN: HTML, accessed July 2, 2007.

35. The work of Miriam Ticktin (2006) and Didier Fassin (2001, 2005) bears witness to the emergence of a new biopolitics where severe illness gives rise to a new expression of compassion for asylum seekers, yet, setting aside for the moment the broader implication, it remains to be seen to what extent this humanitarianization of asylum will become the European norm. So far the common standards advanced in the EU directives suggest otherwise.

Chapter 7. The Border as Intertext: Memory, Belonging, and the Search for a New Narrative

Epigraph: "The Borders of Europe—Seen from the Outside" (2005).

1. These questions were always particularly acute in Ukraine, with the border inscribed in the very name of the country. "Ukraine," as most authors writing about the country note, means "borderland" (Reid 2000; Subtelny 1988; Wanner 1998). But there

is another way to translate it. The term derives from the verb "kraïty," "to cut." It literally means "a piece that is cut." Depending on one's location, outside or inside that piece that has been "cut," one can refer to it respectively as "a borderland" or "a land." This ambivalence is illustrative of the equivocal nature of Ukrainian national identity. I am grateful to Yaroslav Hrytsak for pointing out this notable ambiguity.

2. The Polish case is illustrative. Poland's emissaries to Versailles insisted on the territories that were the object of struggles discussed above and rejected the demarcation line on the San and Bug Rivers proposed by British foreign minister Lord Curzon. Hobsbawm notes that the Allies made "reluctant concessions to the expansionism . . . of Poland," but it is hard not to notice that these concessions precisely contradicted the Wilsonian "principle of nationality" (Hobsbawm 1990: 132).

3. The Polish Minority Treaty, known as *Mały Traktat Wersalski* (The Little Treaty of Versailles), was signed on June 28, 1919, by the United States, Britain, France, Italy, Japan (the Principal Allied and Associated Powers), and Poland. Since it was established before the Riga Treaty which closed the contentious question of Poland's eastern border (the western border was determined at the Paris peace conference), it did not take into account the full extent of ethnic heterogeneity in interwar Poland. It did not list Ukrainians as an eligible minority, which reflects the view that they were not seen as a legitimate national group. The groups listed were Germans, Russians, Hungarians and Austrians, in recognition of the fact that they inhabited the territories of Central European empires incorporated into Poland after World War I. The text of the Treaty is available on the website of the Hungarian Institute in Munich, at http://www.forost.ungarisches-institut .de/pdf/19190628-3.pdf accessed on June 16, 2011.

4. It remains a telling fact and a sad testimony to the vitality of anachronistic-seeming forms of nationalism, that when the phrase "1919 Minorities Treaties" is entered in Polish into Google, the entire first page of records consists of links to various right-wing websites, blogs, and publications that deplore the Versailles order and the "imposition of the detrimental Minorities Treaties" which "allowed foreign powers to meddle in Polish affairs," and granted "unwarranted rights" to "so-called minorities" (Google search, May 16, 2007).

5. In 1999 Czesław Miłosz published in Poland a book entitled *Wyprawa w Dwudziestolecie* (A Journey into the Interwar Period). It contains a vast collection of press clippings and public communiqués which document the highly discriminatory discourse around minorities in the 1920s and 1930s. Miłosz's commentary provided context and argued for a deromanticization of the twenty years of Polish independence between the wars (Miłosz 1999).

6. As Wilson points out, "To the main ideologist of the new [Ukrainian] identity, Dmytro Dontsov (1883–1973), Poland was Ukraine's oppressor, but Russia was its existential antithesis, just as it was that of Europe as a whole" (Wilson 2000: 129). A permanent exhibition at the Historical Museum in Lviv tells the story of the Polish efforts to eradicate education in the Ukrainian language, presents anti-Ukrainian propaganda, and documents the harassment and imprisonment of activists of the national movement.

I went to see the exhibition on the strong recommendation of a local journalist, who praised its truthfulness, but whose sentiments were otherwise far from national martyrology and who had many admiring things to say about the "Polish neighbor."

7. Nevertheless the stereotype of Ukrainians as Nazi collaborators stuck. In *A Biography of No Place* Kate Brown passionately argues against such blanket accusations, at the same time offering a nuanced explanation of the politics of OUN in the context of the Nazi occupation (Brown 2004: 212–19). On collaboration with the Nazis more generally see Snyder (2010: 395–96).

8. Despite that, Motyka objects to labeling the killings an act of genocide, which makes him the enemy in the circles of the "national-Kresy" historians.

9. Incidentally, Andrew Wilson, a (presumably impartial) British historian, does not mention the killings at all. He concludes his section on OUN-UPA by saying, "The complicated history of the OUN-UPA is not well remembered. The fact that the OUN and UPA were able to fight at all is what is now celebrated in Western Ukraine. The Soviet propaganda caricature of the movement before 1943—its initial reliance on the invading Germans and the claim that opponents in the Red Army were largely kith and kin—prevails elsewhere. There is no more divisive symbol in modern Ukraine" (Wilson 2000: 133–34).

10. "By the end of 1947 some 7.6 million Germans had left Poland, roughly half of them as refugees fleeing the Red Army, roughly half as deportees" (Snyder 2010: 323).

11. It is important to note that the ways in which Germans were classified at the time were very different from those common today. For example, Polish propaganda of the time made no distinction between "Germans" (Niemcy) and "Nazis" (called *hitlerowcy* at the time). The two categories were interchangeable, to the extent that some writers insisted on flaunting the rule of capitalizing names of nationalities and writing Niemcy in lower case. Only due to the GDR's status as a friendly state in the Soviet orbit, distinctions were made between "good" socialist Germans and "bad" bourgeois ones. Sixty years later, the complex politics of resentment and reprisal continues to haunt Polish-German relations and, by extension, internal EU politics.

12. Professional Polish and Ukrainian historians agree that the number killed during Akcja Wisła oscillated around one thousand people, including partisans killed in action, persons convicted by martial courts, and those who died in the concentration camp in Jaworzno. Approximately four thousand Ukrainians were imprisoned there (Hrytsak 2000; Motyka 1998).

13. Official Ukrainian census data from 2002 state that Poles make up 0.3 percent of Ukraine's total population: ca. 148,000 people, of whom 20,000–30,000 live in the borderland (depending on which districts are counted as part of it). Polish consular authorities question these data. According to an official I spoke to in Lviv, the total number might be as high as 1.3 million. The causes of the discrepancy are manifold: being of Polish ancestry was a cause of discrimination in the Soviet Union; legacies of Polish-Ukrainian enmity account for the fact that, especially in the borderland, people are reluctant to admit their minority status; many of those the consulate considers ethnically

"Polish" no longer speak the Polish language and identify with neither prewar nor contemporary Poland (data made available by Polish Consulate in Lviv, on file with author).

14. This is according to the Stalinist principle which categorized Soviet-dominated peoples as "national in form, socialist in content." Relative freedom of practicing such elements of cultural identity as folklore and language was the "national form" which did not challenge or alter the socialist content (Verdery 1996: 83–103).

15. See also Holmes 2009 for a discussion of recent Wilsonian scholarship and the deeper genealogies and wider resonances of Versailles.

16. Some of the troubling questions concerning "the right to have rights" of human beings who have lost the protection of a legal sovereign body have been (partially) addressed since the end of World War II through the previously discussed 1951 Geneva Convention Relating to the Status of Refugees and the New York Protocol of 1957, and the creation of the United Nations High Commissioner on Refugees (UNHCR) and the International Criminal Court. As Seyla Benhabib shows, "the right to have rights today means the recognition of the universal status of personhood of each and every human being independently of their national citizenship" (2004: 68). The challenge ahead, she states, is "developing an international regime which decouples the right to have rights from one's nationality status" (68).

17. One example of such events was the 2003 ceremony to commemorate the sixtieth anniversary of the Volhynia killings in the village of Pavlivka, where presidents Leonid Kuchma and Aleksander Kwaśniewski together unveiled a victims' memorial. The inscription was criticized for leaving out details about the perpetrators and the time of the killings. Another important ceremony, which I attended in June 2005, was the reopening of the cemetery of the Polish soldiers and civilians who perished in the Polish-Ukrainian conflict over Lviv in 1918–1919. The necropolis, known as Cmentarz Orląt Lwowskich (Cemetery of the Lviv Eaglets), after decades of devastation and years of conflict between Polish officials and Lviv municipal authorities over commemorative signage, was reopened with the participation of presidents Yushchenko and Kwaśniewski, and was hailed as a momentous event for Polish-Ukrainian reconciliation.

18. The key exponents of such views are organizations of the resettled former inhabitants of Kresy, such as the Society for Volhynia and Polissia, whose educational activities are discussed further in this chapter. A prominent outlet for such views is http://www.kresy.pl, which also features right-wing opinion pieces on other issues.

19. There is also the question of German influence in this part of Europe, taken up in the context of debates around the concept of Mitteleuropa (Rupnik 1990).

20. The poem was originally written in Ukrainian, but in the Roman alphabet rather than the Cyrillic. Translated by Virlana Tkacz and Wanda Phipps, the poem in its entirety, together with other work by Bondar, is available at http://ukraine.poetry internationalweb.org/piw_cms/cms/cms_module/index.php?obj_id=5552, accessed October 5, 2010.

21. Michel-Rolph Trouillot, in his essay on anthropology of the state (2001), describes how in January 1999 Amartya Sen, on his way to a conference in Davos, was

stopped at the Zurich airport for entering Switzerland without a visa. Sen uses his Indian passport, and "the Swiss were worried that he would become dependent on the state, as Indians are likely to be." The visa apparently was delivered to the airport by the conference organizers, and Sen gave his talk, but Trouillot juxtaposes the economics Nobel Laureate's experience with that of unprivileged "aliens" who are routinely refused entry to or expelled from western countries such as Germany, France, and the U.S. "Behind the banality of these millions of encounters between individuals or groups and governments we discover the depth of governmental presence in our lives, regardless of the regimes and the particulars of the social formation" (Trouillot 2001: 125).

22. In *The Native Realm* he confesses, "My allergy to everything that smacks of the 'national' and an almost physical disgust for people who transmit such signals have weighed heavily upon my destiny." That was the case in life, and we might add in death as well. After Miłosz died in 2004, local right-wing activists mounted a protest against burying him at the Skałka monastery in Kraków, a national pantheon reserved for the most prominent dead. The argument was that Miłosz's patriotism was dubious (in an extreme version, that he was not Polish at all) and thus not worthy of the national shrine.

23. Marta Kempny has analyzed a comparable situation among Polish migrants in Belfast, and she examined the role of religion in shaping ethnic identity more generally (Kempny 2010).

24. The important names here are Jerzy Giedroyć (1906–2000), Juliusz Mieroszewski (1906–1976), and Bohdan Osadchuk (1920–2011). All of them were exiled in the postwar period and published in the *Kultura* edited by Giedroyć in Paris. These authors, unequivocally anti-Communist and committed to a continental order based on cooperation of sovereign nation-states, argued that both Poland's and Ukraine's precarious geopolitical positions makes it necessary for the two nations to foster close ties. With Russia as a neighbor and—as they believed—a perennial threat, Polish-Ukrainian conflicts would only facilitate imperial incursions on their territories and allow for a more efficient application of the old tsarist principle of *divide et impera* (Giedroyć 2005). *Kultura* was a major venue for independent Polish and Central European political thought during the Cold War. It was published from 1947 until Giedroyć's death in 2000. Until 1989 it was being smuggled into Poland and distributed among the politically conscious intelligentsia, and circulated among Polish émigrés abroad. For an English-language selection of essays from the journal see Kostrzewa 1990.

25. The Orange Revolution itself began with a wave of mass demonstrations in Kyiv and other cities organized in response to the rigged presidential elections in November 2004. The protests, which united people of three generations and of divergent political views, resulted in a second vote in late December, and ultimately in the victory of opposition candidate Viktor Yushchenko. Yushchenko ran on an unambiguously pro-Western and reformist platform. His opponent, Viktor Yanukhovych, was supported by unpopular incumbent Leonid Kuchma, by the industrial magnates and their constituents from the southeast of Ukraine, and, rather openly, by Russian president Vladimir Putin. Many Western observers saw the weeks-long standoff and popular protests as a

belated coda to the peaceful democratic transitions in Eastern Europe in 1989. The Revolution was scrupulously covered by U.S. and Western European media, but nowhere did it incite as much interest, popular excitement, and political support as it did in Poland. For a detailed account of the events of late 2004 and early 2005 in Ukraine, including the involvement of industrial magnates and foreign consultants, see Wilson 2005.

26. Even political arch-enemies, such as former Solidarity leader Lech Wałęsa and serving president Aleksander Kwaśniewski, struck a truce in the name of the Orange cause. They both made trips to Kyiv to facilitate negotiations between the feuding sides. Achieving a peaceful resolution was not easy. In Ukraine the political split between the pro-Yanukhovych East and Yushchenko's West was pronounced even at the height of the Orange Revolution, despite efforts, ongoing since independence in 1991, to forge a platform that would unify all Ukrainians under one national banner (Riabchuk 2004).

27. The op-ed protesting the exhibition was published on March 30, 2005. http://info.wiadomosci.gazeta.pl/szukaj/wiadomosci/tonące (the link is no longer active).

28. Kwaśniewski, besides his role as a mediator during the Orange Revolution, was generally involved in dialogue with Ukrainian authorities concerning historical animosities and participated in several high-profile events intended as a display of official "Polish-Ukrainian reconciliation." One was the dedication of a monument to the fighters of the Ukrainian national movement in Jaworzno in eastern Poland, in recognition of their martyrdom at the site of the concentration camp for Ukrainian minority activists in the interwar period. Referring to *Gazeta Wyborcza*, the largest Polish daily with a decidedly liberal profile, as "Jews" is a mainstay of casual anti-Semitism.

29. After the parliamentary and presidential elections in Poland in late 2005 and parliamentary elections in Ukraine in early 2006 the rhetoric of friendship, alliance, and cooperation receded. As politics in Poland were dominated by local integralists (Holmes 2000), and Ukraine's own political situation grew ever more uncertain in 2006 and 2007, fostering a neighborly bond appeared to slip off the agenda on both sides.

30. The Lviv based journal *Ji* is a particularly well-known forum for Central European debates; see http://www.ji-magazine.lviv.ua. See also Riabchuk 2004; Hnatiuk 2003.

31. See the website of Archipelag Pogranicza (Borderland Archipelago), http://pogranicze.sejny.pl/?lang=en, for a remarkable example of a creative community engaging with the past and future of the borderland through visual arts, theater, literature, and the cultivation of ideas, by its own publishing house as well as lectures, conferences, and other public events. The Borderland Archipelago is an important institution regionally, in the Sejny area on the Polish-Lithuanian border, but many of its activities make a national and international impact, as, for example, the publication of the first edition of the Polish-language version of Jan Gross's *Neighbors: The Destruction of the Jewish Community in Jedwabne, Poland* (2001), a book that sparked a national debate concerning Polish involvement in the killing of Jews during the Nazi occupation of Poland (Szmagalska 2006).

32. She draws on the writings of historian Daniel Beauvois, whose work on the

relations between tsarist administration, Polish nobility, and peasantry in Volhynia from the late eighteenth to the early twentieth century gives rich evidence of the cruelty and privation suffered by peasants on noble estates. Beauvois likens the dynamic to that of colonial plantations and argues that "the mode of treating local population, and the estate-based economy geared primarily toward export, resembled above all a colonial system" (Beauvois 2005: 725).

33. Janion cites many examples of nineteenth and twentieth-century poetry, fiction, and historiography which praise the centuries-long process of Polish eastward expansion, and extol the strength and resolve of the ruling nobility. Among these writers are the novelist Henryk Sienkiwicz, the nineteenth-century poet Wincenty Pol, historian Bogumił Jasionowski, and the notorious Zofia Kossak-Szczucka, an established writer of the interwar period known for her open anti-Semitism.

34. Institutions involved in such Eastern policy include the Center for Eastern Studies (OSW), Poland-America-Ukraine Cooperation Institute (PAUCI), and a number of other think tanks and NGOs.

35. Similarly, open anti-Semitism has been all but purged from the public discourse, which does not mean that the cultural code wherein it has been rooted has changed (cf. Goldfarb 2007; Szmagalska 2006).

36. Polish involvement in Ukrainian development reproduced the dynamic of "collision and collusion" that was set off in the early 1990s by western aid to Eastern Europe (Wedel 1998).

37. I am leaving out here the related topic of postcolonial critiques of Ukrainian culture, as articulated by such authors as Oksana Zabuzhko and Mykola Riabchuk, that emphasize primarily the Russian and Soviet domination of Ukraine. That experience is arguably more salient and traumatic than the experience of Polish colonization, whose memory is transmitted primarily in Western Ukraine. The question of the extent of the Russian grip on Ukrainian consciousness is also the more expedient one in the light of contemporary politics (Zabuzhko 1996; Riabchuk 2004; Hnatiuk 2003).

Conclusion

Epigraph: Michel Foucault, "Confronting Governments: Human Rights" (1984), in *The Chomsky-Foucault Debate on Human Nature* (New York: New Press, 2006). 212.

1. It merits mentioning, however, that the controversial directive on minimal standards in granting and withdrawing refugee status (Council Directive 2005/85/EC of December 1, 2005) was met with many objections among the MEPs and was ultimately approved without Parliament support (Centrum Stosunków Międzynarodowych 2005: 6).

2. Of course European countries, Poland included, do have laws that provide paths to citizenship for legally residing immigrants. In this sense EU citizenship can also be achieved, for becoming a citizen of any one of the member states automatically grants it.

3. These provisions have been included in the Charter of Fundamental Rights of the European Union (2000/C 364/01), which enshrines political, social, and economic

rights for EU citizens and residents into EU law. It fully entered into force, together with the Lisbon Treaty, on December 1, 2009. The ban on the death penalty is contained in Ch. I, art. 2, par. 2; the prohibition on removal, deportation, and extradition "to a state where there is serious risk that he or she would be subjected to the death penalty, torture or other inhuman and degrading punishment" is Ch. II, Art. 19, par. 2. Poland, the Czech Republic, and the UK opted out of certain provisions of the Charter.

4. This is not to say that it grants freedom from the economic necessity to migrate, as the post-2004 wave of Eastern European mobility has shown.

Bibliography

European Union Documents
All the documents listed below can be retrieved through the free European Union law search engine Eur-Lex, available at http://eur-lex.europa.eu/.

Charter of Fundamental Rights of the European Union (2000/C 364/01)

Common Consular Instructions on Visas for the Diplomatic Missions and Consular Posts (2002/C 313/01)

Council and Commission Action Plan Implementing the Hague Programme on Strengthening Freedom, Security and Justice in the European Union (Council Ref. 9778/2/05)

Council Directive 2004/83/EC of 29 April 2004 On Minimum Standards for the Qualification and Status of Third Country Nationals or Stateless Persons as Refugees or as Persons Who Otherwise Need International Protection and the Content of the Protection Granted

Council Directive 2005/85/EC of 1 December 2005 On Minimum Standards on Procedures in Member States for Granting and Withdrawing Refugee Status

Council Regulation (EC) No 343/2003 of 18 February 2003 Establishing the Criteria and Mechanisms for Determining the Member State Responsible for Examining an Asylum Application Lodged in One of the Member States by a Third-Country National (Dublin Regulation)

Council Regulation (EC) No 539/2001 of 15 March 2001 Listing the Third Countries Whose Nationals Must Be in Possession of Visas When Crossing the External Borders and Those Whose Nationals Are Exempt From That Requirement

Directive 2009/52/EC of The European Parliament and of the Council of 18 June 2009 Providing for Minimum Standards on Sanctions and Measures Against Employers of Illegally Staying Third-Country Nationals

Green Paper on a Community Return Policy on Illegal Residents COM (2002) 175 Final

Green Paper on The Future Common European Asylum System COM (2007) 301 Final

Green Paper on an EU Approach to Managing Economic Migration COM (2004) 0811

Proposal for a Regulation of the European Parliament and of the Council Establishing a European Asylum Support Office COM (2009) 66 Final

Regulation (EC) No 562/2006 of the European Parliament and of the Council of 15 March 2006 Establishing a Community Code on the Rules Governing the Movement of Persons Across Borders (Schengen Borders Code)

The Hague Programme: Strengthening Freedom, Security and Justice in the European Union (2005/C 53/01)

The Stockholm Programme. An Open and Secure Europe Serving and Protecting Citizens 2010/C 115/01

Treaty Establishing a Constitution for Europe 2004/C 310/01 (Failed)

Treaty of Amsterdam Amending the Treaty of the European Union, the Treaties Establishing the European Communities and Certain Related Acts, 1997

Treaty of Lisbon Amending the Treaty on European Union and the Treaty Establishing the European Community, Signed at Lisbon, 13 December 2007

Treaty of Rome Establishing the European Economic Community (1957)

*   *   *

Agamben, Giorgio. 1998. *Homo Sacer: Sovereign Power and Bare Life.* Stanford, Calif.: Stanford University Press.

Agier, Michel. 2008. *On the Margins of the World: The Refugee Experience Today.* Cambridge: Polity.

Aksartova, Sada. 2006. "Why NGOs? How American Donors Embraced Civil Society After the Cold War." *International Journal of Not-for-Profit Law* 8, 3: 15–21.

Alldred, Pam. 2003. "No Borders, No Nations, No Deportations." *Feminist Review* 73: 152–57.

Allina-Pisano, Jessica and Andras Simonyi. 2011. "The Social Lives of Borders: Political Economy at the Edge of the EU." In *Transnational Europe: Promise, Paradox, Limits*, ed. Joan DeBardeleben and Achim Hurrlemann. 222–38. New York: Palgrave Macmillan.

Alvarez, Robert R., Jr. 1995. "The Mexican-U.S. Border: The Making of an Anthropology of Borderlands." *Annual Review of Anthropology* 24: 447–70.

Amnesty International (AI). 2004. Amnesty International Statement to the 88th Session of the Governing Council of the International Organization for Migration (IOM). http://www.amnesty.org/en/library/info/IOR30/025/2004/en.

Anderson, Benedict. 1992. "The New World Disorder." *New Left Review* 193: 3–13.

———. 1991. *Imagined Communities: Reflections on the Origins and Spread of Nationalism.* London: Verso.

Anderson, Bridget. 2001. "Why Madam Has So Many Bathrobes? Demand for Migrant Workers in the EU." *Journal of Economic and Social Geography* 92, 1: 18–26.

———. 2000. *Doing the Dirty Work? The Global Politics of Domestic Labour.* London: Zed Books.

Anderson, James. 2007. "Singular Europe: An Empire Once Again?" In *Geopolitics of European Union Enlargement: The Fortress Empire*, ed. Warwick Armstrong and James Anderson. 9–29. London: Routledge.

Anderson, Malcolm. 1996. *Frontiers: Territory and State Formation in the Modern World.* Cambridge: Polity Press.

Andreas, Peter. 2000a. "Introduction. The Wall After the Wall." In *The Wall Around the West. State Borders and Immigration Controls in North America and Europe*, ed. Peter Andreas and Timothy Snyder. 1–13. Lanham, Md.: Rowman and Littlefield.

———. 2000b. *Border Games: Policing the U.S.-Mexico Divide.* Ithaca, N.Y.: Cornell University Press.

Andreas, Peter, and Timothy Snyder, eds. 2000. *The Wall Around the West: State Borders and Immigration Controls in North America and Europe.* Lanham, Md.: Rowman and Littlefield.

Andrukhovych, Yuri. 2004. *Dvanadtsat' Obruchiv* (Twelve Rings). Kyiv: Vydavnytstvo Krytyka.

———. 2000. "Środkowowschodnie Rewizje" (Central Eastern Revisions). In *Moja Europa: Dwa eseje o Europie zwanej środkową* (My Europe: Two Essays on So-called Central Europe), ed. Andrzej Stasiuk and Yuri Andrukhovych. 9–74. Wołowiec: Czarne.

Anzaldúa, Gloria. 2007. *Borderlands: The New Mestiza = La Frontera.* 3rd ed. San Francisco: Aunt Lute Books.

Appadurai, Arjun. 2001. *Globalization.* Durham, N.C.: Duke University Press.

———. 1996. *Modernity at Large: Cultural Dimensions of Globalization.* Vol. 1. Minneapolis: University of Minnesota Press.

Arendt, Hannah. 1963. *Eichmann in Jerusalem: A Report on the Banality of Evil.* New York: Viking.

———. 1951. *The Origins of Totalitarianism.* 2nd enl. ed. New York: Meridian.

Ash, Timothy Garton. 1999. "The Puzzle of Central Europe." *New York Review of Books* 46, 5: 18.

Bader, Veit. 2005. "The Ethics of Immigration." *Constellations* 12, 3: 131–61.

Balcerowicz, Leszek. 1995. *Wolność i rozwój: Ekonomia wolnego rynku* (Freedom and Development: Free Market Economics). Kraków: Znak.

Balibar, Étienne. 2004. *We, the People of Europe? Reflections on Transnational Citizenship.* Trans. James Swenson. Princeton, N.J.: Princeton University Press.

———. 2002. *Politics and the Other Scene.* London: Verso.

Ballinger, Pamela. 2003. *History in Exile: Memory and Identity at the Borders of the Balkans.* Princeton, N.J.: Princeton University Press.

Barth, Fredrik. 2000. "Boundaries and Connections." In *Signifying Identities: Anthropological Perspectives on Boundaries and Contested Values*, ed. Anthony P. Cohen. 15–37. London: Routledge.

———. 1969. *Ethnic Groups and Boundaries: The Social Organization of Culture Difference.* Results of a Symposium Held at the University of Bergen, 23–26 February 1967. Bergen; London: Universitetsforlaget; Allen and Unwin.

Batory Foundation. 2004. *Monitoring Polskiej Polityki Wizowej* (Monitoring Polish Visa Policy). Warszawa: Fundacja im. Stefana Batorego

Bauman, Zygmunt. 2004. *Wasted Lives: Modernity and Its Outcasts.* Oxford: Polity.

Beauvois, Daniel. 2005. *Trójkąt Ukraiński: Szlachta, carat i lud na Wołyniu, Podolu i Kijowszczyźnie, 1793–1914* (Ukrainian Triangle: The Nobility, the Tsar and the People in Volhynia, Podilia and Kyiv Region, 1793–1914). Lublin: Wydawnictwo UMCS.

Bechtel, Delphine. 2006. "Lemberg/Lwów/Lvov/Lviv: Identities of a 'City of Uncertain Boundaries.'" *Diogenes* (International Council for Philosophy and Humanistic Studies) 53, 2: 62–71.

Beck, Adrian. 2005. "Reflections on Policing in Post-Soviet Ukraine: A Case Study of Continuity." *Journal of Power Institutions in Post-Soviet Societies* 2. http://pipss.revues.org/index294.html.

Bekus-Goncharova, Nelly. 2008. "Living in Visa Territory." *Eurozine.* http://www.eurozine.com/articles/2008-02-22-goncharova-en.html.

Bell, Colin and Sol Encel. 1978. *Inside the Whale: Ten Personal Accounts of Social Research.* Rushcutters Bay, Australia: Pergamon.

Benhabib, Seyla. 2004. *The Rights of Others: Aliens, Residents, and Citizens.* Cambridge: Cambridge University Press.

Berdahl, Daphne. 2000. "Introduction: An Anthropology of Postsocialism." In *Altering States: Ethnographies of Transition in Eastern Europe and the Former Soviet Union,* ed. Daphne Berdahl, Matti Bunzl, and Martha Lampland. 1–14. Ann Arbor: University of Michigan Press.

———. 1999. *Where the World Ended: Re-Unification and Identity in the German Borderland.* Berkeley: University of California Press.

Berdahl, Daphne, Matti Bunzl, and Martha Lampland. 2000. *Altering States: Ethnographies of Transition in Eastern Europe and the Former Soviet Union.* Ann Arbor: University of Michigan Press.

Betts, Alexander. 2005. "International Cooperation Between North and South to Enhance Refugee Protection in Regions of Origin." RSC Working Paper 25. University of Oxford Refugee Studies Centre.

Bhabha, Homi. 1996. "Unsatisfied: Notes on Vernacular Cosmopolitanism." In *Text and Nation: Cross-Disciplinary Essays on Cultural and National Identities,* ed. Laura Garcia Moreno and Peter Pfeifer. 191–207. Columbia, S.C.: Camden House.

Bialasiewicz, Luiza. 2003. "Another Europe: Remembering Habsburg Galicja." *Cultural Geographies* 10, 1: 21.

Biehl, João Guilherme. 2005. *Vita: Life in a Zone of Social Abandonment.* Berkeley: University of California Press.

Bieler, Andreas. 2002. "The Struggle over EU Enlargement: A Historical-Materialist Analysis of EU Integration." *Journal of European Public Policy* 9, 4: 575–97.

Bieniecki, Mirosław, Hanna Bojar, and Joanna Kurczewska. 2005. *Polish-Ukrainian Borderland in a Perspective of Polish Integration with the European Union.* Warszawa: Fundacja im. Stefana Batorego.

Bigo, Didier. 2002. "Security and Immigration: Toward a Critique of the Governmentality of Unease." *Alternatives* 27: 63–92.

Bigo, Didier and Elspeth Guild. 2005. *Controlling Frontiers: Free Movement into and Within Europe*. Aldershot: Ashgate.

Blank, Diana R. 2004. "Fairytale Cynicism in the 'Kingdom of Plastic Bags': The Powerlessness of Place in a Ukrainian Border Town." *Ethnography* 5, 3: 349–78.

Bohmer, Carol and Amy Shuman. 2008. *Rejecting Refugees: Political Asylum in the 21st Century*. Abingdon: Routledge.

Boratyński, Jakub. 2002. "Nie odgradzajmy się od sąsiadów ze Wschodu" (Let Us Not Separate from Our Eastern Neighbors). *Rzeczypospolita* February 7.

Borneman, John. 1998. *Subversions of International Order: Studies in the Political Anthropology of Culture*. Albany: State University of New York Press.

Borneman, John and Nick Fowler. 1997. "Europeanization." *Annual Review of Anthropology* 26: 487–514.

Bornstein, Avram S. 2002. "Borders and the Utility of Violence: State Effects on the 'Superexploitation' of West Bank Palestinians." *Critique of Anthropology* 22, 2: 201–20.

Bourdieu, Pierre. 2000. *Pascalian Meditations*. Stanford, Calif.: Stanford University Press.

———. 1998. *Practical Reason: On the Theory of Action*. Stanford, Calif.: Stanford University Press.

Bowen, John Richard. 2007. *Why the French Don't Like Headscarves: Islam, the State, and Public Space*. Princeton, N.J.: Princeton University Press.

Bowker, Geoffrey C. and Susan Leigh Star. 1999. *Sorting Things Out: Classification and Its Consequences*. Cambridge, Mass.: MIT Press.

Boym, Svetlana. 2001. *The Future of Nostalgia*. New York: Basic Books.

Bridger, Susan and Frances Pine. 1998. *Surviving Post-Socialism: Local Strategies and Regional Responses in Eastern Europe and the Former Soviet Union*. London: Routledge.

Brown, Kate. 2004. *A Biography of No Place: From Ethnic Borderland to Soviet Heartland*. Cambridge, Mass.: Harvard University Press.

Brubaker, Rogers, Magrit Feischmidt, Jon Fox, and Liana Grancea. 2006. *Nationalist Politics and Everyday Ethnicity in a Transylvanian Town*. Princeton, N.J.: Princeton University Press.

Buchowski, Michal. 2006. "The Specter of Orientalism in Europe: From Exotic Other to Stigmatized Brother." *Anthropological Quarterly* 79, 3: 463–82.

Budrowska, Bogusława. 2003. "Kobieta i kariera: Realia polskie" (The Woman and the Career: The Polish Context). In *Szklany sufit: Bariery i ograniczenia karier kobiet* (Glass Ceiling: The Barriers and Limitations in Women's Careers), ed. Anna Titkow. 19–38. Warszawa: ISP.

Bunyan, Tony. 1999. "The Story of Tampere: An Undemocratic Process of Excluding Civil Society." *Statewatch Bulletin* 9, 5: 1–6.

Buyandelgeriyn, Manduhai. 2008. "Post-Post-Transition Theories: Walking on Multiple Paths." *Annual Review of Anthropology* 37: 235–50.

Carens, Joseph. 2008. "The Rights of Irregular Migrants." *Ethics and International Affairs* 22, 2: 163–86.

———. 2003. "Who Should Get In? The Ethics of Immigration Admissions." *Ethics and International Affairs* 17, 1: 95–110.

Carey, Henry F. and Rafal Raciborski. 2004. "Postcolonialism: A Valid Paradigm for the Former Sovietized States and Yugoslavia?" *East European Politics and Societies* 18, 2: 191–235.

Carter, Donald Martin. 1997. *States of Grace: Senegalese in Italy and the New European Immigration.* Minneapolis: University of Minnesota Press.

Case, Holly. 2009. "Being European: East and West." In *European Identity,* ed. Jeffrey T. Checkel and Peter J. Katzenstein. 111–31. Cambridge: Cambridge University Press.

Castañeda, Haide. 2010. "Deportation Deferred: 'Illegality,' Visibility and Recognition in Contemporary Germany." In *The Deportation Regime: Sovereignty, Space and the Freedom of Movement,* ed. Nicholas De Genova and Natalie Peutz. 245–61. Durham, N.C.: Duke University Press.

Castells, Manuel. 1996. *The Rise of the Network Society.* Vol. 1. Cambridge: Blackwell.

Cavanagh, Clare. 2004. "Postcolonial Poland." *Common Knowledge* 10, 1: 82–92.

CBOS (Centrum Badania Opinii Publicznej/Public Opinion Research Center). 2008. *Bilans czterech lat integracji Polski z Unią Europejską* (Summary of the Four Years of EU Integration). BS/66/2008.

———. 2004. *Poparcie dla członkostwa w Unii Europejskiej, opinie o unijnej konstytucji i skutkach niepowodzenia brukselskiego szczytu* (Support for European Union Membership, Opinions Concerning the EU Constitution and the Consequences of the Failure of the Brussels Summit). BS/16/2004.

Centrum Stosunków Międzynarodowych (Center for International Relations). 2005. "*Parlament Europejski zgłosił poprawki do dyrektywy azylowej*" (European Parliament Submitted Amendments to the Asylum Directive). *Biuletyn Migracyjny* 3:6.

Chalfin, Brenda. 2004. "Border Scans: Sovereignty, Surveillance and the Customs Service in Ghana." *Identities* 11, 3: 397–416.

———. 2003. "Working the Border in Ghana: Technologies of Sovereignty and Its Others." Occasional Papers from the School of Social Science 16. Institute for Advanced Study, Princeton, N.J.

Chalmers, Damian. 2006. *European Union Law: Text and Materials.* Cambridge: Cambridge University Press.

Chandler, Andrea. 1998. *Institutions of Isolation: Border Controls in the Soviet Union and its Successor States, 1917–1993.* Montreal: McGill-Queen's University Press.

Chessa, Cecilia. 2004. "State Subsidies, International Diffusion, and Transnational Civil Society: The Case of Frankfurt-Oder and Słubice." *East European Politics and Societies* 18, 1: 70–109.

Chivens, Thomas. 2006. "Intervening Gender: The Policing of Domestic Violence Between the United States and Poland." Manuscript.

Clem, Ralph S. and Marek Jan Chodakiewicz. 2004. "Poland Divided: Spatial Differences in the June 2003 EU Accession Referendum." *Eurasian Geography and Economics* 45, 7: 475.

Cohen, Anthony P. 2000. *Signifying Identities: Anthropological Perspectives on Boundaries and Contested Values*. London: Routledge.

———. 1986. *Symbolising Boundaries: Identity and Diversity in British Cultures*. Vol. 2. Manchester: Manchester University Press.

Comaroff, Jean and John Comaroff. 2003. "Ethnography on an Awkward Scale: Postcolonial Anthropology and the Violence of Abstraction." *Ethnography* 4, 2: 147–79.

Coutin, Susan Bibler. 2005. "Being En Route." *American Anthropologist* 107, 2: 195.

———. 2003. *Legalizing Moves: Salvadoran Immigrants' Struggle for U.S. Residency*. Ann Arbor: University of Michigan Press.

Cracknell, David. 2005. "Crikey! FO Speaks Truth About Europe." *Sunday Times Online Edition*, December 11.

Cunningham, Hilary. 2004. "Nations Rebound? Crossing Borders in a Gated Globe." *Identities* 11, 3: 329–50.

Cunningham, Hilary and Josiah McC. Heyman. 2004. "Introduction: Mobilities and Enclosures at Borders." *Identities* 11, 3: 289–302.

Da Lomba, Sylvie. 2004. *The Right to Seek Refugee Status in the European Union*. Antwerp: Intersentia.

Davidson, Miriam. 2000. *Lives on the Line: Dispatches from the U.S.-Mexico Border*. Tucson: University of Arizona Press.

Davies, Norman. 1982. *God's Playground: A History of Poland*. Vol. 2, *From 1795 to the Present*. New York: Columbia University Press.

Day, Sophie. 2010. "The Re-Emergence of 'Trafficking': Sex Work Between Slavery and Freedom." *Journal of the Royal Anthropological Institute* 16: 816–34.

Dąbrowski, Paweł. 2007. "Abolicja w kontekście nielegalnej migracji do Polski" (Abolition in the Context of Illegal Migration to Poland). *Biuletyn Migracyjny* 13: 1–2.

De Genova, Nicholas. 2010. "The Deportation Regime: Sovereignty, Space, and the Freedom of Movement." In *The Deportation Regime: Sovereignty, Space, and the Freedom of Movement*, ed. Nicholas De Genova and Natalie Peutz. 33–65. Durham, N.C.: Duke University Press.

———. 2002. "Migrant 'Illegality' and Deportability in Everyday Life." *Annual Review of Anthropology* 31, 1: 419–47.

Department of State. 2006. *Trafficking in Persons Report*. Washington, D.C.: Department of State.

———. 2005. *Trafficking in Persons Report*. Washington, D.C.: Department of State.

Dinan, Desmond. 2005. *Ever Closer Union: An Introduction to European Integration*. 3rd ed. Boulder, Colo.: Lynne Rienner.

Dominiczak, Henryk. 1997. *Granice państwa i ich ochrona na przestrzeni dziejów 996–1996* (State Borders and the History of Their Protection 996–1996). Warszawa: Bellona.

———. 1985. *Zarys historii Wojsk Ochrony Pogranicza 1945–1985* (An Outline of the History of Borderland Protection Forces 1945–1985). Warszawa: Bellona.

Donnan, Hastings and Thomas M. Wilson. 1999. *Borders: Frontiers of Identity, Nation and State*. Oxford: Berg.

Drakulić, Slavenka. 1997. *Café Europa: Life After Communism*. New York: Norton.

D'Souza, Dinesh. 2002. "Two Cheers for Colonialism." *Chronicle of Higher Education* 48, 35: B7.

Dudziak, Mary L. and Leti Volpp. 2006. *Legal Borderlands: Law and the Construction of American Borders*. Baltimore: Johns Hopkins University Press.

Dunn, Elizabeth C. 2004. *Privatizing Poland: Baby Food, Big Business, and the Remaking of Labor*. Ithaca, N.Y.: Cornell University Press.

Düvell, Franck. 2007. "Ukraine: Europe's Mexico?" Central East European Migration Country Report 1. Centre for Migration, Policy and Society (COMPAS), University of Oxford.

———. 2006. "Crossing the Fringes of Europe: Transit Migration in the EU's Neighbourhood." Working Paper 33. Centre on Migration, Policy and Society (COMPAS), University of Oxford.

Dzenovska, Dace. 2010. "Public Reason and the Limits of Liberal Anti-Racism in Latvia." *Ethnos: Journal of Anthropology* 75, 4: 425–54.

ECRE. 2007. "Refugee Council and European Council on Refugees and Exiles (ECRE) Joint Response to Select Committee on the European Union Sub-Committee F (Home Affairs): Frontex Inquiry." http://www.ecre.org/component/downloads/downloads/58.html.

Ehrenreich, Barbara and Arlie Russell Hochschild. 2004. *Global Woman: Nannies, Maids, and Sex Workers in the New Economy*. New York: Metropolitan/Owl.

Einhorn, Barbara. 1993. *Cinderella Goes to Market: Citizenship, Gender, and Women's Movements in East Central Europe*. London: Verso.

Elias, Norbert. 1994. *The Civilizing Process*. Oxford: Blackwell.

Elliott, Anthony and John Urry. 2010. *Mobile Lives*. Abingdon: Routledge.

Etkind, Alexander. 2010. "'Memory at War' Cultural Dynamics in Poland, Russia and Ukraine." Project Description. http://www.memoryatwar.org/.

European Commission. 2002. "Candidate Countries Eurobarometer." http://europa.eu.int/comm/public_opinion.

Fanning, Bryan and Fidele Mutwarasibo. 2007. "Nationals/Non-Nationals: Immigration, Citizenship and Politics in the Republic of Ireland." *Ethnic and Racial Studies* 30, 3: 439–60.

Fassin, Didier. 2005. "Compassion and Repression: The Moral Economy of Immigration Policies in France." *Cultural Anthropology* 20, 3: 362–87.

———. 2001. "The Biopolitics of Otherness: Undocumented Foreigners and Racial Discrimination in French Public Debate." *Anthropology Today* 17, 1: 3.

Fassin, Didier and Estelle d'Halluin. 2007. "Critical Evidence: The Politics of Trauma in French Asylum Policies." *Ethos* 35, 3: 300–329.

Favell, Adrian. 2009. "Immigration, Migration and Free Movement in the Making of

Europe." In *European Identity*, ed. Jeffrey T. Checkel and Peter J. Katzenstein. 167–92. Cambridge: Cambridge University Press.

———. 2008a. *Eurostars and Eurocities: Free Movement and Mobility in an Integrating Europe*. Malden, Mass.: Blackwell.

———. 2008b. "The New Face of East-West Migration in Europe." *Journal of Ethnic & Migration Studies* 34, 5: 701–16.

Fediv, Lesya. 2004. "Pole-Axed." *Transitions Online*. http://www.tol.org/client/article/11527-pole-axed.html.

Fekete, Liz. 2004. "Deaths at Europe's Borders." *Race & Class* 45, 4: 75.

Feldman, Gregory. 2008. "The Biometric Subject: Producing Migrants as Migration Problems in Today's European Union." Presentation at American Anthropological Association Annual Meeting, San Francisco.

Ferguson, James. 1999. *Expectations of Modernity: Myths and Meanings of Urban Life on the Zambian Copperbelt*. Perspectives on Southern Africa 57. Berkeley: University of California Press.

———. 1990. *The Anti-Politics Machine: "Development," Depoliticization, and Bureaucratic Power in Lesotho*. Cambridge: Cambridge University Press.

Ferguson, Niall. 2003. *Empire: How Britain Made the Modern World*. London: Allen Lane.

Ferrara, Alessandro. 2007. "Europe as a 'Special Area for Human Hope.'" *Constellations* 14, 3.

Firat, Bilge. 2009. "Negotiating Europe/Avrupa: Prelude for an Anthropological Approach to Turkish Europeanization and the Cultures of EU Lobbying in Brussels." *European Journal of Turkish Studies* 9: 2–18.

Fiut, Aleksander. 1999. "Być (albo nie być) Środkowoeuropejczykiem" (To Be (or Not to Be) Central European). Kraków: Wydawnictwo Literackie.

Fligstein, Neil. 2009. "Who Are the Europeans and How Does This Matter for Politics?" In *European Identity*, ed. Jeffrey T. Checkel and Peter J. Katzenstein. 132–66. Cambridge: Cambridge University Press.

Foucault, Michel. 1991. "Governmentality." In *The Foucault Effect: Studies in Governmentality*, ed. Graham Burchell, Peter Miller, and Colin Gordon. 87–104. Chicago: University of Chicago Press.

———. 1990. *The History of Sexuality*. New York: Vintage.

———. 1980. "The Eye of Power." In *Power/Knowledge: Selected Interviews and Other Writings, 1972–1977*, ed. Colin Gordon. 146–66. Hempstead: Harvester.

———. 1977. *Discipline and Punish: The Birth of the Prison*. New York: Pantheon.

Fraser, Nancy. 2003. "From Discipline to Flexibilization: Rereading Foucault in the Shadow of Globalization." *Constellations* 10, 2: 160–71.

Frelak, Justyna. 2005. "Praca Ukraińców w Polsce: Rekomendacje dla polityki migracyjnej" (The Labor of Ukrainians in Poland: Recommendations for Migration Policy). Analizy i Opinie 38.

Frelak, Justyna and Beata Roguska. 2008. "Powroty do Polski: Wyniki badań" (Returns to Poland: Research Findings). Warszawa: ISP.

Freudenstein, Roland. 2000. "Rio Odra, Rio Buh: Poland, Germany and the Borders of Twenty-First-Century Europe." In *The Wall Around the West: State Borders and Immigration Controls in North America and Europe*, ed. Peter Andreas and Timothy Snyder. 173–84. Lanham, Md.: Rowman and Littlefield.

Frontczak, Dorota. 2009. "Umarła Swieta: Smutna historia pełna cudów (Svieta Died: A Sad Story Full of Miracles)." *Gazeta Wyborcza*, July 20.

Fundacja Inicjatyw Społeczno Ekonomicznych. 2008. *Cudzoziemcy w Polsce.* (Foreigners in Poland). Warszawa: FISE

Fuszara, Małgorzata. 2002. "Nowy kontrakt płci?" (A New Sexual Contract?). In *Kobiety w Polsce na przełomie wieków: Nowy kontrakt płci?* (Women in Poland at the Turn of the Century: A New Sexual Contract?), ed. Małgorzata Fuszara, 7–14. Warszawa: ISP.

Gal, Susan and Gail Kligman. 2000. *The Politics of Gender After Socialism: A Comparative-Historical Essay.* Princeton, N.J.: Princeton University Press.

Garapich, Michał P. 2008. "The Migration Industry and Civil Society: Polish Immigrants in the United Kingdom Before and After EU Enlargement." *Journal of Ethnic & Migration Studies* 34, 5: 735–52.

Geertz, Clifford. 1998. "Deep Hanging Out." *New York Review of Books* 45, 16: 69.

———. 1973. *The Interpretation of Cultures: Selected Essays.* New York: Basic Books.

Geremek, Bronisław. 1990. "Which Way to Europe?" *National Review* 42, 15: 28–32.

Giddens, Anthony. 1985. *The Nation-State and Violence.* Berkeley: University of California Press.

Giedroyć, Jerzy. 2005. *Emigracja Ukraińska. Listy 1950–1982* (Ukrainian Exiles: Letters 1950–1982), ed. Bogumiła Berdychowska and Ola Hnatiuk. Warszawa: Czytelnik.

Giorgi, Gabriel and Karen Pinkus. 2006. "Zones of Exception: Biopolitical Territories in the Neoliberal Era." *Diacritics* 36, 2: 99–108.

Glick Schiller, Nina. 2008. "Who Belongs Where? A Global Power Perspective on Migration." ASA Globalog Immigration, http://blog.theasa.org/?cat=49.

Główny Urząd Statystyczny. 2009. *Rocznik Demograficzny 2009* (Demographic Yearbook 2009). Warszawa: GUS.

Goldfarb, Jeffrey C. 2007. "Why Poland? Jews and Poles, Then and Now." Manuscript.

———. 2006. *The Politics of Small Things: The Power of the Powerless in Dark Times.* Chicago: University of Chicago Press.

Good, Anthony. 2006. *Anthropology and Expertise in the British Asylum Courts.* New York: Routledge-Cavendish.

Green, Sarah F. 2005. *Notes from the Balkans: Locating Marginality and Ambiguity on the Greek-Albanian Border.* Princeton, N.J.: Princeton University Press.

Greenhouse, Carol. 2006. "Fieldwork on Law." *Annual Review of Law and Social Science* 2: 187–210.

Gregory, Derek. 2006. "Troubling Geographies." In *David Harvey, a Critical Reader*, ed. Noel Castree and Derek Gregory. 1–25. Malden, Mass.: Blackwell.

Gross, Jan Tomasz. 2006. *Fear: Anti-Semitism in Poland After Auschwitz: An Essay in Historical Interpretation.* New York: Random House.

———. 2001. *Neighbors: The Destruction of the Jewish Community in Jedwabne, Poland.* Princeton, N.J.: Princeton University Press.

Habermas, Jürgen. 2003. "Toward a Cosmopolitan Europe." *Journal of Democracy* 14, 4: 86.

Habermas, Jürgen and Jacques Derrida. 2003. "February 15, Or What Binds Europe Together: A Plea for a Common Foreign Policy, Beginning in the Core of Europe." *Constellations* 10, 3: 291–97.

Hall, Kathleen. 2002. *Lives in Translation: Sikh Youth as British Citizens.* Philadelphia: University of Pennsylvania Press.

Hann, Chris. 2006. *"Not the Horse We Wanted!" Postsocialism, Neoliberalism, and Eurasia.* Piscataway, N.J.: Transaction Publishers.

———. 2002. *Postsocialism: Ideals, Ideologies, and Practices in Eurasia.* London: Routledge.

———. 1998. "Postsocialist Nationalism: Rediscovering the Past in Southeast Poland." *Slavic Review* 57, 4: 840–63.

Hann, Chris and Elizabeth Dunn. 1996. *Civil Society: Challenging Western Models.* London: Routledge.

Hannerz, Ulf. 1996. *Transnational Connections: Culture, People, Places.* New York: Routledge.

Harvey, David. 2001. "Cosmopolitanism and the Banality of Geographical Evils." In *Millennial Capitalism and the Culture of Neoliberalism*, ed. Jean Comaroff and John Comaroff. 271–309. Durham, N.C.: Duke University Press.

———. 1989. *The Condition of Postmodernity: An Enquiry into the Origins of Cultural Change.* Oxford: Blackwell.

Herm, Anne. 2008. "Recent Migration Trends: Citizens of EU-27 Member States Become Ever More Mobile While EU Remains Attractive to Non-EU Citizens." Eurostat Statistics in Focus 98.

Heyman, Josiah. 2004. "Ports of Entry as Nodes in the World System." *Identities* 11, 3: 303–27.

Hirsch, Marianne. 2008. "The Generation of Postmemory." *Poetics Today* 28, 1: 103–28.

Hnatiuk, Ola. 2003. *Pożegnanie z Imperium: Ukraińskie dyskusje o tożsamości* (Farewell to Empire: Ukrainian Debates on Identity). Lublin: Wydawnictwo UMCS.

Hobsbawm, Eric. 1990. *Nations and Nationalism Since 1780: Programme, Myth, Reality.* Cambridge: Cambridge University Press.

Hochschild, Arlie Russell. 2004. "Love and Gold." In *Global Woman: Nannies, Maids and Sex Workers in the New Economy*, ed. Barbara Ehrenreich and Arlie Russell Hochschild. 15–31. New York: Metropolitan/Owl Books.

Holmes, Douglas R. 2009. "Experimental Identities (after Maastricht)." In *European Identity*, ed. Jeffrey T. Checkel and Peter J. Katzenstein. Cambridge: Cambridge University Press.

———. 2003. "Building Europe: The Cultural Politics of European Integration" (Book Review). *American Anthropologist* 105, 2: 464.

———. 2000. *Integral Europe. Fast-Capitalism, Multiculturalism, Neofascism*. Princeton, N.J.: Princeton University Press.

———. 1993. "Illicit Discourse." In *Perilous States: Conversations on Culture, Politics and Nation*, ed. George E. Marcus. 255–82. Chicago: University of Chicago Press.

Hryniewicz, Justyna. 2005. *Uchodźcy w Polsce: Teoria a rzeczywistość* (Refugees in Poland: Theory and Reality). Warszawa: Adam Marszałek.

Hrytsak, Yaroslav. 2009. *Nowa Ukraina: Nowe interpretacje* (New Ukraine: New Interpretations). Lublin: Kolegium Europy Wschodniej.

———. 2005. "The Borders of Europe—Seen from the Outside." *Eurozine*. http//www .eurozine.com/articles/2005-01-10-hrytsak-en.html.

———. 2000. *Historia Ukrainy 1772–1999: Narodziny Nowoczesnego Narodu* (History of Ukraine 1772–1999: The Birth of a Modern Nation). Lublin: Instytut Europy Środkowo-Wschodniej.

Hughes, Donna M. 2000. "The 'Natasha' Trade: The Transnational Shadow Market of Trafficking in Women." *Journal of International Affairs* 53, 2: 625.

Hughes, Donna M. and Tatyana Denisova. 2003. "Trafficking in Women from Ukraine." https://www.ncjrs.gov/pdffiles1/nij/grants/203275.pdf.

Human Rights Watch (HRW). 2009. *Pushed Back, Pushed Around: Italy's Forced Return of Boat Migrants and Asylum Seekers, Libya's Mistreatment of Migrants and Asylum Seekers*. New York: Human Rights Watch.

———. 2006. *Stemming the Flow: Abuses Against Migrants, Asylum Seekers, and Refugees*. New York: Human Rights Watch.

———. 2005. *Ukraine: On the Margins. Rights Violations Against Migrants and Asylum Seekers at the New Eastern Border of the European Union*. New York: Human Rights Watch.

———. 2003. "An Unjust 'Vision' for Europe's Refugees. Human Rights Watch Commentary on the UK's 'New Vision' Proposal for the Establishment of Refugee Processing Centers Abroad." http://www.hrw.org/backgrounder/refugees/UK/newvision.pdf.

Humphrey, Caroline. 2002. *The Unmaking of Soviet Life: Everyday Economies After Socialism*. Ithaca, N.Y.: Cornell University Press.

Huntington, Samuel P. 1993. "The Clash of Civilizations?" *Foreign Affairs* 72, 3: 22–49.

Huyssen, Andreas. 2003. *Present Pasts: Urban Palimpsests and the Politics of Memory*. Stanford, Calif.: Stanford University Press.

ICPS and IPA. 2006. "White Paper: Ukraine's Policy to Control Illegal Migration." http://www.isp.org.pl/files/18872815360939916001156773716.pdf.

Iglicka, Krystyna. 2003. "Priorytety i kierunki rozwoju polskiej polityki migracyjnej" (Priorities and Directions of Development of Polish Migration Policy). *Analizy i Opinie* 13.

———. 2001. "Shuttling from the Former Soviet Union to Poland: From 'Primitive Mobility' to Migration." *Journal of Ethnic & Migration Studies* 27, 3: 505–18.

———. 1999. "The Economics of Petty Trade on the Eastern Polish Frontier." In *The Challenge of East-West Migration for Poland*, ed. Krystyna Iglicka and Keith Sword. 80–100. New York: St. Martin's.

Iglicka, Krystyna and Robert Rybicki. 2002. "Schengen: Consequences for National Migration Policy. Poland." Policy Report, Institute for Public Affairs, Warsaw.

Iglicka, Krystyna and Keith Sword. 1999. *The Challenge of East-West Migration for Poland*. New York: St. Martin's.

Inda, Jonathan Xavier. 2006. *Targeting Immigrants: Government, Technology, and Ethics.* Malden, Mass.: Blackwell.

International Organization for Migration. 2004. *Migration Trends in Selected Applicant Countries.* Vol. 3, *Poland: Dilemmas of a Sending and Receiving Country.* Vienna: IOM.

Janion, Maria. 2006. *Niesamowita Słowiańszczyzna* (The Amazing Slavic Lands). Kraków: Wydawnictwo Literackie.

Jesień Leszek. 2000. "Border Controls and the Politics of EU Enlargement." In *The Wall Around the West: State Borders and Immigration Controls in North America and Europe*, ed. Peter Andreas and Timothy Snyder. 185–203. Lanham, Md.: Rowman and Littlefield.

Kaelble, Hartmut. 2009. "Identification with Europe and the Politicisation of the EU Since the 1980s." In *European Identity*, ed. Jeffrey T. Checkel and Peter J. Katzenstein. 193–212. Cambridge: Cambridge University Press.

Kaiser, Wolfram and Peter Starie. 2005. *Transnational European Union: Towards a Common Political Space.* London: Routledge.

Kaneff, Deema. 2002. "The Shame and Pride of Market Activity: Morality, Identity and Trading in Postsocialist Rural Bulgaria." In *Markets and Moralities: Ethnographies of Postsocialism*, ed. Ruth Mandel and Caroline Humphrey. Oxford: Berg.

Kapllani, Gazmend. 2010. *A Short Border Handbook.* London: Portobello Books.

Kapuściński, Ryszard. 1995. *Imperium.* New York: Vintage International.

Katz, Michael B. 1996 [1986]. *In the Shadow of the Poorhouse: A Social History of Welfare in America.* New York: Basic Books.

Kaźmierkiewicz, Piotr. 2005. *The Visegrad States Between Schengen and Neighborhood.* Warszawa: ISP.

Kearney, M. 1995. "The Local and the Global: The Anthropology of Globalization and Transnationalism." *Annual Review of Anthropology* 24, 1: 547–65.

Kelly, Tobias. 2006. "'Jurisdictional Politics' in the Occupied West Bank: Territory, Community, and Economic Dependency in the Formation of Legal Subjects." *Law & Social Inquiry* 31, 1: 39–74.

Kempny, Marta. 2010. *Polish Migrants in Belfast: Border Crossing and Identity Construction.* Newcastle upon Tyne: Cambridge Scholars.

Keough, Leyla J. 2006. "Globalizing 'Postsocialism': Mobile Mothers and Neoliberalism on the Margins of Europe." *Anthropological Quarterly* 79, 3: 431–61.

Kieniewicz, J. 1990. "*Polska granicą Europy*" (Poland as the Boundary of Europe). *Przegląd Powszechny* 7, 8: 9–16.

King, Rosemary A. 2000. "United States-Mexico Borderland Narratives: Geopoetic Representations from the Mexican American War to the Present." Ph.D. dissertation, Arizona State University.

Kirişci, Kemal. 2006. "A Friendlier Schengen Visa System as a Tool of 'Soft Power': The Experience of Turkey." *European Journal of Migration & Law* 7, 4: 343–67.

Koch, Erin. 2006. "Beyond Suspicion: Evidence, (Un)Certainty, and Tuberculosis in Georgian Prisons." *American Ethnologist* 33, 1: 50–62.

Kofman, Eleonore. 2000. *Gender and International Migration in Europe: Employment, Welfare and Politics.* London: Routledge.

Konieczna, Joanna. 2003. *Polska-Ukraina, Ukraina-Polska: Paradoksy stosunków sąsiedzkich* (Poland-Ukraine, Ukraine-Poland: The Paradoxes of Neighborly Relations). Warszawa: Fundacja im. Stefana Batorego.

Korczyńska, Joanna. 2005. *Zapotrzebowanie na pracę obcokrajowców Polsce: Próba analizy i wniosków dla polityki migracyjnej* (The Demand for Foreign Labor in Poland: Tentative Analysis and Implications for Migration Policy). Warszawa: Instytut Spraw Publicznych.

Kornai, János. 1992. *The Socialist System: The Political Economy of Communism.* Princeton, N.J.: Princeton University Press.

Kostrzewa, Robert. 1990. *Between East and West: Writings from* Kultura. New York: Hill and Wang.

Kowalski, Marcin. 2005. "*Koniec mafii kolejkowej pod konsulatem we Lwowie?*" (The End of the Queue Mafia at the Lviv Consulate?). *Gazeta Wyborcza,* May 18, 3.

Kowalski, Marcin and Oksana Forostyna. 2005. "Wiza za łapówkę" (Visa for a Bribe). *Gazeta Wyborcza,* May 11, 1.

Krasner, Stephen D. 1999. *Sovereignty: Organized Hypocrisy.* Princeton, N.J.: Princeton University Press.

Krok, K. and M. Smętkowski. 2006. *Cross-Border Cooperation of Poland After EU Enlargement: Focus on Eastern Border.* Warsaw: Wydawnictwo Naukowe Scholar.

Kubicek, Paul. 2007. "Ukraine and the European Neighborhood Policy: Can the EU Help the Orange Revolution Bear Fruit?" *East European Quarterly* 41, 1: 1–23.

Kukathas, Chandran. 2011. "Expatriatism. The Theory and Practice of Open Borders." In *Citizenship, Borders, and Human Needs,* ed. Rogers M. Smith. 324–42. Philadelphia: University of Pennsylvania Press.

Kundera, Milan. 1984. "The Tragedy of Central Europe." *New York Review of Books* 31, 7.

Kűrti, László. 2001. *The Remote Borderland: Transylvania in the Hungarian Imagination.* Albany: State University of New York Press.

Lachmann, Piotr. 1998. "*Granice Pogranicza*" (The Boundaries of the Borderland). *Borussia* 16: 10–21.

Lahav, Gallya and Virginie Guiraudon. 2000. "Comparative Perspectives on Border Control: Away from the Border and Outside the State." In *The Wall Around the West: State Borders and Immigration Controls in North America and Europe,* ed. Peter Andreas and Timothy Snyder. 55–77. Lanham, Md.: Rowman and Littlefield.

Landau, Loren B. 2006. "Immigration and the State of Exception: Security and Sovereignty in East and Southern Africa." *Millennium—Journal of International Studies* 34, 2: 325–48.

Lash, Scott and Jonathan Friedman. 1992. *Modernity and Identity.* Oxford: Blackwell.

Lavenex, Sandra. 2001. "Migration and the EU's New Eastern Border: Between Realism and Liberalism." *Journal of European Public Policy* 8, 1: 24–42.

———. 1999. *Safe Third Countries: Extending the EU Asylum and Immigration Policies to Central and Eastern Europe.* Budapest: Central European University Press.

Ledeneva, Alena V. 2006. *How Russia Really Works: The Informal Practices That Shaped Post-Soviet Politics and Business.* Ithaca, N.Y.: Cornell University Press.

Lemon, Alaina. 1998. "'Your Eyes Are Green like Dollars': Counterfeit Cash, National Substance, and Currency Apartheid in 1990s Russia." *Cultural Anthropology* 13, 1: 22–55.

Levitt, Peggy and Nina Glick Schiller. 2004. "Conceptualizing Simultaneity: A Transnational Social Field Perspective on Society." *International Migration Review* 38, 3: 1002.

Łodzinski, Sławomir. 1998. "Obcy krajowcy. Perspektywy polityki wobec imigrantów w Polsce." (Foreign Natives. Policy Perspectives Concerning Immigrants in Poland). In *Do stołu dla zamożnych: Ruchy migracyjne w Polsce i ich znaczenie dla Polski* (To the Table with the Wealthy: Migrations and Their Significance for Poland), ed. Sławomir Łodziński and Jan Milewski. 174–212. Warszawa: Instytut Krajów Rozwijających Się, WGSR.

Lyon, David. 2002. "Editorial. Surveillance Studies: Understanding Visibility, Mobility and the Phenetic Fix." *Surveillance and Society* 1, 1: 1–7.

Maas, Willem. 2007. *Creating European Citizens.* Lanham, Md.: Rowman and Littlefield.

Magocsi, Paul R. 2002. *Historical Atlas of Central Europe.* Seattle: University of Washington Press.

Makaremi, Chowra. 2008. "Border Detention in Europe: Violence and the Law." Paper presented at ISA 49th Annual Convention, San Francisco, March 26.

Malkki, Liisa. 2007. "Commentary: The Politics of Trauma and Asylum: Universals and Their Effects." *Ethos* 35, 3: 336–43.

———. 1995. *Purity and Exile: Violence, Memory, and National Cosmology Among Hutu Refugees in Tanzania.* Chicago: University of Chicago Press.

Mandel, Ruth and Caroline Humphrey. 2002. *Markets and Moralities: Ethnographies of Postsocialism.* Oxford: Berg.

Massey, Douglas S., Jorge Durand, and Nolan J. Malone. 2002. *Beyond Smoke and Mirrors: Mexican Immigration in an Era of Economic Integration.* New York: Sage.

Matynia, Elżbieta. 2003. "Provincializing Global Feminism: The Polish Case." *Social Research: An International Quarterly* 70, 2: 499–530.

Maziarski, Wojciech. 2001. "Gdzie jest mój sąsiad?" (Where Is My Neighbor?) *Gazeta Wyborcza*, June 1, 7–9.

Merry, Sally Engle. 2006. "Anthropology and International Law." *Annual Review of Anthropology* 35: 99–116.

Michnik, Adam. 2003. "What Europe Means for Poland." *Journal of Democracy* 14, 3: 129–36.

Międzykulturowe Centrum Adaptacji Społeczno-Zawodowej (Intercultural Center for Vocational Adaptation). 2008. "Raport, Wietnamczycy w Polsce: Perspektywy Adaptacji Społeczno-Zawodowej" (Research Report, Vietnamese Nationals in Poland: Perspectives on Social and Vocational Adaptation).

Migreurop. 2009. *Europe's Murderous Borders.* Paris: Migreurop.

Miklósi, Gabor. 2008. "Schengen Blues." *Eurozine.* http://www.eurozine.com/articles/2008-04-09-miklosi-en.html.

Miłosz, Czesław. 1999. *Wyprawa w Dwudziestolecie* (A Journey into the Interwar Period). Krakow: Wydawnictwo Literackie.

———. 1968. *Native Realm: A Search for Self-Definition.* Garden City, N.Y.: Doubleday.

Minca, Claudio. 2006. "Giorgio Agamben and the New Biopolitical Nomos." *Geographiskaler Annaler* B, 88 4: 387–403.

Momsen, Janet Henshall. 1999. "Maids on the Move." In *Gender, Migration and Domestic Service*, ed. Janet Henshall Momsen. 1–20. London: Routledge.

Moore, David Chioni. 2001. "Is the Post in Postcolonial the Post in Post-Soviet? Toward a Global Postcolonial Critique." *Publications of the Modern Language Association of America* 116, 1: 111.

Morokvasic, Mirjana. 2004. "Settled in Mobility: Engendering Post-Wall Migration in Europe." *Feminist Review* 77: 7–25.

———. 1991. "Fortress Europe and Migrant Women." *Feminist Review* 39: 69–84.

Morokvasic-Müller, Mirjana, Umut Erel and Kyoko Shinozaki. 2003. *Crossing Borders and Shifting Boundaries.* Vol. 1, *Gender on the Move.* Opladen: Leske & Budrich.

Morris, Lydia. 2010. *Asylum, Welfare and the Cosmopolitan Ideal: A Sociology of Rights.* Abingdon: Routledge.

Motyka, Grzegorz. 2011. *Od rzezi wołyńskiej do akcji "Wisła": Konflikt polsko-ukraiński 1943–1947* (From the Volhynia Massacre to Action "Wisła": The Polish-Ukrainian Conflict 1943–1947). Kraków: Wydawnictwo Literackie.

———. 2008. "Zapomnijcie o Giedroyciu: Polacy, Ukraińcy, IPN" (Forget About Giedroyć: Poles, Ukrainians and the Institute of National Remembrance). *Gazeta Wyborcza,* May 26.

Najder, Zbigniew. 2003. "Political Consequences of the Post-Enlargement Implementation of Schengen Rules." Policy Report, Institute of Public Affairs, Warsaw.

Niklewicz, Konrad. 2005. "Komisja Europejska forsuje pomysł stworzenia wspólnej polityki migracyjnej w UE" (European Commission Pushes for Establishing a Common Immigration Policy in the EU). *Gazeta Wyborcza*, March 11.

No Border. 2004. "Presentation of the No Border Network." http://noborder.org/about.php#2003.

O'Dowd, Liam. 2003. "The Changing Significance of European Borders." In *New Borders for a Changing Europe: Cross Border Cooperation and Governance*, ed. James Anderson, Liam O'Dowd, and Thomas M. Wilson. 13–36. London: Frank Cass.

Okólski, Marek. 2001. "Incomplete Migration: A New Form of Mobility in East and Central Europe: The Case of Polish and Ukrainian Migrants." In *Patterns of Migration in Central Europe*, ed. Claire Wallace and Dariusz Stola. 105–27. Houndmills: Palgrave Macmillan.

———. 1999. "Recent Migration in Poland: Trends and Causes" In *The Challenge of East-West Migration for Poland*, ed. Krystyna Iglicka and Keith Sword. 15–44. London: Macmillan.

Ong, Aihwa. 1999. *Flexible Citizenship: The Cultural Logics of Transnationality*. Durham, N.C.: Duke University Press.

Ong, Aihwa and Stephen J. Collier. 2005. *Global Assemblages: Technology, Politics, and Ethics as Anthropological Problems*. Malden, Mass: Blackwell.

Ost, David. 2005. *The Defeat of Solidarity: Anger and Politics in Postcommunist Europe*. Ithaca, N.Y.: Cornell University Press.

Pagden, Anthony. 2002. *The Idea of Europe: From Antiquity to the European Union*. Washington, D.C.; Cambridge: Woodrow Wilson Center Press; Cambridge University Press.

Parreñas, Rhacel Salazar. 2004. "The Care Crisis in the Philippines: Children and Transnational Families in the New Global Economy." In *Global Woman: Nannies, Maids and Sex Workers in the New Economy*, ed. Barbara Ehrenreich and Arlie Russel Hochschild. 34–53. New York: Holt.

Pawlicki, Jacek. 2005. "Za dwa lata zniknie granica z Unią" (In Two Years the Border with the Union Will Vanish). *Gazeta Wyborcza*, January 26.

Pelkmans, Mathijs. 2006. *Defending the Border: Identity, Religion, and Modernity in the Republic of Georgia*. Ithaca, N.Y.: Cornell University Press.

Petryna, Adriana. 2005. "Ethical Variability: Drug Development and Globalizing Clinical Trials." *American Ethnologist* 32, 2: 183–97.

———. 2002. *Life Exposed: Biological Citizens After Chernobyl*. Princeton, N.J.: Princeton University Press.

Phillips, Sarah D. 2008. *Women's Social Activism in the New Ukraine: Development and the Politics of Differentiation*. Bloomington: Indiana University Press.

———. 2005. "Civil Society and Healing: Theorizing Women's Social Activism in Post-Soviet Ukraine." *Ethnos: Journal of Anthropology* 70, 4: 489–514.

Phizacklea, Annie. 1983. *One Way Ticket: Migration and Female Labour*. London: Routledge.

Pine, Frances. 2006. "Lost Generations and the Problem of Reproduction: Emerging Inequalities in Kinship in Poland." Presentation at Max Planck Workshop, Global Connections and Emerging Inequalities in Europe, July 6–7.

———. 2002a. "Retreat to the Household? Gendered Domains in Postsocialist Poland." In *Postsocialism: Ideals, Ideologies and Practices in Eurasia*, ed. C. M. Hann. 95–113. London: Routledge.

———. 2002b. "Dealing with Money: Złotys, Dollars and Other Currencies in the Polish Highlands." In *Markets and Moralities: Ethnographies of Postsocialism*, ed. Ruth Mandel and Caroline Humphrey. 75–100. Oxford: Berg.

Pocock, J. G. A. 2002. "Some Europes in Their History." In *The Idea of Europe: From Antiquity to the European Union*, ed. Anthony Pagden. 55–72. Washington, D.C.: Woodrow Wilson Center Press.

Rabinow, Paul. 2003. *Anthropos Today: Reflections on Modern Equipment.* Princeton, N.J.: Princeton University Press.

Redlich, Shimon. 2002. *Together and Apart in Brzezany: Poles, Jews, and Ukrainians, 1919–1945.* Bloomington: Indiana University Press.

Reid, Anna. 2000. *Borderland: A Journey Through the History of Ukraine.* Boulder, Colo.: Westview Press.

Reszka, Paweł. 2004. "*Ukraińscy angliści w szkołach na Lubelszczyźnie*" (Ukrainian English Teachers in Schools in the Lublin Area). *Gazeta Wyborcza*, October 17.

Riabchuk, Mykola. 2005. "Schengen: A Fortress of Rules." *Eurojournal.* http://eurojournal.org/more.php?id=200_0_1_0_M8.

———. 2004. *Dwie Ukrainy* (Two Ukraines). Wrocław: Kolegium Europy Wschodniej.

Ries, Nancy. 2002. "'Honest Bandits' and 'Warped People': Russian Narratives About Money, Corruption and Moral Decay." In *Ethnography in Unstable Places: Everyday Lives in Contexts of Dramatic Political Change*, ed. Carol J. Greenhouse, Elizabeth Mertz, and Kay B. Warren. 276–315. Durham, N.C.: Duke University Press.

———. 1997. *Russian Talk: Culture and Conversation During Perestroika.* Ithaca, N.Y.: Cornell University Press.

Riles, Annelise. 2006. "Anthropology, Human Rights, and Legal Knowledge: Culture in the Iron Cage." *American Anthropologist* 108, 1: 52–62.

Robins, Kevin. 2003. "Peculiarities and Consequences of the Europe-Turkey Border." *European Studies* 19: 233–50.

Rumford, Chris. 2006. "Theorizing Borders." *European Journal of Social Theory* 9, 2: 155–69.

Rupnik, Jacques. 1990. "Central Europe or Mitteleuropa?" *Daedalus* 119, 1: 249–78.

Sahlins, Peter. 1989. *Boundaries: The Making of France and Spain in the Pyrenees.* Berkeley: University of California Press.

Said, Edward W. 1994 [1979]. *Orientalism.* New York: Vintage.

Sampson, Steven. 1996. "The Social Life of Projects: Importing Civil Society to Albania." In *Civil Society: Challenging Western Models*, ed. C. M. Hann and Elizabeth C. Dunn. 121–42. London: Routledge.

Sanders, Todd and Harry West. 2003. "Power Revealed and Concealed in the New World Order." In *Transparency and Conspiracy: Ethnographies of Suspicion in the New World Order*, ed. Harry G. West and Todd Sanders. 1–37. Durham, N.C.: Duke University Press.

Sassen, Saskia. 2011. "Global Migration and Economic Needs." In *Citizenship, Borders, and Human Needs*, ed. Rogers M. Smith. 56–91. Philadelphia: University of Pennsylvania Press.

———. [1991] 2001. *The Global City: New York, London, Tokyo.* Princeton, N.J.: Princeton University Press.

———. 1999. *Guests and Aliens.* New York: New Press.

———. 1996. *Losing Control? Sovereignty in an Age of Globalization.* New York: Columbia University Press.

Schatral, Susanne. forthcoming. "Categorisation and Instruction: The IOM's Role in Preventing Human Trafficking in the Russian Federation." In *Perpetual Motion? Transformation and Transition in Central, Eastern Europe and Russia,* ed. Tul'si Bhambry et al. London: School of Slavonic and East European Studies, University College.

Schweizer, Harold. 2008. *On Waiting.* London: Routledge.

Schwell, Alexandra. 2006. "Boundaries in Border Police Cooperation: The Case of the German-Polish Border." In *Borderland Identities: Territory and Belonging in North, Central and East Europe,* ed. Madeleine Hurd. 255–88. Eslov: Gondolin.

Scott, James C. 1998. *Seeing Like a State: How Certain Schemes to Improve the Human Condition Have Failed.* New Haven, Conn.: Yale University Press.

Scott, James W. 2005. "The EU and 'Wider Europe': Toward and Alternative Geopolitics of Regional Cooperation." *Geopolitics* 10: 429–54.

Seeberg, Peter. 2010. "European Neighbourhood Policy, Post-Normativity, and Pragmatism." *European Foreign Affairs Review* 15: 663–79.

Shearman, Peter and Matthew Sussex. 2004. *European Security After 9–11.* Aldershot: Ashgate.

Shenker, Jack. 2011. "Aircraft Carrier Left Us to Die, Say Migrants." *The Guardian,* May 8.

Shokalo, Oleksander. 2005. "Intehratsia chy povernennia dodomu?" (Integration or Return Home?) *Dzerkalo Tyzhnia* 12, 540: 5–6.

Shore, Cris. 2006. "'Government Without Statehood'? Anthropological Perspectives on Governance and Sovereignty in the European Union." *European Law Journal* 12, 6: 709–24.

———. 2000. *Building Europe: The Cultural Politics of European Integration.* London: Routledge.

Shore, Cris and Marc Abélès. 2004. "Debating the European Union: An Interview with Cris Shore and Marc Abélès." *Anthropology Today* 20, 2: 10–14.

Shore, Cris and Susan Wright. 1997. *Anthropology of Policy: Critical Perspectives on Governance and Power.* London: Routledge.

Siemaszko, Ewa and Władysław Siemaszko. 2000. *Ludobójstwo dokonane przez nacjonalistów ukraińskich na ludności polskiej Wołynia* (Genocide Perpetrated by Ukrainian Nationalists on the Polish Population of Volhynia). Warszawa: Von Borowiecky.

Silverstein, Paul A. 2005. "Immigrant Racialization and the New Savage Slot: Race, Migration, and Immigration in the New Europe." *Annual Review of Anthropology* 34: 363–84.

Simon, Suzanne. 2007. "Framing the Nation: Law and the Cultivation of National Character Stereotypes in the NAFTA Debate and Beyond." *Political and Legal Anthropology Review (PoLAR)* 30, 1: 22–45.

Słubik, Katarzyna. 2011. "Abolicja nie dla wszystkich" (Abolition Not for Everyone). *Biuletyn Migracyjny* 31: 8–9.

Smith, Rogers M., ed. 2011. *Citizenship, Borders, and Human Needs.* Philadelphia: University of Pennsylvania Press.

Snyder, Timothy. 2010. *Bloodlands: Europe Between Hitler and Stalin.* New York: Basic Books.

———. 2003. "The Causes of Ukrainian-Polish Ethnic Cleansing 1943." *Past and Present* 179: 197–234.

———. 2000. "Conclusion: The Wall Around the West." In T*he Wall Around the West: State Borders and Immigration Controls in North America and Europe*, ed. Peter Andreas and Timothy Snyder. 219–27. Lanham, Md.: Rowman and Littlefield.

Spivak, Gayatri Chakravorty. 1988. "Can the Subaltern Speak?" In *Marxism and the Interpretation of Culture*, ed. Cary Nelson and Lawrence Grossberg. 271–313. Urbana: University of Illinois Press.

Stasiuk, Andrzej. 2004. *Jadąc do Babadag* (Going to Babadag). Wołowiec: Wydawnictwo Czarne.

Stasiuk, Andrzej and Yuri Andrukhovych. 2000. *Moja Europa: Dwa eseje o Europie zwanej Środkową* (My Europe. Two Essays on So-called Central Europe). Wołowiec: Czarne.

Stolcke, Verena. 1995. "Talking Culture." *Current Anthropology* 36, 1: 1–24.

Stoler, Ann L. 2008. "Imperial Debris: Reflections on Ruins and Ruination." *Cultural Anthropology* 23, 2: 191–219.

———. 2002. *Carnal Knowledge and Imperial Power. Race and the Intimate in Colonial Rule.* Berkeley: University of California Press.

Strojny, Aleksander et al. 2005. *Ukraina Zachodnia* (Western Ukraine). Warszawa: Bezdroża.

Subtelny, Orest. 1988. *Ukraine: A History.* Toronto: University of Toronto Press with Canadian Institute of Ukrainian Studies.

Szczepanikova, Alice, Marek Canek, and Jan Grill. 2006. *Migration Processes in Central and Eastern Europe. Unpacking the Diversity.* Prague: Multikulturni Centrum Praha.

Szerepka, Leszek and Marta Jaroszewicz. 2007. *Wyzwania migracyjne w państwach sąsiedztwa wschodniego Unii Europejskiej* (Migration Challenges in the Eastern Neighborhood of the European Union). Warszawa: Ośrodek Studiów Wschodnich.

Szmagalska, Karolina. 2006. "The Refusal to Mourn: Confronting the Facts of Destruction of the Jewish Community in Jedwabne." In *Diaspora and Memory: Figures of Displacement in Contemporary Literature, Arts and Politics*, ed. Marie-Aude Baronian, Stephan Besser, and Yolande Jansen. 125–37. Amsterdam: Rodopi.

Szmagalska-Follis, Karolina. 2011. "The Awkward Divide: Paradoxes of Transnationality on the Polish-Ukrainian Border." In *Transnational Europe: Promise, Paradox, Limits*, ed. Joan DeBardeleben and Achim Hurrlemann. 239–56. New York: Macmillan.

———. 2009. "Are the European Union's New Boundaries like the Iron Curtain? Borders and Freedom of Movement in Poland and Ukraine." *International Journal of Politics, Culture, and Society* 22, 3: 385.

———. 2008. "Repossession: Notes on Restoration and Redemption in Ukraine's Western Borderland." *Cultural Anthropology* 23, 2: 329–60.

Tarasiewicz, Małgorzata. 1991. "Women in Poland: Choices to Be Made." *Feminist Review* 39: 182–85.

Ticktin, Miriam. 2006. "Where Ethics and Politics Meet: The Violence of Humanitarianism in France." *American Ethnologist* 33, 1: 33–49.

Titkow, Anna. 2003. *Szklany sufit: Bariery i ograniczenia karier kobiet* (The Glass Ceiling: The Barriers and Limitations in Women's Careers). Warszawa: ISP.

———. 2001. "Interes grupowy polskich kobiet: Zakres wątpliwości i szanse artykulacji" (The Group Interest of Polish Women: The Scope of Uncertainty and Possibilities of Articulation). In *Kobiety w Polsce na przełomie wieków: Nowy kontrakt płci?* (Women in Poland at the Turn of the Century: A New Sexual Contract?), ed. Małgorzata Fuszara. 39–64. Warszawa: ISP.

Todorova, Maria Nikolaeva. 1997. *Imagining the Balkans*. New York: Oxford University Press.

Tomaszewski, J. 1991. *Mniejszości narodowe w Polsce w XX wieku* (National Minorities in Twentieth-Century Poland). Warsaw: Spotkania.

———. 1985. *Rzeczpospolita wielu narodów* (The Republic of Many Nations). Warszawa: Czytelnik.

Torpey, John C. 2000. *The Invention of the Passport: Surveillance, Citizenship, and the State*. Cambridge: Cambridge University Press.

Toruńczyk, Barbara. 1987. "*O królach i duchach: Z opowieści wschodnioeuropejskich.*" (Of Kings and Ghosts: Eastern European Narratives) *Zeszyty Literackie* 20.

Trouillot, Michel-Rolph. 2001. "The Anthropology of the State in the Age of Globalization." *Current Anthropology* 42, 1: 125–38.

Uehling, Greta. 2004. "Irregular and Illegal Migration Through Ukraine." *International Migration* 42, 3: 77–109.

United Against Racism. 2011. "List of 15551 Documented Refugee Deaths Through Fortress Europe." http://www.unitedagainstracism.org/pdfs/listofdeaths.pdf

United Nations High Commissioner for Refugees (UNHCR). 2006. *Convention and Protocol Relating to the Status of Refugees with an Introductory Note by the Office of the United Nations High Commissioner for Refugees*. Geneva: UNHCR.

Urry, John 2007. *Mobilities*. Cambridge: Polity.

Verdery, Katherine. 2002a. "Seeing Like a Mayor: Or, How Local Officials Obstructed Romanian Land Restitution." *Ethnography* 3, 1: 5–33.

———. 2002b. "Whither Postsocialism?" In *Postsocialism. Ideals, Ideologies and Practices in Eurasia*, ed. C. M. Hann. 15–28. London: Routledge.

———. 1999. *The Political Lives of Dead Bodies: Reburial and Postsocialist Change*. New York: Columbia University Press.

———. 1996. *What Was Socialism, and What Comes Next?* Princeton, N.J.: Princeton University Press.

Volkov, Vadim. 2002. *Violent Entrepreneurs: The Use of Force in the Making of Russian Capitalism.* Ithaca, N.Y.: Cornell University Press.

Wagstyl, Stefan. 2002. "A Symbolic Step for Former Communist States." *Financial Times*, November 19, 2.

Walker, Neil. 2004. "The Legacy of Europe's Constitutional Moment." *Constellations* 11, 3: 368–92.

Wallace, Claire. 2002. "Opening and Closing Borders: Migration and Mobility in East-Central Europe." *Journal of Ethnic & Migration Studies* 28, 4: 603–25.

Walters, William. 2010. "Deportation, Expulsion and the International Police of Aliens." In *The Deportation Regime. Sovereignty, Space and the Freedom of Movement*, ed. Nicholas De Genova and Natalie Peutz. 69–100. Durham, N.C.: Duke University Press.

———. 2006. "Border/Control." *European Journal of Social Theory* 9, 2: 187–203.

———. 2002. "Mapping Schengenland: Denaturalizing the Border." *Environment and Planning D: Society and Space* 20: 561–80.

Wang, Horng-Iuen. 2004. "Regulating Transnational Flows of People: An Institutional Analysis of Passports and Visas as a Regime of Mobility." *Identities: Global Studies in Culture and Power* 11: 351–76.

Wanner, Catherine. 2003. "Advocating New Moralities: Conversion to Evangelicalism in Ukraine." *Religion, State & Society* 31, 3: 273.

———. 1998. *Burden of Dreams: History and Identity in Post-Soviet Ukraine.* University Park: Pennsylvania State University Press.

Wasilewska, Olga. 2008. "Schengen zatkało wschodnich sąsiadów" (Schengen Clogged the Eastern Neighbors). *Gazeta Wyborcza*, July 9, 19.

Wedel, Janine R. 1998. *Collision and Collusion: The Strange Case of Western Aid to Eastern Europe, 1989–1998.* New York: St. Martin's.

Wenzel, Michal. 2009. *Stosunek do obcokrajowców w Polsce* (Attitudes to Foreigners in Poland). Warsaw: Instytut Spraw Publicznych.

Werbner, Pnina. 2008. "Introduction. Towards a New Cosmopolitan Anthropology." In *Anthropology and the New Cosmopolitanism: Rooted, Feminist and Vernacular Perspectives*, ed. Pnina Werbner. 1–29. Oxford: Berg.

West, Barbara A. 2001. *The Danger Is Everywhere! The Insecurity of Transition in Postsocialist Hungary.* Prospect Heights, Ill.: Waveland.

Wilson, Andrew. 2005. *Ukraine's Orange Revolution.* New Haven, Conn.: Yale University Press.

———. 2000. *The Ukrainians: Unexpected Nation.* New Haven, Conn.: Yale University Press.

Wolff, Larry. 1994. *Inventing Eastern Europe: The Map of Civilization on the Mind of the Enlightenment.* Stanford, Calif.: Stanford University Press.

Yar, Majid. 2003. "Panoptic Power and the Pathologization of Vision: Critical Reflections on the Foucauldian Thesis." *Surveillance and Society* 1, 3: 254–71.

Yúnez-Naude, Antonio. 2011. "Rural Migration and Economic Development with

Reference to Mexico and the United States." In *Citizenship, Borders, and Human Needs*, ed. Rogers M. Smith. 39–55. Philadelphia: University of Pennsylvania Press.

Zabuzhko, Oksana. 1996. *A Kingdom of Fallen Statues: Poems and Essays.* Ed. Marco Carynnyk. Toronto: Wellspring.

Zarycki, Tomasz. 2004. "Uses of Russia: The Role of Russia in the Modern Polish National Identity." *East European Politics and Societies* 18, 4: 595–627.

Zielonka, Jan. 2006. *Europe as Empire: The Nature of the Enlarged European Union.* Oxford: Oxford University Press.

Zolberg, Aristide. 1999. "Matters of State: Theorizing Immigration Policy." In *The Handbook of International Migration: The American Experience*, ed. Charles Hirshman, Philio Kasinitz, and Josh DeWind. 71–93. New York: Russell Sage.

Index

Acknowledgments

This book grows out of my lifelong obsession with borders. I must have first become aware of their power when as a five-year-old I was refused a passport by the then-communist Polish authorities. My father and I were due to travel to the United States to accompany my mother, who had been granted a post-doctoral fellowship at an American university. Unfortunately, at the time, in the early 1980s, the Party was still reluctant to let citizens out of the already imploding socialist paradise. Our passport applications were rejected on the grounds that our departure was "not in the interest of the socialist homeland." Several months of bureaucratic tussle ensued and eventually my father and I were able to travel. Since then I have been an avid collector of border experiences, which in time inspired the research that led to this book.

My deepest thanks go to all the people in Poland and Ukraine who gave me access to their personal and professional lives and shared their understandings and perspectives on the social and legal changes in which they were immersed. I especially want to acknowledge the busy women and men for whom negotiating the new border of the European Union is an everyday challenge, but who found the time in their hectic lives to share their stories with me. Their real names do not appear in this book, but what I was able to learn about their lives thoroughly informs it.

In Ukraine I would have been lost without the patient help, support and hospitality of Olena Borovets and her family, Andriy Bondarenko, Nadia and Khrystyna Chushak, Halyna Krouk and Father Mykhailo Piniakha and his family. I thank Yaroslav Hrytsak, Ihor Markov, Sofia Mamchur, Vava Baczynska as well as Andriy Pavlyshyn. I am also grateful for the assistance provided by the Lviv unit of Amnesty International, especially by Svitlana Marintseva. Big thanks are due to Ihor Gnat at the Lviv Centre of Social Adaptation, and to the staff of the UNHCR office in Kyiv; likewise to the consuls at the Polish Consulates in Lviv and in Lutsk. I must also note and thank my countless anonymous travel companions on the cross-border buses and *marshrutki* who did not mind chatting with me on our shared journeys and who taught me a great deal about everyday life on the border.

In Poland, I am grateful to the many border guards, especially at the Border Guard headquarters in Warsaw and at the units on the eastern border, and to officials at the Office for Repatriation and Aliens, Ministry of Foreign Affairs, and Customs Service whose names do not appear in this text, but who have assisted me in innumerable ways, most of all by enduring my presence and questions in their offices and at border checkpoints. My interpretation of some of the issues I discussed with them probably differs from theirs. That, however, does not change the fact that I am thankful not just for their willingness to talk to me, but also for the good spirit of most of these encounters. I am also deeply indebted to Father Piotr Kuszka in Warsaw, Father Stefan Batruch in Lublin, and Piotr Kaźmierczak, Justyna Frelak, Joanna Fomina and Mirek Bieniecki at the Institute for Public Affairs, as well as to Viktor Chumak at the International Centre for Policy Studies. The places I visited and the events I participated in thanks to their kind invitations and assistance informed my thinking in critically important ways. I thank Magda Kmak at the Helsinki Foundation for Human Rights, Ernest Zienkiewicz at the Warsaw UNHCR, and Stanisław Stępień at the South Eastern Institute in Przemyśl. I appreciate also the help of Przemek Osiak, Jacek Jarymowicz, Ksenia Meyza, Ola Hantiuk, Rostyslav Kramar, Marek Cynkar, Miron Kertyczak, Joanna Konieczna, and Volodymyr Pavliv. The friendship of Agnieszka Kościańska and Michał Petryk sustained me through fieldwork and beyond. I thank also Bogna Burska for our summer reunions and much more, and Krzysztof Miękus for his help with selecting the cover image.

Many mentors and colleagues at various stages encouraged and stimulated my obsession with borders and cheered on as I progressed with this project. I thank Adriana Petryna for her wisdom, compassion, and generosity as a teacher and critic. Without the congenial atmosphere at the New School for Social Research and the unwavering intellectual support and direction provided by Jeff Goldfarb, Ann Stoler, and Douglas Holmes (across institutional boundaries) this project could not have been completed. Other teachers to whom I am grateful include Judith Friedlander, Ari Zolberg, Vera Zolberg, Harry West, David Plotke, Ann Snitow, Richard Bernstein, and, at Princeton, John Borneman. Robert Kostrzewa was always a kind and helpful presence. The Transregional Center for Democratic Studies was a fantastic platform for the exchange of ideas, discussions, and encounters that left a deep imprint on this work. I thank all of my TCDS friends. My very special gratitude goes to Elżbieta Matynia. This project benefited from her support and inspiration in countless ways.

As I went along, many people gave feedback on various fragments of this text, both as readers and as participants in workshops and conferences. I was particularly fortunate to have participated in the New Social Science Training Work-in-Progress Series at the New School for Social Research; the Anthropology of Law Workshop at the Birkbeck School of Law; the Global Connections and Emerging Inequalities in Europe workshop at the Max Planck Institute in Halle; the Conference on Transnational Europe: Promise, Paradox, Limits at Carleton University; the workshop on Justice and Security in Canada and the EU at the University of Toronto; the Conference on Citizenship, Borders, and Human Needs at the University of Pennsylvania; and the Managing Migration workshop at the National University of Ireland Maynooth. Michael Herzfeld's "Nation State and Its Intimacies" seminar in Warsaw deserves a special mention for the week-long discussions it stimulated. My interlocutors at these events are too numerous to list, but I am grateful to the organizers and everyone who took the time to engage with and comment on my work. The input of audiences and readers helped clarify and improve it, but of course the responsibility for any errors or misinterpretations remains solely mine. I thank my dear friends and colleagues Erin Koch, Anne Galvin, Simanti Dasgupta, Irit Dekel, Michael Weinman, Amy Sodaro, Christiane Wilke, Yuri Contreras, Maureen Murney, and Thom Chivens for the caring attention they gave to my work.

During my time at the Penn Program on Democracy, Citizenship, and Constitutionalism, I had the privilege of working with Rogers Smith, who challenged me to think in new directions and helped build my confidence that this project was of interdisciplinary interest. I feel fortunate to have been part of DCC events in the academic year 2007/2008, when the theme was "Borders, Citizenship, and Human Needs." At the University of Pennsylvania I have cherished the opportunity to engage with the wider intellectual community, especially with Kathleen Hall, Sarah Paoletti, Asif Agha, Gregory Urban, and Deborah Thomas, and with the undergraduate and graduate students who often challenged me to think through unexpected points and connections. A big thank you is due also to Elspeth Wilson, Dave Karpf, and Larysa Carr.

I thank colleagues and students at the Anthropology Department of the National University of Ireland Maynooth, where I was based while completing the final work on this manuscript. I am grateful to Abdullahi El-Tom and other members of the department for the support I received during a particularly hectic time in my life. I thank Tom Strong and Andrew Levitt for their friendship and the many fabulous meals in Dublin. In Lancaster, yet another home base, I thank Sue Penna and Nayanika Mookherjee.

My research and writing endeavors that led to this book have been supported by the Wenner Gren Foundation's Wadsworth Fellowship, the Alexander and Ilse Melamid and Dr. Ruth Westheimer Fellowships, and the Law and Social Science Program of the National Science Foundation. I am grateful to these funders for making my training, fieldwork, and writing possible.

I want to thank my editor, Peter Agree, for his trust in this project and for his extraordinary kindness, patience, and clarity in guiding it to completion. Julia Rose Roberts and Alison Anderson at Penn Press have also been wonderfully helpful and patient.

Two chapters in this book include parts of an essay that appeared in *Transnational Europe: Promise, Paradox, Limits*, edited by Joan DeBardeleben and Achim Hurrelman (New York: Palgrave Macmillan, 2011). An earlier version of Chapter 5 appeared in *Citizenship, Borders, and Human Needs*, edited by Rogers M. Smith (Philadelphia: University of Pennsylvania Press, 2011).

Finally, my thanks go to my dearest friends and family in Warsaw and New York. I thank Libby Newman for being my partner in the never-ending quest to find the right balance. I thank Magda Gubała-Ryzak, Celina Imielińska, Ewa Księżycka and Henryk Majczyński, and Fabrizio and Eugenia Follis for their warmth and unfailing hospitality, thanks to which I could periodically recharge my batteries. Without the help of three wonderful women, Sarah Stuart, Barbara Grelik, and Eugenia Hommel, who helped look after my baby son, this work could not have been completed. Danuta Zagrodzka, my aunt, and my two grandmothers, Wanda Zagrodzka and Walentyna Szmagalska, passed away as I worked on this project. All three of them were strong women who inspired me in different ways, and I will forever cherish their memory. My long-departed grandfather, Wacław Zagrodzki, would have applauded my interest in Ukraine. My beloved parents, Jolanta Zagrodzka and Jerzy Szmagalski, provided inexhaustible support and encouragement in addition to all manner of hugely important practical help. They taught me that borders are there to be crossed. I dedicate this book to them. Above all, I thank Luca Follis, who has been my most patient and caring reader, partner, and friend, and I thank our son Benjamin for being the perpetually smiling source of joy from day one.